CHRONICLES
OF THE
ANCIENT
WORLD

CHRONICLES OF THE
ANCIENT

WORLD

JOHN HAYWOOD

Quercus

CONTENTS

Introduction 6

INTRODUCTION

The greater part of human history is unchronicled. For hundreds of thousands of years humans lived in small mobile communities based on extended family groups, hunting, fishing and gathering wild plant foods. Cultural and technological change was slow. It is almost unimaginable in the modern age, but generations passed without anyone inventing anything new.

THEN, AROUND 10,000 YEARS AGO in the Middle East, environmental changes caused by the end of the last Ice Age made hunting and gathering an increasingly insecure way of life. People responded by settling down in permanent villages and becoming farmers. It was a development that changed everything, setting humanity on a course that led directly to the development of the world's first civilizations and, with them, the beginning of recorded history.

Before farming, people were entirely dependent on the natural productivity of the environment for their food supplies. This imposed strict limits on population growth. Despite periodic crop failures, farmers found that most years they could produce more food than they needed to support themselves and their families. They could have more children and, with more hands, more land could be cultivated and even more food could be produced. A succession of technological innovations, such as the plough, irrigation and metal tools, and selective breeding to improve crops and domestic animals, led to great increases in productivity and bigger food surpluses and even faster population growth.

Surplus food was the first form of wealth and it gave great power to whoever could control it. Surplus food also allowed increasing numbers of people to be spared from farming to specialize in other occupations, such as craft production, warfare, trade or religion. The pace of cultural and technological change began to increase and has rarely faltered since. These changes provided the impulse behind the development of more hierarchical class-based forms of society. As population grew the scale of those societies increased too, outgrowing the bonds of kinship, leading to the development of organized religions and the first institutions of government to establish common values and rules for living. The size of settlements increased, from villages of hundreds of people, to towns of thousands, and eventually cities of tens of thousands of people. In hunter-gatherer societies people could easily memorize the knowledge they needed for daily life and their customs and religious and historical traditions were passed down from generation to generation by word of mouth. As farming communities grew in size and complexity, unaided human memory became increasingly inadequate for ensuring the smooth running of social and economic life. Some means was needed of storing information permanently outside the human mind: writing.

Writing was first used 5,500 years ago in Uruk, the first community large enough to be considered a city, on the fertile and densely populated plains of Sumeria in southern Mesopotamia (now part of Iraq). A few hundred years later writing evolved independently in Egypt's Nile river valley. The development of these writing systems marks the true beginning of ancient history. Before this our knowledge of ancient societies is based entirely on archaeology, the study of the material remains of past cultures. This can tell us much but it has no voice. We can look in wonder at prehistoric monuments like Stonehenge but no amount of archaeological excavation will ever tell us for certain exactly what they meant to the people who built and used them. The invention of writing allows the people of the ancient world to speak directly to us and tell us about their customs and beliefs and the great events that shaped their lives. Fortunately, the ancient civilizations used

BELOW **Times of prosperity.** *The 'Standard of Ur' (see pp. 32–3) dating from c. 2600–2400 BC, has two sides depicting War and Peace. This section is taken from the Peace side and shows servants delivering animals for a banquet.*

durable writing materials, such as clay tablets and stone steles, but it still seems little short of miraculous that we can still read documents written by scribes who died over 5,000 years ago. How much of the mass of digital information stored in electronic formats on computer hard disks today will still be available for people to read 5,000 years in the future?

It was no accident that these developments happened first in the Middle East (or as archaeologists call it, the Near East): this was the region of the world that was richest in wild plants and animals suitable for domestication (the process of selective breeding that improves their usefulness for food production). Wheat,

ABOVE **Alexander the Great** *forces Darius III to flee at the Battle of Gaugamela, one of many humiliating defeats for the Persian king during Alexander's formidable campaign.*

barley, peas, lentils, vines, olives, cattle, pigs, sheep and goats were all first domesticated in this region. Farming would develop independently in many other regions of the world but none got off to such a flying start. The most fertile soils of the Middle East were in Sumeria, the southern part of Mesopotamia, the flood plain of the Tigris and Euphrates rivers in present-day Iraq. Because of the region's low rainfall, it was only after the development of irrigation techniques around 5500 BC that farmers began to settle the plains and exploit their fertile soils. The population rose rapidly and by 3000 BC Sumeria was densely populated and dotted with prosperous cities, each of which was an independent state.

There was a price to pay for Sumeria's precocious development, however. Salts left behind in the poorly drained soils when irrigation water evaporated under the hot sun gradually damaged their fertility, reducing crop yields and sending the Sumerian cities into decline. In the second millennium BC, primacy passed to the states of Babylon and Assyria in central and northern Mesopotamia, where higher rainfall meant that farmers relied less on irrigation. In this millennium too, ancient Egypt entered its most splendid period as an imperial power. Although it developed only a few centuries after Sumerian civilization, ancient Egyptian civilization proved much more durable. Rainfall was just as low in the Nile valley but farmers did not suffer the same fertility problems as the reliable Nile floods washed away salt build-ups and fertilized the fields with fresh silt every year.

In the first millennium BC the centres of power continued to shift. In the 6th century BC both Mesopotamia and Egypt came under the control of the vigorous new Persian kingdom which developed on the Iranian plateau. But the Persian advance westwards was halted early in the next century by the Greeks, whose own astonishingly inventive civilization laid the intellectual foundations of our own. Persia itself was conquered in the 330s BC by Alexander the Great, who spread the influence of Greek civilization across the Middle East as far as India. Alexander's empire fragmented after his death and the disunited Greeks were unable to resist the advance of a new great power from the western Mediterranean, Rome, which by 30 BC had brought most of the ancient world under its rule.

The decline and fall of the Roman empire is the last chapter in the history of the ancient world. In the 4th century, its culture was transformed by the spread of Christianity, and in the 5th its western provinces, including Rome itself, were occupied by Germanic barbarians from northern Europe. The deposition of the last emperor of the west by a barbarian general in 476 is seen by many historians as marking the end of the ancient world and the beginning of the Middle Ages. Yet, like all artificial divisions in history, this disguises the real continuity between the ancient world, the Middle Ages and, ultimately, our own times.

THE FIRST DYNASTIES

3500–2000 BC

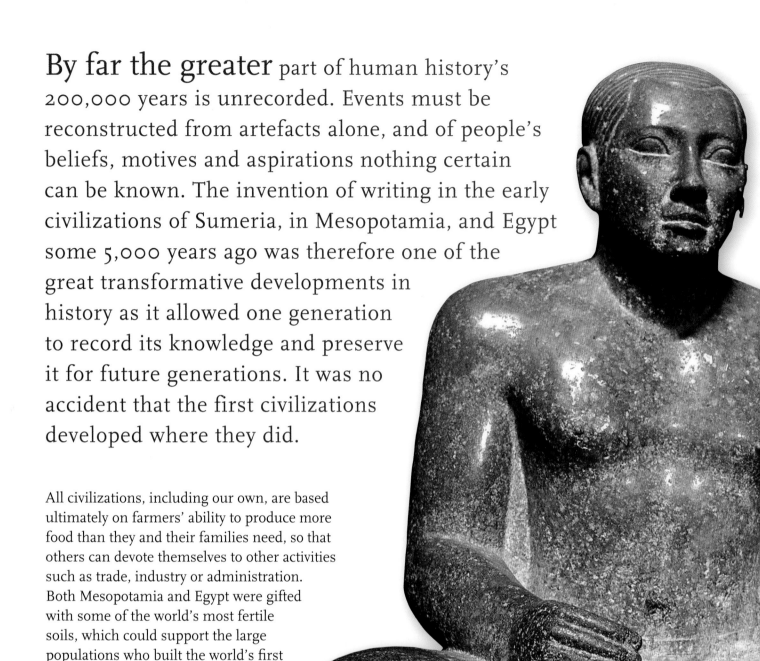

By far the greater part of human history's 200,000 years is unrecorded. Events must be reconstructed from artefacts alone, and of people's beliefs, motives and aspirations nothing certain can be known. The invention of writing in the early civilizations of Sumeria, in Mesopotamia, and Egypt some 5,000 years ago was therefore one of the great transformative developments in history as it allowed one generation to record its knowledge and preserve it for future generations. It was no accident that the first civilizations developed where they did.

All civilizations, including our own, are based ultimately on farmers' ability to produce more food than they and their families need, so that others can devote themselves to other activities such as trade, industry or administration. Both Mesopotamia and Egypt were gifted with some of the world's most fertile soils, which could support the large populations who built the world's first cities and forged its first kingdoms.

PREVIOUS PAGES **Gilgamesh, legendary king of Uruk** *in Sumeria, the world's first city, shown in this 8th-century BC Assyrian relief wrestling a lion. Gilgamesh was famed for his strength and wisdom, his affair with Ishtar, the goddess of love and war, and his ultimately unsuccessful search for personal immortality.*

THE FOUNDATION OF URUK

In Uruk [King Gilgamesh] built walls, a great rampart, and the temple of blessed Eanna for the god of the firmament Anu, and for Ishtar, the goddess of love. Look at it still today: the outer wall where the cornice runs, it shines with the brilliance of copper; and the inner wall, it has no equal. Touch the threshold, it is ancient. Approach Eanna the dwelling of Ishtar, our lady of love and war, the like of which no latter-day king, no man alive can equal. Climb upon the wall of Uruk; walk along it, I say; regard the foundation terrace and examine the masonry: is it not burnt brick and good? The seven sages laid the foundation.

THE EPIC OF GILGAMESH, COMPOSED *c.* 2000 BC

c. 3500 BC

THE MOTHER OF CITIES ✦ The first urbanized civilization was born in the region of southern Mesopotamia, known in ancient times as Sumer or Sumeria. Now lying mostly in Iraq, Mesopotamia, meaning 'the land between the rivers', is the flood plain of the Tigris and Euphrates rivers. Southern Mesopotamia has a very hot arid climate and it remained a virtually uninhabited desert until *c.* 5500 BC when the development of irrigation made it possible for farmers to settle the region and unlock the potential of its fertile alluvial soils. The population grew rapidly as cultivation intensified, and by *c.* 4300 BC small towns were developing across the area. By *c.* 3500 BC the fastest growing of these, Uruk or Warka, with a population of tens of thousands, had become the world's first city. Such a large community was impossible to govern efficiently by word of mouth and unaided human memory. By 3300 BC administrators in the city had developed a form of

13

LEFT **Egyptian scribe.** *This granite funerary statue shows Petamenope (c. 650 BC), the librarian and archivist of the temple of Amun at Karnak. Scribes enjoyed high status and could become very wealthy: Petamenope could afford to build himself a large and elaborately decorated tomb in the Valley of the Kings.*

ABOVE **The Warka Vase.** *This votive alabaster vase, discovered at Uruk (Warka), is one of the earliest surviving works of narrative relief sculpture, dating to c. 3200–3000 BC. The lower tier shows growing grain and sheep and oxen. In the second tier a procession of naked men carry votive offerings of fruit and grain, and in the top tier the procession is shown ending in the temple of Inanna, the Sumerian fertility goddess.*

WRITING

The invention of writing in *c.* 3500 BC in Sumeria marks the beginning of the end of prehistory and the beginning of recorded history. The Sumerian writing system used a pictographic script, derived from an earlier recording system that used different-shaped clay tokens to stand for different commodities, such as grain or cattle.

The meaning of most pictographic symbols is obvious. The symbol for barley was a simplified picture of an ear of barley; that for an ox was a simplified bull's head. Signs were combined to express more complex ideas. For example, the combination of a head and a bowl meant 'to eat'. The symbols were inscribed on wet clay tablets which were allowed to dry for storage in archives. By around 2900 BC the symbols had become more abstract and were now inscribed using a rectangular-ended reed stylus that made wedge-shaped impressions from which the script gets its name, cuneiform ('wedge-shaped'). In cuneiform a sign could also stand for the phonetic value of the word so that they could be combined to make other words. If this system was used in English, the sign for 'man' could be combined with the sign for 'age' to make another word: 'manage'. Syllable signs were also introduced so that cuneiform was able accurately to record all elements of human speech. Cuneiform was written from left to right. For nearly 2,500 years, cuneiform was the most widespread script used in the Middle East, being adopted by the Babylonians, Assyrians, Elamites, Hittites and Persians among other peoples.

Writing, using a hieroglyphic script, came into use in Egypt between 3200 BC and 3000 BC. The earliest hieroglyphs were based on motifs used to decorate pottery. Although, like Sumerian pictographic, hieroglyphic uses pictures to represent words, their meaning is not obviously related to their appearance. There were two main types of hieroglyph. Some were logograms which represented complete words or concepts. Others represented consonants which could be used to spell out words like letters in an alphabet. Hieroglyphic (meaning 'sacred carving') was used only for monumental commemorative and religious inscriptions and other formal writing. Around 2600 BC a simplified cursive form of writing called hieratic ('priestly') came into use for religious texts and official documents. This could be written quickly with brush and ink on paper made from the papyrus reed.

One feature that cuneiform and hieroglyphic had in common was that they took a long time to learn: hieroglyphic had around 800 symbols while the different variants of cuneiform had anything from 400 to 1,000. Literacy was therefore confined to the elite who could afford to have their children educated. As practitioners of a relatively rare skill, scribes enjoyed high social status and could rise high in the ranks in government, the priesthood or the military. Nevertheless, teachers, such as this Egyptian schoolmaster, still needed to remind their pupils of the ultimate benefits of going to school:

Be a scribe, who is freed from forced labour, and protected from all work. He is released from hoeing with the hoe, and he need not carry a basket. It spares him from plying the oar, and it is free from vexation. He has not many masters, nor a host of superiors. ... The scribe, he directs every work that is this land.

ABOVE **Land deal.** *This slate tablet from Uruk, dating to c. 3100 BC, records a transfer of property between the two individuals represented in the Sumerian pictographic script, the world's first writing system.*

pictographic writing from an earlier system of clay tokens which was widely used across Mesopotamia. The script was inscribed on soft clay tablets, which were allowed to dry and could be stored in archives. Thanks to Mesopotamia's dry climate, thousands of these early documents have survived, buried in the ruins of Uruk and the dozens of other Sumerian cities which had grown up on the plain by 3000 BC.

It is clear that Sumeria remained primarily an oral culture because writing was, for centuries, used only for recording taxes paid, rations issued and other economic transactions. The only exceptions are teaching materials such as word lists. Not even the names of rulers were recorded. Though much has been learned about the region's social structure and economy, reconstructing the early political history of Sumeria from these documents is as difficult as it would be to reconstruct the political history of the modern world from bundles of tax returns, invoices and credit card bills. Each Sumerian city had its own independent government, which was always based in a temple precinct. A city's ruler was, in theory, its patron god. The city itself was regarded as the property of the god, who, it was believed, actually dwelt in its temple. In practice, the government was headed by an *en* (or, if it was a woman, a *nin*), a priestly figure who acted as the earthly administrator of the god's estates and as intercessor for his or her human subjects. Archaeological excavations show that temples physically dominated Sumerian cities, emphasizing the importance of a city's relationship with its god. Temples acted as storehouses where surplus agricultural production, offered in the name of the city gods, was gathered before being redistributed as rations to administrators and craft workers or traded for raw materials, such as timber, stone and metals, which were not available locally. The Sumerian people themselves remain something of a mystery. Their own name for themselves was 'the Black-Headed People'. Their language was unrelated to any other known language, so their origins will probably never be known.

15

c. 3000 BC

KING NARMER UNIFIES EGYPT ✦ The ancient kingdom of Egypt was the world's earliest territorial kingdom. Several small kingdoms began to form in Egypt around 3500 BC as the Nile valley began to fill up with settlers fleeing desertification in the Sahara. Competition for space in the narrow confines of the valley led to the stronger kingdoms taking over the weaker ones. By c. 3100 BC only two were left: the kingdoms of Upper (southern) and Lower (northern) Egypt. By this time the Egyptians had begun to develop their system of hieroglyphic writing, but for several centuries this was used only for recording names and short lists. As a result, the names of a few early kings of Upper Egypt are known, but little more. Around 3000 BC one of these kings, Narmer, marched north into Lower Egypt and conquered it, creating for the first time a unified kingdom of Egypt.

Narmer's achievement is commemorated in pictorial form in low relief carvings on a cosmetics palette made from a 60-centimetre (2-ft) tall slab of fine-grained grey siltstone. This remarkable object shows nothing less than the birth of a civilization. The king's name appears on both sides of the palette in the earliest example of a *serekh*. This is a symbolic representation of a palace, the central institution of Egyptian royal government, which contained the hieroglyphs spelling out the king's name and gave him protection from evil. The *serekh* evolved into the simpler cartouche, an elliptical shape with a horizontal line at the bottom which served the same

> *The remarkable Narmer Palette shows nothing less than the birth of a civilization.*

protective function and is one of the most distinctive features of ancient Egyptian royal inscriptions. Apart from one other word, the king's name is the only writing which appears on the palette.

On one side, the palette shows Narmer wearing the white crown that symbolized Upper Egypt and preparing to smite a defeated enemy with a raised mace while he stands over the corpses of two other fallen enemies. This image of might remained a standard part of Egyptian royal iconography for the next 3,000 years. In front of Narmer is a falcon, the symbol of the sky god Horus who was closely associated with Egyptian royalty. The close association between Narmer and Horus probably means that the king was regarded as an incarnation of the god. The ideology of divine kingship that was so central to ancient Egyptian civilization was therefore already established at its very beginning. On the other

OPPOSITE **The Narmer Palette.** *This slate cosmetics palette commemorates the unification of Egypt by King Narmer c. 3000 BC. This side of the palette shows the triumphant king, wearing the white crown of Upper Egypt, smiting an enemy with a mace. The falcon represents the sky god Horus who was the focus of a royal cult, in whose temple at Hierakonpolis the palette was found. The bulls represent royal strength. The small figure behind the king is a servant, carrying his sandals. The rectangular box at the top is a* serekh, *a symbolic representation of a palace containing the hieroglyph of the king's name.*

THE KING LISTS

The earliest form of history writing in Mesopotamia and Egypt was the king list. Though brief, often giving little more than the kings' names, the lengths of their reigns and their genealogy, these were highly political documents, written to serve the interests of ruling dynasties by establishing their legitimacy.

One of the earliest of these lists is the Sumerian King List, which was compiled shortly after the destruction of Ur in 2004 BC. Several copies, all inscribed on clay tablets, have survived. Although the list contains much material that is obviously legendary it also expresses the Sumerian understanding of the way history worked. The Sumerians were aware of the way one city achieved a position of pre-eminence only to be supplanted by a rival, whose pre-eminence proved to be equally transient. Sumerians saw this pattern as the work of the gods. Kingship, they believed, was a gift of the gods. They had first bestowed it on Eridu, which Sumerians believed was the place of the creation. When Eridu and its rulers fell from favour, kingship, and with it political pre-eminence, was transferred to Bad-tibira, then Larak, Sippar and so on over thousands of years. The list was compiled in Isin to support its claim to be Sumeria's pre-eminent city against its rival Larsa, whose kings are pointedly omitted. The list mentions only one female ruler, Ku-bau, 'the innkeeper' of Kish.

> *When kingship had first come down from heaven,*
> *Eridu became the seat of kingship. At Eridu,*
> *Alulim reigned as king for 28,800 years. Alalgar*
> *reigned for 36,000 years: two kings reigned for*
> *64,800 years. Eridu was abandoned and its*
> *kingship was taken to Bad-tibira.*
>
> SUMERIAN KING LIST, ADAPTED FROM S.N. KRAMER,
> *THE SUMERIANS*, (1963)

RIGHT **Ancient bestseller.** *The Weld-Blundell prism, discovered at Larsa in 1922, is the most complete surviving copy of the Sumerian King List, a list of the pre-eminent kings of Sumeria from the creation of the world to the 19th century BC. The list includes much legendary material including an early account of the great flood sent by the gods to destroy humankind. The four-sided clay tablet was pierced vertically so that it could be mounted on a frame and rotated while it was being read.*

side of the palette Narmer is shown again, this time wearing the red crown that symbolized Lower Egypt. The fact that he is shown on the palette wearing both crowns implies that he was ruler of both Upper and Lower Egypt. In later royal iconography, the two crowns were combined to form the *shemty*, the double crown of Upper and Lower Egypt. On this side too there is a triumphal parade of standard bearers, more slaughtered enemies, and a portrayal of the king as a raging bull smashing the walls of a fortified town and trampling an enemy. A hollow on this side, formed by the entwined necks of two mythological beasts, was the part of the palette that was actually used for mixing cosmetics. Ancient Egyptian cosmetics, which were worn by both men and women, contained rare minerals imported from as far afield as Afghanistan, so elaborate mixing palettes of this sort were status symbols; worthy objects to carry important messages. The Narmer palette was excavated in 1895 from the ruins of the temple of Horus at Narmer's capital of Hierakonpolis ('city of the falcon'), where it had probably been placed by the king himself as a thank-offering to the god for his victory.

ANCIENT EGYPTIAN HISTORICAL PERIODS

+ *Predynastic Period 5300–3000 BC*
+ *Early Dynastic Period 3000–2649 BC*
+ *Old Kingdom 2649–2134 BC*
+ *First Intermediate Period 2134–2040 BC*
+ *Middle Kingdom 2040–1640 BC*
+ *Second Intermediate Period 1640–1532 BC*
+ *New Kingdom 1532–1070 BC*
+ *Third Intermediate Period 1069–664 BC*
+ *Late Period 664–332 BC*
+ *Ptolemaic Period (Greek rule) 332–30 BC*
+ *Roman Period 30 BC–AD 395*

c. 2920 BC

THE FIRST DYNASTY ✦ The next king known to have ruled Egypt was Hor-Ahu ('fighting falcon'), who was also known as Men or Menes. Hor-Ahu's name associates him closely with Horus, suggesting that, like Narmer, he was from Upper Egypt. The exact relation, if any, between Narmer and Hor-Ahu is unknown. Recently discovered king lists suggest that Hor-Ahu was Narmer's son but uncertainties about the dates of both men's reigns mean that they could have lived as much as a century apart. Though not much is known about Hor-Ahu's reign, he did found a dynasty that continued to rule Egypt for six generations after his death. For this reason he is considered the founder of Egypt's first historical dynasty. Hor-Ahu's other major achievement was the foundation of Memphis as a new capital city in Lower Egypt. Strategically situated where the narrow Nile valley begins to widen out into the broad fertile Delta, Memphis remained Egypt's capital for the next 900 years. According to later traditions, Hor-Ahu reigned for 62 years, meeting his end when he was attacked by a hippopotamus while out hunting.

c. 2649 BC

EGYPT'S OLD KINGDOM PERIOD BEGINS ✦ Hor-Ahu's successors in the First Dynasty faced frequent conflicts between Upper and Lower Egypt and these finally brought the dynasty down c. 2770 BC. The Second Dynasty (c. 2770–c. 2649 BC) also struggled to keep Upper and Lower Egypt united. During the reign of the last Second Dynasty king, Khasekhemy, a rebel army from the north almost captured Hierakonpolis before it was defeated. Savage southern reprisals – killing, it was claimed, 47,000 northerners – seems to have finally ended separatism in Lower Egypt. This, together with the effective administration the First and Second Dynasty kings had built, laid the foundations for a great expansion of Egyptian power into Sinai and Nubia, which began with the accession of Sanakhte, the first king of the Third Dynasty, c. 2649 BC.

The founder of Egypt's first historical dynasty, Hor-Ahu reigned for 62 years, meeting his end when he was attacked by a hippopotamus while out hunting.

Sanakhte's accession is taken to mark the beginning of Egypt's Old Kingdom period. This was the first of ancient Egypt's three periods of imperial greatness and strong royal government, known to historians as the Old Kingdom (c. 2649–2134 BC), Middle Kingdom (2040–c. 1640 BC) and New Kingdom (1532–1070 BC), each of them separated by shorter periods of division and weak government known as Intermediate Periods. The Old Kingdom saw a marked expansion in the use of writing but such texts as have survived are mainly religious: the rulers of the period left no records of their deeds.

c. 2630 BC

THE FIRST PYRAMID IS BUILT FOR KING DJOSER ✦ The Old Kingdom is sometimes also called the 'pyramid age' after the gigantic royal tombs that are its most remarkable monuments. The first pyramid was begun soon after the accession of Sanakhte's successor, his brother Djoser (r. c. 2630–c. 2611 BC). Previously, Egyptian kings and nobles had been buried in *mastabas* ('benches'). These were low, flat-roofed buildings, built of a mixture of mud brick (adobe) and stone, which contained a burial chamber. Egyptians did not waste any of their limited area of fertile riverside land on cemeteries, so mastabas were always built on the edge of the desert plateau which overlooked the Nile valley, from where they would have appeared simply as low humps. As part of the ongoing consolidation of royal authority, Djoser wanted a tomb that exalted the majesty of the king far above that of even his wealthiest subjects.

Djoser's pyramid was built at Saqqara, not far from the royal capital at Memphis. The project was masterminded by the royal vizier, Imhotep, the first architect whose name is known to history. Imhotep was later deified for his achievements. Imhotep began Djoser's pyramid as a huge stone *mastaba*, which

ABOVE **The step pyramid at Saqqara.** *The development of the pyramid began with the construction of the so-called step pyramid for King Djoser by his chief minister, the vizier Imhotep. Imhotep's vision for his king's tomb was evolutionary rather than revolutionary, being a* development of the traditional mastaba tombs in which wealthy Egyptians were buried. Mastabas had the form of a rectangular platform. Imhotep simply stacked one mastaba on top of another to create a tomb of imposing majesty that far overshadowed those of his wealthiest subjects.

he then heightened by adding six further platforms, giving the building the stepped appearance from which it gets its popular name, the 'step pyramid'. A complex of stone buildings built around the pyramid contained a mortuary chapel where food and prayers were offered to the dead king, and a courtyard where the king could celebrate the *sed* festival. This was a ritual race which was run by the Egyptian kings in the 30th year of their reigns to show that they still had the vigour to rule. Djoser never undertook this: he died in the 19th year of his reign and was buried in a chamber under his pyramid. A mummified foot found in the burial chamber, which like almost all Egyptian royal tombs was robbed in antiquity, is thought to be all that remains of the king.

Before the construction of Djoser's pyramid complex, the Egyptians had no traditions of monumental stone architecture. The resources and labour needed to complete such an innovative project in what can have been no more than about 18 years must have been vast. That it was possible stands testimony to the power of the monarchy to command the resources and labour of the kingdom, and to the administrative efficiency of its civil servants.

c. 2600 BC

THE GIFT OF A VASE ✦ 'Mebaragesi *lugal* (king) of Kish'. This simple four-word inscription, marking a votive alabaster vase as the gift of a king, is the oldest royal inscription yet known from Mesopotamia. More, and longer, inscriptions soon followed, commemorating not only votive gifts but victories in battle, alliances, legislation and genealogies, providing the first information about political events in the region. Until this time, the rulers of the city states had remained anonymous: their names and actions went unrecorded. The appearance of royal inscriptions marks the emergence of dynasties of kings ruling over the city states, who saw a permanent record of their actions as a source of legitimacy.

The driver of this important change in government was probably increasing conflict between the Sumerian city states over resources, especially access to water. Under these circumstances, war leaders were able to achieve permanent power as kings. By usurping the *ensis'* role as intercessor with the city gods, the kings concentrated both military and religious authority in their own hands. Royal palaces were built next to the temples as a physical expression of the kings' close relationship to the gods. As usurpers, kings were understandably more anxious

OPPOSITE **The Sphinx at Giza.** *Sphinxes are mythical beasts with the body of a lion, a human head, and, in some cases, feathered wings. In ancient Greek mythology sphinxes were malevolent but in Egyptian and Mesopotamian traditions they were benevolent, protective, beings. In Egypt they were closely associated with the sun-god Ra. Because of their protective character, sculptures of sphinxes were commonly incorporated into temple complexes and tombs, and many pharaohs were portrayed as sphinxes. The most famous Egyptian sphinx is the Great Sphinx at Giza, thought to portray Khafre, builder of the second of the pyramids of Giza.*

to establish their legitimacy before their subjects and the gods. Kings needed to demonstrate to their subjects that, like the *ensis* they had sidelined, they ruled as servants of the gods. If things went well for the city and harvests were good, this proved that the gods were with the king, demonstrating his legitimacy. Any disaster – a flood, a failed harvest or a defeat in war – implied that the king did not enjoy divine favour, throwing his legitimacy into question. When a king placed an inscription on a temple offering, or on a statue of himself in respectful prayer, he was anxiously trying to make sure the gods did not forget how well he was serving them and abandon him.

c. 2550 BC

CONSTRUCTION OF THE GREAT PYRAMID ✦ Djoser's immediate successors built step pyramids. The first attempt to build a true pyramid was made in the reign of King Huni (*c.* 2599–*c.* 2575 BC). Built on poor foundations, it fell down. His successor, Snofru (*c.* 2575–*c.* 2551 BC), the founder of the Fourth Dynasty, was the first to build a true pyramid but only at his second attempt (his first attempt is the so-called 'bent pyramid' of Dahshur).

BELOW **The Great Pyramids of Khufu** *(right), Khafre (centre) and Menkaure (left) at Giza. Pyramids were originally encased in a gleaming shell of smooth white limestone. Only Khafre's pyramid retains any of its original casing; the rest was looted in the Middle Ages for the buildings of nearby Cairo. The three small pyramids were built for Menkaure's queens.*

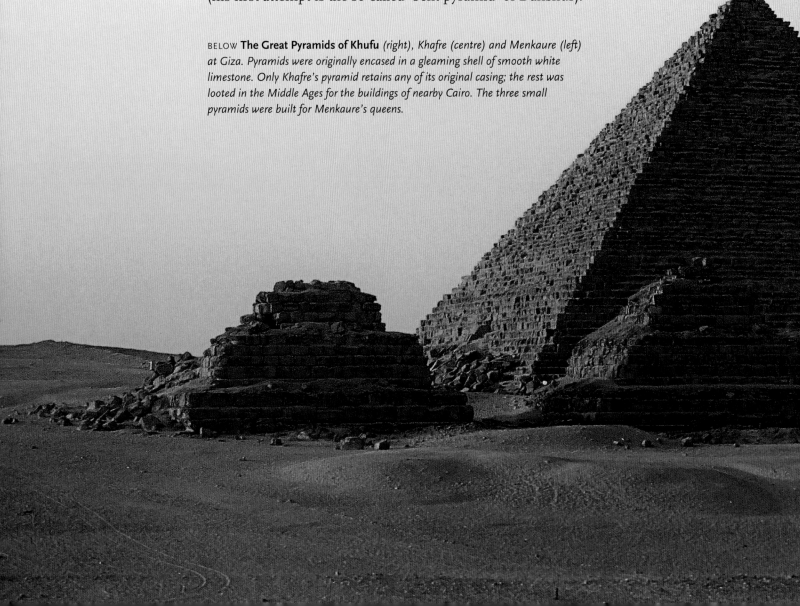

Pyramid building reached its climax under Snofru's son Khufu (r. *c.* 2551–*c.* 2528 BC), and his son and grandson Khafre (r. *c.* 2520–*c.* 2494 BC) and Menkaure (r. *c.* 2490–*c.* 2472 BC), who built the three great pyramids at Giza. At 146 metres (481 ft) high, Khufu's Great Pyramid remained the world's tallest human structure for over 3,800 years until it was finally overtopped by the 160-metre (524-ft) tall spire of Lincoln cathedral in 1311. It is estimated that Khufu's pyramid was built of about 2.5 million limestone blocks, each weighing on average 2.5 tons. A workforce of around 6,000 craftsmen and 20,000 conscripted labourers spent 20 years quarrying, shaping and moving the blocks into place using technology no more complex than stone hammers, soft copper chisels, sleds and levers. Khafre's pyramid is only slightly smaller than his father's at 135 metres (448 ft) high but it appears to be taller because it was built on higher ground. Menkaure's pyramid was a much more modest 70 metres (228 ft) tall, probably a sign that his father's and grandfather's vast pyramids had put a near intolerable strain on the kingdom's resources.

Khufu's Great Pyramid remained the world's tallest human structure for over 3,800 years until it was finally overtopped by the 160-metre (524-ft) spire of Lincoln cathedral in 1311.

Pyramids were associated with the cult of the sun god Ra, and their flared shape is believed to represent the rays of the sun up which the deceased king ascended to join the gods. If the pyramids offered the kings a route to immortality, it is far less obvious what was in it for the ordinary Egyptians who either worked directly on the pyramids, or who provided the supplies to feed the workers and paid taxes to fund it. However, Egyptians at this time believed that only the king was guaranteed an afterlife but that, as a god, he could grant an afterlife to his loyal subjects. By helping to ensure the king's immortality, the people, therefore, also helped ensure their own afterlives too.

c. 2400 BC

EANNATUM OF LAGASH CONQUERS UMMA ✦ As a result of conflicts over land and water, many of the smaller Sumerian cities had become tributaries of the larger cities and their kings had been demoted to governors. One of these conflicts, between the cities of Lagash and Umma, ran for over a century. Lagash's ultimate victory over Umma was commemorated by its triumphant king, Eannatum, in words and pictures on a monument known as the Vulture Stele, only fragments of which survive.

The stele has two sides, a 'historical' side and a 'mythological' side. The historical side shows scenes of battle against the rival city of Umma, with Eannatum leading a phalanx of helmeted spearmen; the king, again, leading a parade of warriors carrying battleaxes and spears in a four-wheeled chariot; vultures carrying off the heads of the slain; and the funeral ceremony of Lagash's fallen warriors. An inscription praises Eannatum's leadership and justifies his aggression on the grounds that Umma had seized some of Lagash's territory: 'Eannatum struck at Umma. The bodies were soon 3,600 in number ... I, Eannatum, like a fierce storm wind, I unleashed the tempest!' The mythological side of the stele shows Ningursu, the patron god of Lagash, symbolically slaughtering the city's enemies. A long inscription describes the peace agreement between the rulers of the two cities, their sacred oaths, and calls down the wrath of the gods upon Umma should it rebel.

OPPOSITE **King Menkaure.** *The slate sculpture portrays Menkaure wearing the white crown of Upper Egypt. He is flanked on his right by Hathor, the goddess of love and motherhood, wearing her symbols of cow's horns and a sun disc. To his left is a personification of Hathor's name with her standard over her head. The face of both representations of Hathor is that of Menkaure's queen Khamerernebty II.*

THE PYRAMID TEXTS

The Pyramid Texts are the world's oldest religious literature. They are collections
of spells which were carved on the walls of royal tombs and sarcophagi to reanimate
the king's body after his death and to protect and guide him as he made the
perilous ascent to join the gods in heaven.

The oldest of the texts date to *c.* 2345 BC and their
archaic language makes them difficult to interpret.
Originally exclusively for the use of the king, after
the end of the Old Kingdom the texts evolved into
the 'Book of the Dead', which guided all Egyptians
to the afterlife.

A spell to protect the deceased on his journey to the sky

28 *Thou hast thine heart Osiris* [the god of the afterlife];
thou hast they feet, Osiris; thou hast thine arm, Osiris.
He [the king] *hath his own heart; he hath his own feet;*
he hath his own arm. A ramp to the sky is built for him,
that he may go up to the sky thereon. He goeth upon the
smoke of the great exhalation [incense]. *He flieth as a*
bird, and he settleth as a beetle on an empty seat that is
the ship of Ra [the sun god]: *'Stand up, get thee*

forth, thou without … that he may sit in thy seat.
He roweth in the sky within thy ship, O Ra, and he
cometh to land in thy ship, O Ra. When thou ascendest
out of the horizon, he is there with his staff in his hand,
the navigator of thy ship, O Ra. Thou mountest up to
sky and art far from the earth.

TRANS. FROM *THE LITERATURE OF THE ANCIENT EGYPTIANS*
BY ADOLF ERMAN.

ABOVE **Part of a hieroglyphic funerary inscription** *from the tomb*
of Irukaptah, Sakkara.

OPPOSITE **Pyramid texts.** *The tomb chamber in the pyramid of King*
Unas (r. 2375–2345 BC) is inscribed with the Pyramid texts. The world's
oldest known religious literature, the texts are a collection of prayers
and spells to protect and guide the king to his afterlife with the gods.
The texts evolved into the 'Book of the Dead', which guided everyone's
souls to the afterlife.

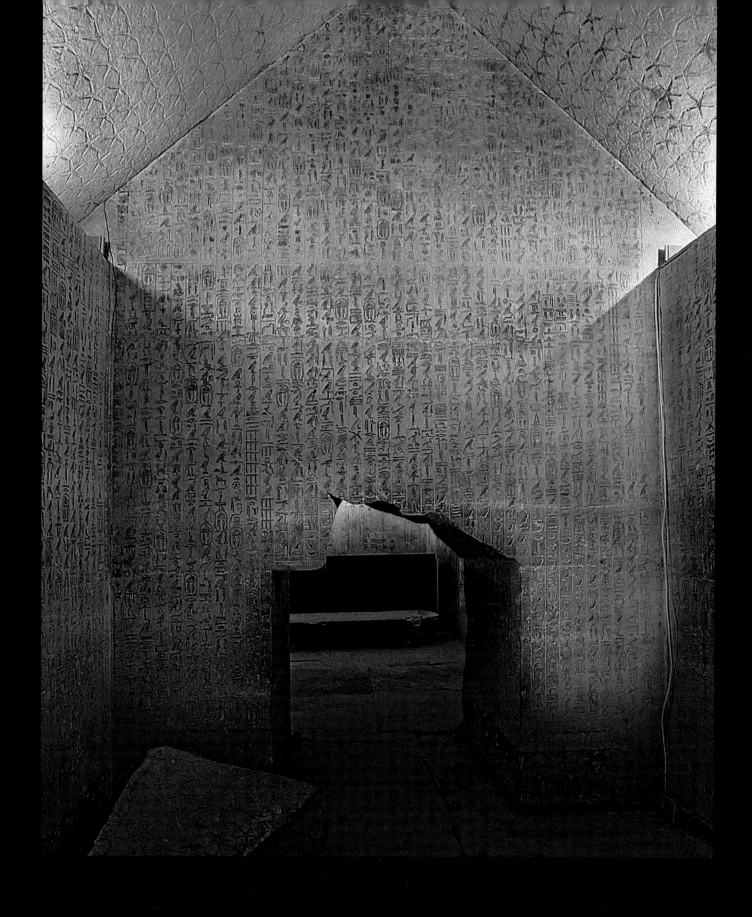

c. 2360 BC

THE EARLIEST KNOWN LAW CODE ✦ Laws and customs to regulate social behaviour and avoid, or resolve, conflicts of interest are universal to all human societies. In preliterate societies, laws and customs were committed to memory and passed down by word of mouth from one generation to another. The size and complexity of urbanized civilizations greatly increased the possibilities of social conflict and required rulers to take a much more formal role in law-giving. The earliest known manifestation of this is the law code issued by King Urukagina of Lagash *c.* 2360 BC. No contemporary copy of Urukagina's code has survived but it is known from extracts preserved in later Mesopotamian law codes.

Urukagina was concerned to prevent the exploitation of the poor by the rich in an increasingly unequal society. One of his laws decrees that the rich must pay in silver when buying from the poor. Another decrees that the rich cannot force the poor to sell their land, livestock, grain or other food against their will. Poor families who had been enslaved by the rich because of debt were freed. Widows and orphans were exempted from taxes. To prevent exploitation by the priesthood, the funeral expenses of the poor were to be paid for by the city, including the cost of the ritual offerings of food and drink for the deceased's journey into the underworld. The humanity of Urukagina's laws extended to punishment, and the death penalty

LEFT **The Vulture Stele of King Eannatum.** *Detail of a stele celebrating the conquest of the Sumerian city of Umma by King Eannatum of Lagash, showing a phalanx of helmeted spearmen on the march (c. 2400 BC). The soldiers' main weapons are spears and axes. They wear helmets of metal or perhaps leather, and shaggy sheepskin skirts.*

was rarely applied. Other measures dealt with corrupt practices by palace officials. Urukagina addressed his laws not to his subjects but to Ningursu, Lagash's patron deity. Justice pleased the gods, and the gods in turn would support the just king.

c. 2350 BC

TO THE EDGE OF THE WORLD ✦ The age of the independent Sumerian city states was brought to an end by Lugalzagesi, the king of Uruk, who overthrew Urukagina of Lagash and went on to conquer the rest of Sumer. Lugalzagesi's power was not confined to Sumer. One of his campaigns took him northwest along the Euphrates River before crossing the Syrian desert to reach the coast of the Mediterranean Sea, which was considered by the Sumerians to be the edge of the world.

c. 2334 BC

SARGON THE GREAT BECOMES KING OF AKKAD ✦ Lugalzagesi's career of conquest was brought to an abrupt end by Sargon the Great. Sargon was the king of Akkad (or Agade), a city in central Mesopotamia whose exact location has never been identified: ancient sources describe it as being 'in front of' Babylon. Later legend supplied Sargon with a suitably noble pedigree but he was in fact a usurper, a high official who seized the throne of Kish from his employer King Ur-Zababa and then moved his capital to Akkad. Because Sargon's name (Šarru-kīnu) means 'the true king' it was probably not his birth name but one he

31

ABOVE **Vase of Entemena.** *This silver vase was dedicated to the Sumerian storm god Ningursu by Entemena, the second successor to Eannatum as ruler of Lagash. The vase is decorated with images of the thunderbird, which was closely associated with Ningursu.*

OVERLEAF **Sumeria at war.** *Scene from the so-called 'Standard of Ur', actually the sound box of a musical instrument, found in a grave in the Royal Cemetery of Ur. The scene, made from shell, red limestone and lapis lazuli set in bitumen, shows a king (centre of the top tier) leading his army to war. On the lower tier, in the earliest representation of wheeled vehicles being used in warfare, vanquished enemies are shown being crushed under the solid wooden wheels of war wagons drawn by teams of asses.*

adopted to establish his legitimacy after his usurpation. Sargon's first conquest was Lugalzagesi's Uruk, after which he imposed his rule on all of Sumer. Lugalzagesi was led off into captivity wearing a wooden collar. Sargon then campaigned in the east, conquering Elam (approximately Khuzestan in southern Iran) and parts of the Iranian plateau. Next, Sargon followed Lugalzagesi's route north, conquering the cities of Mari and Ebla in Syria, the 'Cedar Forest' (the Lebanon Mountains) and the 'Silver Mountains' (the Taurus Mountains in southern Turkey). Sargon died *c.* 2278 and was succeeded in turn by his sons Rimush (r. *c.* 2278–2270 BC) and Manishtushu (r. *c.* 2269–2255 BC), both of whom were able soldiers like their father.

Sargon's conquests created a new type of state: an empire – a multi-ethnic hegemonic state. As Sargon lacked the resources and administrative expertise to impose direct rule throughout his empire, conquered kings were demoted to vassals and required to pay annual tribute to Akkad. This form of overrule, which remained typical of Mesopotamian empires for the next 1,500 years, was inherently weak. Empires could expand rapidly under strong military kings who could enforce the obedience of their vassals. Vassals contributed troops and supplies for further campaigns, feeding more conquests. If a weak king came to the throne, however, it was easy for vassals to declare independence and stop paying tribute. Deprived of the tribute which sustained it, the empire quickly crumbled.

Sargon's career is the first sign of a shift in the balance of power in Mesopotamia towards the north. Through the third millennium new city states arose in central

34

ABOVE **Sargon the Great.** *Cast copper sculpture from Nineveh thought to depict the Akkadian king Sargon the Great or his grandson Naram-Sin (late third millennium BC). The sculpture shows the great care Mesopotamian men took of their beards, oiling them and styling them by using tongs and curling irons to create ringlets and layered patterns.*

THE BABYLONIAN LEGEND OF SARGON

Sargon the mighty, king of Akkad, am I. *My mother was an en-priestess, I never knew my father. My father's brother lives in the highlands. My home city is Azupiranu [not a real city], which lies on the bank of the Euphrates. She conceived me, my en-priestess mother, and secretly gave birth to me, set me in a wicker basket made watertight with bitumen. She cast me into the river, from which I could not get out. The river bore me away, carrying me to Akki the water drawer. Akki the water drawer when lowering his bucket lifted me up. Akki the water drawer raised me as his adopted son. Akki the water drawer set me to work with him as a gardener. While I was still a gardener, the goddess Ishtar grew fond of me. And so for 44 years I reigned as king, ruling and governing over the black-headed people [the Sumerians].*

AUTHOR'S OWN REWRITING OF THE TEXT BASED ON COMPARISON OF THREE DIFFERENT TRANSLATIONS

and northern Mesopotamia. These states were greatly influenced by Sumerian culture, adopting their writing systems, gods, mythology and political ideologies, but their inhabitants spoke Semitic languages related to Hebrew and Arabic. Sargon showed respect for Sumerian culture, using Sumerian and his own Semitic Akkadian language side-by-side in his inscriptions, but it would be the Semitic languages which prevailed in the long term.

c. 2254 BC

NARAM-SIN THE GOD-KING ✦ The Akkadian empire reached its peak under Sargon's grandson, Naram-Sin, who became king around 2254 BC. Mesopotamian kings claimed to rule as agents of the gods but this was not enough for Naram-Sin. He declared that he actually was a god and adopted the hubristic title 'king of the four quarters, king of the universe'. On his commemorative steles he was portrayed wearing horns, a symbol of divinity in Mesopotamian art. According to later Mesopotamian tradition Naram-Sin's presumptuousness offended Enlil, the god who granted kingly authority, who sent hordes of Gutian tribesmen from the Zagros mountains to the east to ravage Mesopotamia, causing his empire to collapse. It is true that no later Mesopotamian king ever claimed to be a god but in reality Naram-Sin defeated the Gutian invasions and passed on his empire intact to his son Shar-Kali-Shari when he died in *c.* 2217 BC.

Deprived of the tribute which sustained it, the empire quickly crumbled.

35

c. 2244 BC

KING PEPI'S PET DWARF ✦ After the construction of the great pyramids of Giza the authority of the Egyptian kings entered a slow decline. Royal wealth was steadily depleted by the luxuries placed in royal tombs for the king to enjoy in the afterlife and the land which was granted to the mortuary temples, where regular offerings were made, again for the kings to enjoy in the afterlife. As royal authority declined power became increasingly decentralized to local governors called nomarchs (from *nome* – a province) and other nobles who used their newfound wealth to build lavish tombs for themselves. Proud of their achievements, these nouveau riche inscribed their autobiographies on the walls of their tombs, providing the earliest accounts of the lives of non-royal people. One of these self-commemorating nobles was Harkhuf, a caravan leader from Aswan on Egypt's southern border. Harkhuf led armed trading expeditions south into Nubia and Darfur to find gold, ebony, ivory, incense and slaves. None of these was more valuable than a dwarf Harkhuf captured during an expedition to Darfur in the second year of the 94-year-long reign of King Pepi II (he came to the throne aged six and lived to be 100). A good judge of character, Harkhuf sent word ahead to the royal court at Memphis to tell the young king about the dwarf. Delighted, the young king sent word back ordering that the greatest care be taken of the dwarf. As Harkhuf's ship sailed down the Nile towards Memphis, the dwarf was given a chaperone to make sure he did not fall overboard and get eaten by a crocodile. Attendants checked on him ten times a night to make sure no harm came to him. Pepi was delighted by the dwarf but it is not recorded how long he continued to live his pampered life before the king lost interest in his new pet.

Mesopotamian kings claimed to rule as agents of the gods but this was not enough for Naram-Sin. He declared that he actually was a god and adopted the hubristic title 'king of the four quarters, king of the universe'.

c. 2193 BC

FALL OF THE AKKADIAN EMPIRE ✦ Shar-Kali-Shari's reign was one of mounting troubles, with continuous attacks by the Gutians and rebellions against the high taxes which were imposed to pay for the defence of the empire. The final straw was probably a long drought which began c. 2200 BC, causing a devastating famine and the complete abandonment of some cities. A Sumerian poem called 'The Curse of Agade' describes the sufferings of the people: 'For the first time since cities were built, the fields produced no grain. ... He who slept on the roof, died on the roof. He who slept in the house had no burial, the people flailed at themselves in hunger.' Following Shar-Kali-Shari's death in c. 2193 BC Mesopotamia collapsed into 80 years of political anarchy. No king was able to keep his throne for long before he was overthrown by a usurper, prompting a Sumerian chronicler to ask 'Who was king? Who was not king?' Akkad did not long survive the end of its empire. Deserted, its mud-brick buildings crumbled to dust and even its site was forgotten; the memory of the empire survived, however, to inspire later generations of Mesopotamian conquerors.

RIGHT **Golden falcon.** *This Old Kingdom period golden falcon's head from Hierakonpolis in Upper Egypt represents the sky god Horus. The early kings of Egypt were regarded as incarnations of Horus but during the Old Kingdom this belief was superseded by the belief that the king was an incarnation of the sun god Ra. The falcon is wearing a crown with the uraeus, the rearing cobra, which was a symbol of royal authority.*

Following Pepi's death in 2152 BC, his son Merenre II reigned for little more than a year before he was murdered. Chaos followed. Seventy kings are said to have reigned in as many days. Pyramid building ceased.

c. 2150 BC

FAMINE IN EGYPT ✦ Mesopotamia was not the only area to experience a devastating famine in the years around 2200 BC. Relief carvings showing emaciated people and animals made during the long reign of Pepi II show that Egypt too was suffering. Ancient Egypt depended entirely on the annual flood of the Nile, which rose at the beginning of August, following summer rains in the East African highlands, and fell in the autumn leaving the fields moist and fertilized by fresh silt. Under normal circumstances Egypt had the most productive agriculture in the ancient world. However, if the summer rains failed, the Nile would not flood and famine would afflict the land. Egyptian kings gained authority from the belief that they were divine and could summon the flood. A succession of low floods could, therefore, damage a king's authority because it was a sign that he had lost the favour of the gods. Pepi's authority had not been strong to begin with and it could not survive starvation on this scale. As he aged he gradually became an irrelevance as the nomarchs became, in effect, independent rulers. Following Pepi's death in 2152 BC, his son Merenre II reigned for little more than a year before he was murdered. Chaos followed. Seventy kings are said to have reigned in as many days. Pyramid building ceased. Finally, around 2134 BC Egypt broke up into rival states, bringing the Old Kingdom period to an end.

2112 BC

SUMERIAN RENAISSANCE ✦ While Egypt tore itself apart, political stability was returning to Mesopotamia under Ur-Nammu (r. 2112–2095 BC), king of the Sumerian city of Ur. Ur-Nammu was originally the governor of Ur, appointed by Utuhegal of Uruk, the king who finally ended the Gutian threat to Mesopotamia. When Utuhegal drowned in an accident,

LEFT **Boy king with his mother.** *Calcite statuette showing the young king Pepi II sitting on the knees of his mother, queen Meryreankhnes. Pepi's reign was the longest in Egyptian history: he came to the throne around 2246 BC and lived to be 100 years old. Disastrous famines afflicted the later years of his reign and after his death in 2152 BC royal authority collapsed.*

Ur-Nammu declared independence and became king of Ur. Ur-Nammu subsequently built an empire which comprised all of Sumer and extended into northern Mesopotamia and east into Elam. Conquest certainly played a part in Ur-Nammu's empire building but his own inscriptions give the impression that diplomacy and marriage alliances also played a big part. He also made much of Ur's importance as a cult centre of the moon god Nanna. Ur-Nammu's most important legacy was the ziggurat he built in honour of Nanna at Ur. Among the most distinctive of Mesopotamian monuments, ziggurats are elevated temple platforms. Ziggurats may have been built before Ur-Nammu's reign but his is the oldest to have survived. Because the Mesopotamians built mainly in mud brick, time has not been kind to the ziggurats. Once they fell out of use in the last centuries BC, they gradually crumbled into undistinguished piles of mud and dust.

ABOVE **Reconstruction of the ziggurat of Ur.** *Now reduced by wind and rain to undistinguished piles of mud and dust, in their heyday Mesopotamian ziggurats were impressive buildings, rivalling the pyramids of Egypt in size. When built c. 2100 BC, the ziggurat of Ur consisted of three tiers rising over 100 feet above the surrounding town which it would have dominated. When restored in the 5th century BC by the Babylonian king Nabonidus another four tiers were added. The temple on the highest tier was dedicated to Ur's patron deity, the moon god Nanna, whose home it was.*

FAMINE IN EGYPT

I arrived in Lower Egypt and collected as much food as I could for you. The Nile, is it not in fact very low? Alas, the food I have collected is in proportion to the flood. Here, they have even begun to eat people. There is no one anywhere to whom nourishment is given. You must hold out until I return. I intend to spend the season of shemu [March–July] here.

Letter of the priest Heqanakte to his family in Thebes. Adapted from Breasted v. 1

2040 BC

EGYPT REUNITED ✦ As in Narmer's time, Egypt was reunified from the south. After Egypt split up in 2134 BC, Lower Egypt came under the control of a weak royal dynasty which based itself at Herakleopolis. Around the same time Intef, the nomarch of Thebes, claimed the title of king of Upper Egypt. In reality, he controlled little more than Thebes itself. However, Intef's successors gradually pushed their frontier north, battling independent nomarchs and the Herakleopolitan kings while building up a strong central government for their own kingdom. By 2060 BC, when Mentuhotep II (r. 2060–2010 BC) became king, the Theban dynasty truly did control all of Upper Egypt. Mentuhotep's reign began with a setback following the rebellion of the nomarch of Abydos. After Mentuhotep crushed the rebellion he embarked on a succession of campaigns against the Herakleopolitans, which ended with reunification of the whole of Egypt in 2040 BC, an event which marks the foundation of the Middle Kingdom. Mentuhotep marked his victory by adopting the title 'Uniter of the Two Lands'. A model army of wooden figurines of Egyptian spearmen and Nubian archers found in the tomb of Mesehti, one of Mentuhotep's generals, typifies the martial spirit of the age. A mass tomb discovered in the 1920s close to Mentuhotep's temple at Thebes containing the remains of 60 soldiers who were killed in battle in Nubia is one of the earliest known war cemeteries. The later years of Mentuhotep's 50-year reign were peaceful and saw prosperity return to Egypt after the long years of warfare.

2004 BC

THE ELAMITES SACK UR ✦ The destruction of their city's temple was the most terrible calamity that could befall ancient Mesopotamians as it was believed that the gods literally dwelt there. If a temple was destroyed, its god was rendered homeless and was forced to abandon the city and its people. Without their god's protection, what would become of them? In wars between Mesopotamian states,

OPPOSITE **King of Ur.** *Cast copper foundation figurine of King Amar-Sin of Ur (r. 2046–2038 BC) carrying a basket of building materials on his head. Sumerians rulers placed such figurines, which probably symbolically represented the king laying the first brick, in the foundations of new temples. Amar-Sin was the grandson of Ur-Nammu, the founder of the Sumerian renaissance. Amar-Sin was remembered as a particularly active builder, commissioning the restoration of many ancient Sumerian monuments, including at the city of Eridu, which Sumerians believed was the place where the god Enki had created the world.*

kings respected the gods of rival states, for fear of provoking their anger, and even embellished the temples of conquered cities. This was a highly political act, a direct appeal by the conqueror for the god to legitimize his rule through signs of divine favour, and a visible reminder to the conquered people of their subjection. The peoples who lived in the regions neighbouring Mesopotamia felt no such restraints however. In 2004 BC an army of Elamites, from the Khuzestan region of southwest Iran, invaded, captured and sacked Ur after a long siege. The victors killed or enslaved many of the city's people and left its temples in ruins. Ur's empire collapsed after the Elamite attack and no Sumerian city ever again achieved such a position of political dominance in Mesopotamia. Within 200 years, power had shifted irrevocably to the north.

Sumeria's failure to recover from the Elamite invasion was due to long-term environmental degradation caused by poor irrigation practices. As irrigation water evaporated from the fields under the hot Mesopotamian sun, it left behind mineral salts which, because of the low natural

THE RUINS OF UR

Your city which has been made into ruins –
    you are no longer its mistress,
Your righteous house which has been given
    over to the pickaxe – you no longer inhabit it,
Your people who have been led to slaughter –
    you are no longer their queen.

LAMENTATION OVER THE DESTRUCTION OF UR, ADDRESSED TO THE GODDESS NINGAL, THE WIFE OF UR'S PATRON DEITY, THE MOON GOD NANNA, WHOSE TEMPLE WAS ONE OF THOSE DESTROYED IN THE ELAMITE ATTACK rainfall, built up in the soil, gradually destroying its fertility. This was a slow-motion disaster, taking centuries to run its course. The Sumerians responded to declining fertility by introducing salt-tolerant strains of wheat and increasing cultivation of date palms, which are also salt-tolerant. However, as yields continued to decline Sumeria slowly became less and less able to support dense urban populations. By around the time of Christ, most Sumerian cities had been abandoned and their fields had reverted to desert. With its higher natural rainfall, farmers in central and northern Mesopotamia did not rely so heavily on irrigation and so did not suffer the same problems. The cities in these areas continued to grow, overtaking those in Sumeria in size and wealth by the beginning of the second millennium BC.

ABOVE **Royal helmet.** *This golden ceremonial helmet belonged to Meskalamdug, an early king of Ur who ruled sometime around the 25th century BC. It is just one of many gold objects discovered in the king's tomb in the Royal Cemetery of Ur when it was excavated by* the pioneering British archaeologist Leonard Wooley in 1924. Meskalamdug's name is known only from inscriptions in the helmet, a golden bowl placed in the king's hands when he was buried, and a single bead found in the northern Mesopotamian city of Mari.

LEFT **Ram in a thicket (*c.* 2500 BC).** *One of a pair of gilded goats found in the 'Great Death Pit' at the Royal Cemetery of Ur. The figures were made of gilded wood with decorations of lapis lazuli, shell, and red limestone. Unusually for Mesopotamia, this grave contained the remains of 74 servants who were drugged and killed before being buried with their ruler, whose name is unknown.*

THE
WIDENING
WORLD

2000–1000 BC

Civilizations exert a powerful influence on their neighbours through war, trade, migration and other social contacts. Between 2000 BC and 1000 BC the influence of the Mesopotamian and Egyptian civilizations began to spread throughout the Middle East and even across the Mediterranean Sea to Europe. The Minoan civilization flourished on Crete until conquered by the younger Mycenaean civilization of the Greek mainland.

In the Middle East, Sumeria declined and was overshadowed by the new Mesopotamian powers of Babylon and Assyria, and the Hittite empire of Anatolia. Egypt reached the height of its power. Yet civilizations fall as well as rise. Towards the end of the period waves of migrations caused economic and political dislocation across the region. Greece fell into a 'dark age' for hundreds of years, the Hittite empire collapsed, Babylon and Assyria battled migrating desert tribes, and, in Egypt, the power of the pharaohs was shattered and never recovered.

c. 2000 BC

PALACES OF CRETE ✦ Europe's earliest civilization, the Minoan, developed on the mountainous Aegean island of Crete. The beginning of the civilization, named for Minos, a legendary king of Crete, was marked by the building of palaces at Knossos, Phaistos, Mallia and Khania *c.* 2000 BC, each of which was the capital of a small kingdom. Unlike Egypt and Mesopotamia, Crete had no fertile flood plains or great rivers which could be tapped for irrigation. Cretan farming was based on the 'Mediterranean triad' of wheat, olives and vines. Olives and vines grew well on Crete's rough mountainsides

46

PREVIOUS PAGES **Might personified.** *Detail of a monumental statue of the Egyptian pharaoh Ramesses II 'the Great' (r. 1290–1224 BC) from the great temple of Luxor. A consummate self-publicist, Ramesses also commissioned the famous temples at Abu Simbel (see p. 77).*

LEFT **Snake goddess.** *Discovered during excavations of the Minoan palace of Knossos, this figurine has been variously interpreted as a priestess or a fertility goddess. In the eastern Mediterranean, snakes were often seen as symbols of renewal and rebirth because they periodically shed their skin.*

OPPOSITE **Palace of Knossos.** *At its peak in c.1700–1400 BC the Minoan palace at Knossos, Crete, covered 6 acres (24,000 square metres) and contained over 1,300 rooms connected by a maze of passages. The palace was decorated with brightly coloured frescoes.*

and produced two valuable and easily stored commodities – olive oil and wine – that were traded with Egypt and other places around the Mediterranean. The small areas of fertile valley land were used for growing wheat, while flocks of sheep kept on the island's extensive mountain pastures inspired a flourishing textile industry supplying Egyptian markets.

As well as being residences for rulers, Minoan palaces were religious, economic and administrative centres, with shrines, audience chambers and storerooms where food surpluses and trade goods were gathered for redistribution. The palaces' great central courtyards were used for communal feasts and religious rituals, including a bull-leaping ceremony. The size and complexity of the palaces is thought to have given rise to the Greek legend of the Labyrinth in which King Minos kept the Minotaur, a monster that was half-human and half-bull. For administration, the Minoans used a hieroglyphic script and a simpler consonantal script known as Linear A. Neither has been deciphered, suggesting that the Minoans spoke a language unrelated to other known languages.

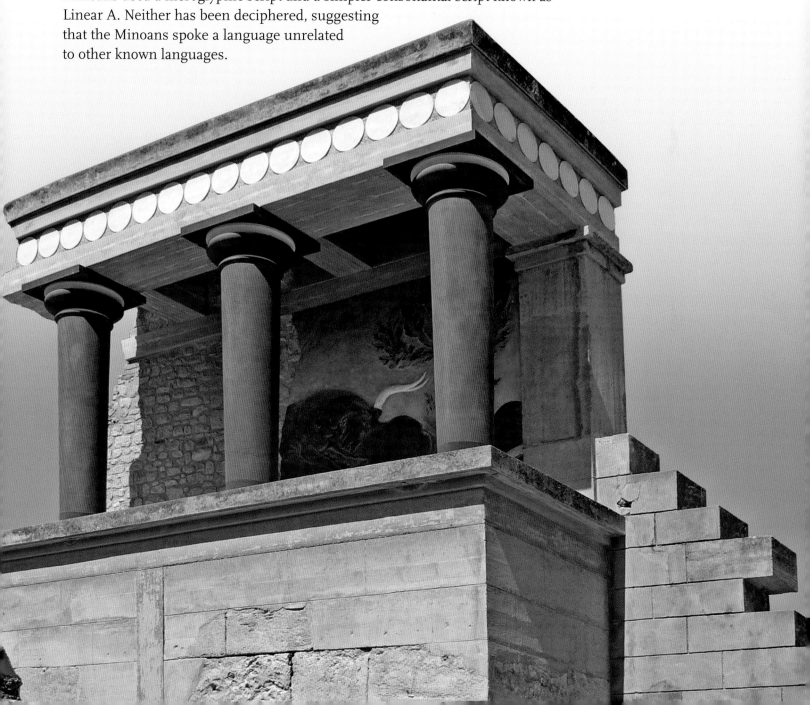

CALENDARS AND CHRONOLOGIES

Ancient Mesopotamians used a calendar based on a year of 12 lunar months (28–9 days each). Each month began with the first sighting of the crescent of the new moon. The first month of the year was Nisannu, which fell in March or April.

Because the lunar year has only 354 days the calendar slipped out of line with the seasons by 11 days every year. Many Mesopotamian festivals were linked to events in the agricultural cycle, so a thirteenth month was intercalated every few years to stop the lunar year falling too far behind the solar year. The ancient Egyptians used a calendar based on 12 months of 30 days each plus five extra days at the end of the year to keep it in line with the seasons. The Egyptian year began with the heliacal rising of the star Sothis (Sirius) at the beginning of August, which heralded the all-important Nile flood.

Both the Mesopotamians and the Egyptians lacked fixed points, such as the birth of Christ in the Christian calendar, for dating events. Events were normally dated with reference to the accession of the reigning king. Remarkably complete king lists survive for both Egypt and Mesopotamia going right back into the third millennium BC, but the lengths of their reigns were not always recorded. This means that, though the relative chronology of recorded events is known, historians face great difficulties establishing an absolute chronology. Because of the uncertainties historians have calculated several different chronologies for both ancient Mesopotamia and ancient Egypt. There are four chronologies in use by historians of ancient Mesopotamia, all of them calculated from observations of the planet Venus recorded in the eighth year of the reign of King Ammisaduqa of Babylon. These fix the date of the king's accession to either 1702 ('high'), 1646 ('middle'), 1582 ('low') or 1550 BC ('ultra low'). The most widely used, and the one used here, is the 'middle' chronology. The chronology used for ancient Egypt is the one known as the 'conventional chronology', which has been compiled from ancient king lists. Dates are only known precisely from 664 BC. From the beginning of the New Kingdom period (c. 1532 BC) until 664 BC there is a margin of error of up to about ten years either way. Moving back in time from the beginning of the New Kingdom period, the margin for error gradually widens and could be as much as 150 years during the Early Dynastic period.

LEFT **Egyptian Zodiac.** *A low relief carving showing the 12 constellations of the zodiac from a chapel dedicated to the underworld god Osiris at Dendera in Egypt. The heavens are shown supported by the four pillars of the sky, depicted as women, and falcon-headed spirits, probably representing the sky-god Horus. Along the rim of the circle are 36 spirits representing the 360 days (which were grouped into 'weeks' of ten days) of the Egyptian lunar year. The relief dates to c. 50 BC.*

1962 BC

DEATH ON THE NILE ✦ The early Middle Kingdom saw its share of coups and attempted coups. In 1962 BC King Amenhemet I, a former official who had overthrown King Mentuhotep III in a military coup in 1991 BC, was murdered by his bodyguard as he slept. Despite the death of the king, the plot, hatched by the palace women and a number of courtiers, failed. To ensure a smooth succession to the throne, Amenhemet had made his son Senusret I co-ruler in 1971 BC. While Amenhemet concentrated on administration, the younger man led Egypt's armies in campaigns in Nubia and Libya. At the time of the attempted coup Senusret was away with an army fighting in Libya. When a loyal messenger brought news of his father's murder, Senusret hurried back to the capital with a small following, restored order and ensured that his father received a proper burial in the pyramid he had built at Lisht.

In a story known as *The Instructions of Amenhemet*, which was written during Senusret's reign, Amenhemet's ghost visits his son to give him advice on rulership and describe his murder:

> *It was after supper, when night had fallen. I sought rest for I was weary. I lay on my bed, gave my thoughts release and so I fell asleep. The rebels began to whisper and take arms, intending treachery. I awoke to the sound of fighting and like the desert serpent I waited there, motionless but alert. The attack was led by the captain of my bodyguard. If I had quickly taken weapons in my hand, I would have made the wretches retreat with a charge! But no one is mighty in the night, no one can fight alone; no success will come without a helper. Look, my injury happened while I was without you, when the entourage had not yet heard that I would hand over to you ... I did not foresee it, and my heart had not taken thought of the disloyalty of servants.*

ADAPTED FROM BREASTED V. I

49

RIGHT **Bull-leaping competition.** *Bulls appear to have played an important part in Minoan religion. Several frescoes in the Minoan palace at Knossos depict youths in a bull-leaping competition or ritual which involved the participant grasping a charging bull by the horns, vaulting over its back, and landing neatly on his feet behind it. This fresco dates to c. 1450–1375 BC.*

1878 BC

A GOOD SHEPHERD ✦ Egypt's Middle Kingdom rulers laid less emphasis than their Old Kingdom predecessors on grand monuments to secure their immortality. The chaos at the end of the Old Kingdom damaged the prestige of the monarchy. The king was still seen as a god on earth but Egyptians no longer believed that he alone was guaranteed an afterlife. During late Old Kingdom times the worship of Osiris, the god of fertility and the ruler of the underworld, became popular. Osiris did not expect moral perfection from his followers. The souls of irredeemably wicked people would be consumed by the demon Ammut but all others could expect a blissful afterlife in the 'Field of Reeds', a lush paradise beyond the western horizon. All that was needed was to follow the correct burial practices and to possess the right spells for the soul to complete the journey through the underworld. Although Middle Kingdom rulers continued to be buried under pyramids, these were comparatively modest affairs, built with a core of cheap mud brick and only a veneer of stone on the outside. Middle Kingdom rulers instead rebuilt the status of the monarchy by directing resources towards the earthly welfare of their subjects through agricultural improvements such as the great Bahr Yusuf canal, which diverted Nile waters into the Faiyum Depression. Beginning with the accession of Senusret III in 1878 BC Middle Kingdom rulers adopted a new iconography. Gone was the bland god-like serenity of the Old Kingdom rulers' portrait sculptures, replaced by careworn expressions. The king was now the good shepherd, shouldering the heavy burden of caring for his people's welfare.

> *Osiris did not expect moral perfection from his followers. The souls of irredeemably wicked people would be consumed by the demon Ammut but all others could expect a blissful afterlife in the 'Field of Reeds'.*

c. 1862 BC

EGYPT CONQUERS NUBIA ✦ The traditional southern frontier of ancient Egypt was at the First Cataract (a series of difficult-to-navigate rapids and shoals) of the Nile at Aswan. To the south was Nubia, now part of Sudan, which the Egyptians also knew as Kush. The people of Nubia were black Africans whose culture was heavily influenced by Egypt's. During the Old Kingdom period, Egyptian expeditions, such as those led by Harkhuf (see p. 36), plundered

OPPOSITE **The burden of kingship.** *Egypt's Middle Kingdom rulers rebuilt the monarchy's shattered authority by demonstrating their commitment to their subjects' welfare both in public works and iconography. This granite sculpture of Senusret III (r. 1878–1841 BC)* *depicts the king as a serious and thoughtful man, wearied by his heavy responsibilities. A good soldier, Senusret spent much of his reign campaigning successfully in Nubia, using the loot to restore temples neglected since the fall of the Old Kingdom.*

Nubia's resources at will. Following the fall of the Old Kingdom, a Nubian kingdom developed based on the city of Kerma, near the Third Cataract of the Nile. Middle Kingdom rulers reacted with campaigns of conquest to seize direct control of Nubian resources. These campaigns culminated in the reign of Senusret III, with the conquest of all of Lower Nubia (the area between the First and Second Cataracts of the Nile). A chain of over a dozen forts were built to defend the newly conquered lands. Senusret erected a commemorative stele at Semna, south of the Second Cataract, boasting of his conquests and exhorting his successors to defend them.

c. 1813 BC

THE BIRTH OF ASSYRIA ✦ In the period of weakness following the fall of Ur in 2004 BC, Amorite tribes from the Syrian desert seized control of many Mesopotamian cities. It was under Amorite rulers that Assyria and Babylon, the two kingdoms whose rivalry was to dominate much of the next 1,200 years of Mesopotamian history, first came to prominence. Ashur, the main city of Assyria, was a prosperous trade centre when it came under the rule of the Amorite Shamshi-Adad in c. 1813 BC. An excellent soldier and administrator, Shamshi-Adad was the younger son of an Amorite king from western Syria. Excluded from succession to his father's kingdom, Shamshi-Adad conquered his own. First seizing the city of Shubat-Enlil (Tell Lailan) in northern Syria, he used this as a base to conquer Ashur and the equally prosperous city of Mari on the Euphrates. Further campaigns extended his power to almost all of northern Mesopotamia. Shamshi-Adad shared power with his two sons. The elder, Ishme-Dagan, a good soldier who made his father proud, was given Assyria to rule; the younger, the petulant and immature Yasmah-Addu, was given Mari, where he soon immersed himself in the pleasures of wine and women and outraged his father by his neglect of government. Neither son prospered after their father's death in c. 1781 BC. Yasmah-Addu was soon expelled from Mari by its former ruler Zimri-Lim. More surprisingly, Ishme-Dagan failed to live up to his early promise and held on to Assyria for only about 11 years before he was expelled by the powerful Babylonian king Hammurabi. Assyria was reduced to a minor kingdom until the 14th century BC when its power recovered under a series of able kings who consciously emulated Shamshi-Adad's example of strong military rulership.

1792 BC

HAMMURABI BECOMES KING OF BABYLON ✦ Babylon was a minor city in central Mesopotamia when it came under Amorite rule c. 1894 BC. Its rise to become one of the great powers of the ancient world was due entirely to its sixth Amorite ruler, Hammurabi (c. 1792–1750 BC). When Hammurabi inherited the

ABOVE **Dancing girls.** Ancient Egyptians of all classes wore the minimum of clothing. Men typically wore only a simple linen skirt and went bare-chested and bare-foot, while women wore light ankle length linen sheath dresses held up by one or two shoulder straps. Cloth was rarely dyed. Children went naked until puberty and female dancers commonly performed nude, as depicted in this 14th-century BC fresco. Egyptians of both sexes wore make-up, and shaved their bodies and heads and wore elaborate wigs instead. This arose from the belief that hair was appropriate only to animals, not humans.

throne from his father Sin-Muballit *c.* 1792 he did so as a vassal of Shamshi-Adad. To the south was another powerful ruler, Rim-Sin (r. 1822–1763 BC) of Larsa, who dominated Sumeria. It was against Rim-Sin that Hammurabi won his first victory when, early in his reign, he seized the Sumerian cities of Isin and Uruk. For the next 20 years Hammurabi concentrated on improving his kingdom's defence and irrigation systems, and on building diplomatic alliances with neighbouring rulers. After the death of Shamshi-Adad in 1781 BC, Zimri-Lim of Mari supported Hammurabi in his wars with Ishme-Dagan, the rival city of

THE LAWS OF HAMMURABI

Today Hammurabi is remembered not for his conquests but for his law code, which he probably issued in the 21st year of his reign (*c.* 1771 BC).

The code originally had 282 sections but sections 66 to 99 are now lost and the 13th section was deliberately left blank because the Babylonians considered 13 to be an unlucky number. The code is not a complete legal system as it is mainly concerned with commercial, family and property law, and with slavery, fees, prices and wages. One of the principles of the code is the presumption of innocence, with both plaintiff and accused being given the opportunity to give evidence. Following the tradition established by the Sumerians, Hammurabi described his code's purposes as 'to cause justice to prevail in the land, to destroy the wicked and the evil, that the strong may not oppress the weak'. However, in its reliance on brutal retaliatory punishments involving the mutilation and death of the guilty or members of their families, it stands in stark contrast to the more humane punishments of Sumerian codes.

Eshnunna and the powerful Elamite kingdom to the east. In 1764 BC Hammurabi finally secured his eastern border when he defeated a coalition of Elamites, Gutians and other hill peoples. In 1761 BC he overthrew Rim-Sin of Larsa and brought all of Sumeria under his control. This established Hammurabi as the most powerful single ruler in the region and he immediately turned on his ally Zimri-Lim, defeating him in 1760 BC and destroying Mari in 1757 BC. Babylon's last significant rival in Mesopotamia, Eshnunna, was conquered in 1755 BC, after Hammurabi's forces had diverted its water supply. Babylonian power went into a period of gradual decline after Hammurabi's death *c.* 1750 BC but during his time as ruler the city had emerged as Mesopotamia's leading culture, a position it retained, through all the peaks and troughs of its political fortunes, until the 4th century BC.

The code was inscribed on a polished basalt stele which also showed Hammurabi standing reverently before Shamash, the god of justice. Fragments of the code are also known from copies made on clay tablets. Although the code includes instructions for plaintiffs to consult it, it is likely that Hammurabi ordered the stele to be made mainly for the benefit of the gods, so they might see what a just ruler he was. The stele's original location is, however, unknown: it was found far from Babylon, at Susa in modern Iran, where it was taken as loot by the Elamites after they sacked the city *c.* 1159 BC.

LEFT **The stele of Hammurabi.** *The black basalt stele shows the Babylonian king Hammurabi standing before Shamash the Mesopotamian god of justice above a long inscription of his law code. The stele was probably originally displayed in a temple, rather than in public, as a reminder to the gods of Hammurabi's concern for justice.*

Excerpts from the laws of Hammurabi

3 *If any one brings an accusation of any crime before the elders, and does not prove what he has charged, he shall, if it be a capital offense charged, be put to death.*

22 *If any one commits a robbery and is caught, then he shall be put to death.*

129 *If a man's wife is taken in adultery with another man, both shall be bound and thrown into the river, but the husband may pardon his wife and the king his slaves.*

195 *If a son strikes his father, his hands shall be cut off.*

196 *If a man puts out the eye of another man, his eye shall be put out.*

197 *If he breaks another man's bone, his bone shall be broken.*

229 *If a builder has built a house for a freeman and has not made his work sound, so that the house falls down and causes the death of the owner of the house, that builder shall be put to death.*

230 *If it causes the death of the son of the owner of the house, they shall kill the son of that builder.*

1915 TRANSLATION ADAPTED FROM L.K. KING

c. 1700 BC

CRETE UNITED ✦ Around 1700 BC the Minoan palaces were destroyed by fires, which were probably the result of wars between the palace kingdoms. Though all the palaces were rebuilt, only Knossos regained its former splendour, suggesting that its rulers had conquered the whole island, reducing the other centres to tributary status. The influence of Knossos came to extend far beyond Crete. Later sources describe how King Minos' fleets dominated the Aegean and imposed tribute on the Greeks. Minoan colonies were founded on several Aegean islands and they had their own quarter in the Egyptian port of Avaris in the Delta.

1640 BC

EGYPT INVADED ✦ The Middle Kingdom reached its peak in the reign of Senusret III's son Amenemhet III (r. 1844–1797 BC) but after his death it declined rapidly. Of the 70 kings recorded in the next 160 years, none ruled for longer than 14 years. Senusret III had led campaigns in the Levant, forcing the Canaanite and other Semitic peoples who lived there to become vassals of Egypt. As the Middle Kingdom weakened, immigrants from the Levant began to settle in the Nile Delta, and the Nubian kingdom of Kerma extended its control as far north as the First Cataract. Finally, c. 1640, the Middle Kingdom was brought to an end when the Hyksos ('Desert Princes') invaded from the Levant and conquered Lower Egypt, which they ruled from the port of Avaris in the Delta. Upper Egypt remained under the control of an Egyptian dynasty based at Thebes. Egypt was a very conservative society and its technological development lagged far behind that of the Middle East. As a result of Hyksos influence, Egyptians adopted the use of wheeled vehicles, including the war chariot, bronze technology, new weapons such as the scimitar and the powerful composite bow, an improved potter's wheel, the vertical loom, new crops and domestic animals, including the horse and the zebu (Asian humpbacked cow), new musical instruments and new fashions in dance and clothing.

As a result of Hyksos influence, Egyptians adopted the use of wheeled vehicles, including the war chariot, bronze technology, new weapons such as the scimitar and the powerful composite bow, an improved potter's wheel, new crops and new musical instruments.

OPPOSITE **Minoan boxers.** *A heavily restored fresco showing two boys boxing, from the Minoan city of Akrotiri on the island of Thera. This and many other frescos were preserved when the city was buried in ash from a catastrophic volcanic eruption which blew the island apart in 1628 BC. The site has been described as a Minoan Pompeii.*

ANCIENT TECHNOLOGY

The development of a settled farming way of life in the ancient Middle East around 8000 BC had a profound impact on technological development, freeing it from the constraints imposed by the need of nomadic and semi-nomadic hunter-gatherer groups for artefacts that were easily portable, such as simple stone tools and hunting weapons, fish hooks, nets and harpoons, and fibre ropes and baskets.

Over the next 4,000 years, farming peoples developed a wide range of new technologies so that, *c.* 3500 BC, the peoples of the Middle East possessed almost all the technical skills that formed the basis of civilized life before the Industrial Revolution: building construction, carpentry, pottery, metalworking, wheeled vehicles, shipbuilding and sails, spinning and weaving, and food processing techniques including brewing and baking. Glass was also invented in the Middle East but not until *c.* 1600 BC.

Metalworking was the most complex technology used by ancient civilizations. Metals such as gold and copper, which occur in their native form, were used to make jewellery and small tools from *c.* 8700 BC. By around 6000 BC metalworkers had discovered how to extract copper, gold, silver and lead from ore by smelting in kilns that were first invented for baking pottery. These metals were all too soft to replace stone tools in everyday use. It was only with the invention of bronze, a hard alloy of copper and arsenic or tin, *c.* 3800 BC, that the Stone Age really began to come to an end. Another advance which occurred around the same time was the invention of the lost wax method of metal casting, which allowed complex shapes to be made of metal. Bronze remained the main metal used to make tools until the late second millennium BC when the skill of ironworking was developed, probably in Anatolia. Even more important, at the time, than metalworking were the discovery of irrigation techniques and the invention of the plough, which together allowed a great intensification of agriculture and increase in food production, without which urban life would have been impossible.

LEFT **Egyptians plough and sow.** *Ancient Egyptians and Mesopotamians used a very simple type of plough known as the ard or scratch plough. This was little more than a pointed stick, often reinforced with a stone or metal tip, which merely cut the surface of earth. To break the ground completely it was necessary to cross-plough fields at 90°. The more efficient mouldboard plough, which could both cut and turn the soil, was invented somewhere in the Middle East c. 1000 BC.*

1628 BC

VOLCANIC ERUPTION DEVASTATES THE AEGEAN ✦

In 1628 BC one of the most violent volcanic eruptions of recent geological history blew apart the Aegean island of Thera (Santorini). Earthquakes and tsunamis caused widespread damage on Crete, and the Minoan colony of Akrotiri on Thera was buried under massive ash falls. As centuries later at Pompeii, the ash preserved the buildings it had buried. Excavations at Akrotiri in the 1960s and 1970s found perfectly preserved frescoes on the walls of houses, which still stood to their original heights. No traces of bodies were found, suggesting that the inhabitants had warning of the eruption and were able to escape in time. Many historians believe that the destruction of Thera may have given rise to the legend of the lost land of Atlantis, which was first recorded in the works of the Athenian philosopher Plato (470–399 BC). Claiming Egyptian priests as his ultimate source, Plato described Atlantis as a large island in the Atlantic Ocean west of the Pillars of Hercules (the Straits of Gibraltar): its magnificent capital was carved from the living rock by the sea god Poseidon. After the Atlanteans set about enslaving all the peoples of the Mediterranean, the gods decided to punish them for their arrogance and, in a single moment, Atlantis was destroyed by an earthquake and sank beneath the sea.

c. 1595 BC

THE HITTITES SACK BABYLON ✦

Hammurabi's dynasty continued to rule Babylon until 1595 BC when the Hittites, under their king, Mursilis I, captured and sacked the city, beginning a 'dark age' that lasted almost two centuries. The Hittites were an Indo-European people who had migrated into central Anatolia, probably from southeastern Europe, around 1800 BC. Mursilis launched his attack from Aleppo, in Syria, which he had captured after a long siege. With the capture of Babylon, Mursilis seemed about to become the most powerful ruler in the Middle East but before he could consolidate his conquests he was

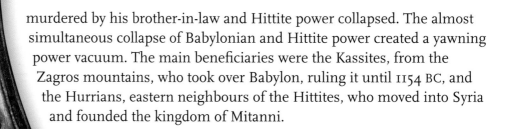

murdered by his brother-in-law and Hittite power collapsed. The almost simultaneous collapse of Babylonian and Hittite power created a yawning power vacuum. The main beneficiaries were the Kassites, from the Zagros mountains, who took over Babylon, ruling it until 1154 BC, and the Hurrians, eastern neighbours of the Hittites, who moved into Syria and founded the kingdom of Mitanni.

1532 BC

HYKSOS EXPELLED FROM EGYPT ✦ Using the new military technology the Hyksos had introduced to Egypt, the Theban king Seqenenre II (d. 1555 BC) began a long struggle to expel them. However, he probably failed to make much impression on the Hyksos. Examination of his mummy has shown that he died violently in battle: he was struck down by an axe blow to the head and then had his throat cut. His son Kamose (r. 1555–1550 BC) continued the war, enjoying some success in his short reign, and it was brought to a triumphant conclusion by his brother Ahmose I (r. 1550–1525 BC), who led a great war fleet into the Delta and captured Avaris in 1532 BC after a series of battles. Ahmose's victory marks the beginning of the New Kingdom, the period in which Egypt reached the peak of its power and influence. Ahmose was the last native Egyptian ruler to build a pyramid for his tomb. Pyramids had always been closely associated with the sun god Ra, but his importance in Egyptian religion had declined as the cult of Osiris gained popularity. The religious symbolism of the pyramid had lost its potency. Ra was replaced as the god most closely associated with royalty by Amun, the patron god of Thebes, who came to be regarded as the king of the gods. In time, Ra's identity was completely absorbed by Amun, who became known as Amun-Ra. It was also in the New Kingdom period that Egyptian kings adopted the title 'pharaoh'. Meaning 'great palace', the title was a sign of the central role the royal household played in government and of the total identification of the king with the Egyptian state.

ABOVE **Hyksos axed.** *This ceremonial golden battle axe belonged to the warrior pharaoh Ahmose I, who expelled the Hyksos from Egypt and founded the New Kingdom. The axe is decorated with inlays of lapis lazuli, carnelian, amazonite and glass.*

OPPOSITE **Embracing the afterlife.** *Wall painting from the tomb of Tutankhamun showing the king embracing Osiris, the god of the underworld. Standing behind the king is his ka, or vital essence. Egyptians believed that the ka entered the body at birth and left the body at death. The ka needed to be sustained after death by offerings of food and drink, the essence of which it consumed.*

1504–1492 BC

CONQUESTS OF THUTMOSE I ✦ Thutmose I continued the tradition of strong military leadership established by the Theban kings. During his short reign, Thutmose conquered Nubia as far south as the Fifth Cataract, and the whole of the Levant, establishing his northern frontier on the Euphrates river in Syria. The only river Egyptian soldiers had ever seen was the north-flowing Nile. They were astonished to see that the Euphrates flowed south: it seemed to them that it was flowing 'uphill' and against nature. Thutmose's conquest of Nubia was motivated by the traditional Egyptian desire to control its resources. The conquest of the Levant was inspired by the desire for a secure northern frontier, in order to prevent any repetition of the Hyksos occupation of the Delta. While Nubia was subjected to full colonial government under a viceroy, in the Levant local rulers were left in place under the supervision of Egyptian officials and garrisons.

1473 BC

A FEMALE PHARAOH SEIZES POWER ✦ On his death in 1492 BC Thutmose was succeeded by a son by a minor wife, Thutmose II (r. 1492–1479 BC). To strengthen his claim to the throne Thutmose II married his domineering half-sister Hatshepsut. Aware of Hatshepsut's desire for power, Thutmose declared his young son by a harem girl, Thutmose III, to be king shortly before his death in 1479 BC. Hatshepsut subsequently acted as regent for her stepson but used the position to advance her own supporters. Around 1473 BC she finally seized power, mounting a propaganda offensive to legitimize her rule. Hatshepsut claimed that she had been conceived by the god Amun to be pharaoh and was portrayed with all the trappings of kingship, right down to a false beard. She even claimed, falsely, that she had been crowned pharaoh in the presence of her father, Thutmose I. Apart from being one of the few women to rule Egypt in her own right, Hatshepsut is best known for sending a trading expedition down the Red Sea to acquire incense from the land of Punt (East Africa); a record of this was carved on the walls of her mortuary temple near Thebes.

> *Hatshepsut claimed that she had been conceived by the god Amun to be pharaoh and was portrayed with all the trappings of kingship, right down to a false beard.*

OPPOSITE **Return from Punt.** *This detail from a low relief frieze in Queen Hatshepsut's mortuary temple at Thebes shows Egyptian soldiers returning from a maritime trading expedition to the land of Punt, in East Africa. The Egyptians gave themselves a strong negotiating hand by ensuring that their occasional trading expeditions to sub-Saharan Africa were well armed. The expedition returned with 31 living myrrh trees, a source of incense, whose roots had been carefully wrapped to protect them during the voyage home. The trees were planted outside the queen's mortuary chapel, where the stump of one of them can still be seen.*

VICTORY DENIED

By taking an unexpected route through the mountains, Thutmose III took the rebel city of Megiddo by surprise. One of Thutmose's officers, Thanuny, describes how the king deployed his army in three divisions and routed the rebel forces in battle, only for indiscipline in the Egyptian ranks to allow the survivors to escape and prolong the war.

Early the next morning, command was given to the whole army to move. His majesty went forth in a chariot of electrum, arrayed with his weapons of war, like Horus the Smiter, lord of power, like Montu [a war god] of Thebes, while his father Amun strengthened his arms. The southern wing of his majesty's army was on a hill south of the brook of Kina, the northern wing was at the northwest of Megiddo, while his majesty was in the centre, with Amun the protector of his members, and the valour of his limbs. Then his majesty prevailed against the enemy at the head of his army, and when they saw his majesty prevailing against them, they fled headlong to Megiddo in fear, abandoning their horses and chariots of gold and silver. The people hauled them up, pulling them by their clothing into the city. ... Now, if only his majesty's army had given their hearts to plundering the things of the enemy, they would have captured Megiddo at that moment.

1456 BC

THE BATTLE OF MEGIDDO ✦

In 1458 BC Hatshepsut died, possibly murdered on the orders of Thutmose III, who now finally began to rule in his own right. He did everything he could to erase his stepmother's memory, destroying or burying her monuments and omitting her from official king lists. Hatshepsut was no soldier and during her reign many of her father's conquests slipped from Egyptian control. The greatest warrior pharaoh in Egypt's history, Thutmose III energetically restored the Egyptian empire, leading at least 17 military campaigns in the remaining 33 years of his reign. Many of Egypt's vassals in the Levant had transferred their allegiance to the kingdom of Mitanni in northern Syria. Thutmose made restoring Egyptian control of the area his priority, winning his first great victory over a coalition of Canaanite kings led by the king of Kadesh at Megiddo (the Armageddon of the Bible, now in Israel) in 1456 BC. The Megiddo campaign has special significance as the earliest in recorded history for which a detailed account survives, including the tactics used, the numbers of casualties and prisoners, and a list of plunder, which included over 900 chariots.

The account of the campaign was

OPPOSITE **Thutmose III makes offering to Amun.** *Ahmose I's successors promoted the cult of Amun, the patron god of their home city of Thebes. Amun's identity was merged with that of the sun-god Ra and as Amun-Ra became regarded in the New Kingdom as the most important of the gods.*

THE TROJAN WAR

Among the greatest achievements of ancient Greek culture were Homer's epic poems about the heroes of the Trojan War, *The Iliad* and *The Odyssey*.

Homer's epics were composed in the 8th century BC, drawing on ancient traditions passed down by word of mouth for generations. The war was supposedly caused when the Trojan prince Paris abducted Helen, the wife of king Menelaus of Sparta. Menelaus' brother Agamemnon, the king of Mycenae, led the Greeks in a campaign to win Helen back but the city fell only after a ten-year siege, and then only by Odysseus' ruse of feigning retreat while leaving behind a gigantic wooden horse in which Greek soldiers were hiding. When the Trojans unwisely took the horse into the city, the hidden soldiers emerged at night and opened the gates to the rest of the Greek army who had secretly returned under cover of darkness. Excavations at the site of Troy have revealed a fortified city that was rebuilt many times between

its foundation *c.* 3000 BC and it final abandonment in the 4th century AD. The city commanded an important trade route from the Mediterranean to the Black Sea and the expansionist Mycenaeans might well have attacked Troy to eliminate a commercial rival. Greeks of the Classical period believed that the Trojan War had taken place *c.* 1184 BC but modern historians favour a date of *c.* 1260–1240 BC, on the basis of archaeological evidence that Troy was violently destroyed at this time.

BELOW **The Trojan Horse.** *The appeal of the story of the Trojan wars has never faded and has inspired countless artworks through the ages. This painting by the Florentine artist Giovanni di Ser Giovanni (1406–86) gives the story a contemporary Renaissance Italian setting.*

Thutmose's army, and was inscribed on the wall of the great temple of Karnak near Thebes. The rebels had garrisoned the three passes which gave access to Megiddo. Thanuny describes how Thutmose, against the advice of his officers, achieved surprise by leading the army over the narrowest and most difficult pass, routing the enemy force which held it and arriving unexpectedly before Megiddo the same evening.

Indiscipline among the Egyptian troops lost Thutmose the chance to capture Megiddo quickly so he ordered the city to be surrounded with a wooden palisade: it finally surrendered after a seven-month siege but the king of Kadesh escaped.

c. 1450 BC

MYCENAEAN CONQUEST OF CRETE ✦ Around 1450 BC a wave of destruction swept over Minoan Crete. Almost all the island's known palaces, towns and villages were destroyed or damaged by fire. Only at Knossos was the destruction limited. In the aftermath, new burial customs, new gods, new art forms, a new script and a new language were introduced to the island – all evidence that the destruction was caused by foreign invaders who had conquered the island and established a ruling dynasty at Knossos. The conquerors were Mycenaean Greeks from the mainland.

The Mycenaeans take their name from Mycenae, a hilltop citadel in the Peloponnese, which features in Homer's *Iliad* as the capital of King Agamemnon, who led the Greeks in the Trojan War. The earliest evidence for the emergence of the Mycenaean civilization is richly furnished shaft graves at Mycenae, dating to between 1650 BC and 1550 BC. The finds from these graves, including bronze weapons, gold vessels and spectacular gold death masks, reveal the Mycenaeans as a wealthy, warlike, aristocratic people. Mycenaean Greece was divided into about 20 independent kingdoms, each ruled from a fortified citadel. The Mycenaeans were expansionist: as well as conquering Crete, they established colonies throughout the Aegean, on the coast of Anatolia and in Cyprus, and went on plundering raids against Egypt and the Hittite kingdom.

ABOVE **Royal burial site.** *The circular enclosure at Mycenae known as Grave Circle A encompassed six richly furnished shaft graves containing a total of 19 bodies. Among the finds were five golden masks including the famous 'Mask of Agamemnon', gold cups and jewellery, and bronze weapon, many with gold fittings, all evidence of a wealthy and aristocratic culture. The graves were in use from around 1600–1500 BC.*

1353–1335 BC

REIGN OF THE HERETIC PHARAOH ✦ One of the very few sharp breaks in the cultural continuity of ancient Egyptian civilization occurred during the reign of the pharaoh Amenophis IV (r. 1353–1335 BC). Rejecting the conservative traditions of Egyptian culture, Amenophis launched a religious revolution aimed at replacing his country's traditional polytheism with a monotheistic cult of the Aten or sun disc. In the fifth year of his reign he changed his name from Amenophis ('Amun is Pleased') to Akhenaten ('Servant of the Aten'), and founded a new capital which he called Akhetaten ('Horizon of the Aten'), now known as el-Amarna. Akhenaten proscribed the traditional cults, abolished their priesthoods and confiscated their property.

Akhenaten's religion recognized the Aten as the only god, who manifested himself to humanity as the sun: the giver of life and creator of all things. Temples to the Aten were open to the sky, so that worshippers could see his manifestation as the sun disk. There were no mysteries and no priesthood: the pharaoh was the sole intermediary between the Aten and humanity and, much as in Old Kingdom times, it was only through his intercession that his subjects could enjoy an afterlife. This relationship provides a clue that Akhenaten was not motivated by religious enthusiasm alone but by a desire to strengthen royal authority by marginalizing the wealthy and politically powerful Theban priesthood of the chief god Amun. Akhenaten's reign also marked a break with established artistic traditions, and saw the introduction of a new, informal style of official art. Atenism seems, however, to have won few coverts outside the immediate royal circle and excavations have revealed that even at Akhetaten people continued to revere the traditional gods in secret. While Akhenaten devoted all his energies to establishing the Aten cult, everyday administration and foreign policy came under the control of his father-in-law Ay and the general Horemheb.

HYMN TO THE ATEN (VERSE 1)

Thou dost appear beautiful on the horizon of heaven,
O living Aten, thou who wast the first to live,
When thou hast risen on the eastern horizon,
Thou hast filled every land with thy beauty.
Thou art fair, great, dazzling, high above every land;
Thy rays encompass the lands to the very limit of all thou hast made.
Being Ra, thou dost reach to their limit
And curb them for thy beloved son;
Though thou art distant, thy rays are upon the earth;
Thou art in their faces, yet thy movements are unknown.

AUTHORSHIP UNKNOWN BUT POSSIBLY AKHENATEN HIMSELF (TRANS. D. WINTON THOMAS, DOCUMENTS FROM OLD TESTAMENT TIMES, 1961).

71

1325 BC

TOMB OF TUTANKHAMUN ✦

Tutankhamun, the most famous of all the pharaohs, would be virtually unknown today but for the sensational discovery of his almost intact tomb in the Valley of the Kings in 1922. Akhenaten's son by a minor wife, Tutankhamun was only about 8 years old when he came to the throne and still only about 17 when he died. Although some scholars speculate that he may have been murdered, the exact cause of Tutankhamun's early death has not yet been established, despite intensive investigation of his mummy. During his short reign Tutankhamun was dominated by Ay and Horemheb, both of whom succeeded him in turn after his death. Originally called Tutankhaten ('Living Image of the Aten'), he changed his name to Tutankhamun ('Living Image of Amun') in the second year of his reign, signalling a restoration of the old religion. Tutankhamun died before an appropriately sized tomb could be built for him, so he was buried instead in an already completed tomb that was intended for a courtier. Many of Tutankhamun's magnificent grave goods and even his sarcophagus were second-hand.

RIGHT **Queen Nefertiti.** *Painted limestone bust of Akhenaten's senior wife Nefertiti, made by the sculptor Thutmose c. 1345 BC. The naturalism that characterizes this magnificent sculpture is a consequence of the artistic revolution that accompanied Akhenaten's religious revolution, which saw the rejection of the formality of traditional Egyptian art. After Akhenaten's death, traditional artistic forms were quickly revived.*

Despite ingenious attempts to hide and defend them – with booby traps, curses and security patrols – almost every Egyptian royal tomb was plundered in ancient times. Tutankhamun's tomb was no exception: it was robbed twice soon after the pharaoh's death. However, the entrance to the tomb was accidentally buried under spoil from the excavation of a new royal tomb and lost before the robbers could remove more than a fraction of its valuables. The goods that were left behind included the boy-king's solid gold inner coffin, gold death mask and 170 pieces of jewellery: this represents what was hurriedly gathered together for the burial of a rather unimportant pharaoh. A stronger ruler who had lived long enough to prepare properly for his death, and had a larger tomb to fill, would likely have been buried in far greater splendour.

1285 BC

BATTLE OF KADESH ✦ During Akhenaten's reign, Egypt's grip on the Levant began to slip. The Canaanites reasserted their independence and the Hittites extended their empire south into Syria. The pharaoh Sethos I (r. 1306–1290 BC) brought Canaan back under Egyptian control but the Hittites retained a firm hold on Syria. Seeing an opportunity to restore Egyptian rule as far north as the Euphrates, Sethos' son, Ramesses II (r. 1290–1224 BC) invaded Syria in 1285 BC with a 20,000-strong army, which was divided into four divisions named after the gods Amun, Ra, Ptah and Seth. Such a large army moved slowly, giving the Hittite king Muwatallis plenty of time to prepare. As Ramesses approached the fortified Hittite-held city of Kadesh in southern Syria, two captured Hittite spies informed him that Muwatallis' army was still far to the north. Ramesses advanced quickly with the

ABOVE **Wedjet's eye.** *A protective amulet from Tutankhamun's tomb in the form of the eye of Horus, also known as a 'Wedjet eye'. The eye is flanked by the vulture goddess Nekhbet, protector of Upper Egypt, and the snake goddess Wedjet, protector of Lower Egypt. The amulet is made of gold inlaid with lapis lazuli, shell and carnelian.*

OVERLEAF **Tutankhamun conquers.** *This magnificent image of military kingship, from a chest discovered in Tutankhamun's tomb, shows the young king leading his army in a chariot against a horde of Nubians. Because of his age, it is unlikely that Tutankhamun actually took part in any battles.*

Ramesses was a consummate propagandist and self-publicist. His present-day reputation as Egypt's greatest pharaoh owes much to the dozens of self-aggrandizing monuments, such as the great temple at Abu Simbel, and self-glorifying inscriptions he had made.

Amun division and had set up camp outside Kadesh when two more Hittite spies were captured. Under torture they revealed that the first two spies had been sent with false information. In reality, Muwatallis was camped just the other side of Kadesh with an army of over 36,000 men and 2,500 chariots. Almost at once, Muwatallis struck at the Ra division, while it was still on the march towards Kadesh, scattering it completely, then wheeled round and charged into Ramesses' camp. The Hittites threatened to overwhelm the Egyptians but Ramesses rallied his forces, buying enough time for reinforcements to arrive and attack the Hittites who, thinking victory was assured, had stopped to loot the Egyptian camp. Attacked from two sides, Muwatallis began to withdraw, sending in a fresh chariot division to cover his retreat. Ramesses counterattacked and the Hittite charioteers suffered heavy casualties as they fled in disorder across a river to safety. Nightfall brought the battle to a close and the two armies returned to the same positions they had held before the start of the battle. The following morning, they fought another indecisive engagement but afterwards the balance of advantage still lay with Muwatallis. Kadesh had strong fortifications and a flooded moat and it could not safely be besieged with Muwatallis' army still in the field and undefeated. The campaign ended with a truce and Ramesses returned to Egypt having achieved nothing.

Ramesses was a consummate propagandist and self-publicist. His present-day reputation as Egypt's greatest pharaoh owes much to the dozens of self-aggrandizing monuments, such as the great temple at Abu Simbel, and self-glorifying inscriptions he had made during his exceptionally long reign. In inscriptions, paintings and relief carvings placed in temples throughout Egypt, Ramesses shamelessly presented the Battle of Kadesh as a great victory rather than the narrow escape from disaster that it really was: copying his triumphant inscriptions became a popular exercise for generations of schoolboys training to become scribes. Years of warfare followed between Egypt and the Hittites, with neither side achieving a clear advantage over the other. Finally, recognizing the futility of the conflict, the two powers agreed to a peace

THE WORLD'S OLDEST SURVIVING PEACE TREATY

But now Ramesses, the great king, the king of the country of Egypt, has established this bond by treaty on a silver tablet with Hattusili, the great king, the king of the country of Hatti, his brother, starting from this day, to settle forever among them a good peace and a good fraternity. He is a brother to me and he is at peace with me; and I am a brother to him and I am forever at peace with him. Look, we are united and a bond of fraternity already exists among us and of peace, and it is better than the bond of fraternity and of peace that existed between the country of Egypt and the country of Hatti.

EXTRACT FROM THE HITTITE TEXT ON A CLAY TABLET EXCAVATED FROM THE ROYAL ARCHIVES AT HATTUSA. TEXT ADAPTED FROM BREASTED V. 3

ABOVE **Royal colossus.** *Four colossal statues of Ramesses II flank the entrance to the great temple at Abu Simbel in Nubia. The temple, dedicated to Amun, Ra-Horakhty, Ptah and the deified Ramesses, was cut out of the rock of a cliff overlooking the Nile. Nearby, a smaller temple, dedicated to the goddess Hathor and Ramesses'* *chief wife Nefertari, was also cut into the cliff. Ramesses constructed the temples to stamp his authority on the always rebellious Nubians. When the construction of the Aswan Dam in the 1950s threatened to submerge the temples, they were laboriously dismantled and reconstructed at a higher level under artificial hills.*

treaty in about 1268 BC. Remarkably, both the Hittite and Egyptian copies of the treaty still survive, sealed with gifts and marriage alliances. An important factor in the entente was probably a mutual fear of Assyria which, at that time, was the dominant power in Mesopotamia under its warlike king Shalmaneser I (r. 1273–1244 BC).

c. 1200–1100 BC

DARK AGE ✦ During the 12th century BC waves of migrations caused political chaos, destruction and economic dislocation throughout the eastern Mediterranean and Middle East. All of the main centres of the Mycenaean civilization were destroyed by unknown invaders, writing fell out of use and Greece entered a 'dark age' which lasted for 400 years. The Hittite empire collapsed, it is thought, under attack from migrating Phrygians from southeast Europe. Cities throughout the Levant, Syria and Babylonia were also sacked: some of the attackers were Aramaean nomads from the Syrian desert. Babylonia was also attacked by Chaldaean nomads from the Arabian desert. Assyria struggled to fend off attacks by Mysians and Urartians from the north and Aramaeans from the west. Egypt was attacked by a mysterious group of migrating peoples who are known to modern historians as the Sea Peoples. The Sea Peoples came from all around the Mediterranean: the Shardana probably came from Sardinia; the Teresh may have been Etruscans from Italy; the Ekwesh and Peleset were probably refugees from the fall of the Mycenaean civilization; and the Lukka were Anatolian peoples displaced by the Phrygians. By the time they reached Egypt, the Sea Peoples had already ravaged the coasts of Cyprus and the Levant but the pharaoh Ramesses III defeated them in a great naval battle when they invaded the Delta in 1180 BC. The Peleset and other survivors withdrew and settled in Canaanite territory, which became known, after them, as Palestine: in the Bible they are known as the Philistines.

c. 1070 BC

END OF THE NEW KINGDOM ✦ A downside of the abandonment of Akhenaten's solar cult was the restoration of the power and influence of the Theban priesthood of Amun. By the 12th century BC the temple of Amun at Karnak, outside Thebes, owned two-thirds of all the temple lands in Egypt, 90 per cent of Egypt's shipping and 80 per cent of its factories, giving it a stranglehold over the economy. The priesthood had become hereditary so the pharaoh had no control over appointments. The pharaohs' obvious powerlessness to rein in the over-mighty priests undermined royal authority. After the death of Ramesses III, Egypt's last great warrior pharaoh, in 1163 BC, Nubia and the Levant drifted out of Egyptian control. The decline of Egypt's prestige is well illustrated by the story of Wenamun, a temple official sent by Ramesses XI (r. 1100–1070 BC) to Byblos in Lebanon to buy cedar wood. In earlier times, Wenamun would have been an honoured guest and he would have been given whatever the pharaoh had asked for. Now, Wenamun recorded in the report he wrote about his mission, he was told that if he wanted wood, he would have to pay for it: '[The king of Byblos] *said to me: "If the ruler of Egypt were the owner of my property, and I also were his servant, he would not send silver and gold, saying 'Do the command of Amun'. It was not the payment of tribute which they exacted of my father. As for me, I am myself neither your servant nor am I the servant of him that sent you"'* (trans. Breasted v. 3). Unfortunately for Wenamun he had been robbed on his way to Byblos, so he returned home empty-handed. Following Ramesses' death in 1070 BC, Egypt was divided into two states, with Upper Egypt under the rule of the chief priests of Amun, and Lower Egypt ruled by a dynasty based at Tanis in the Delta. Ramesses' death is taken to mark the end of the New Kingdom and the beginning of the Third Intermediate Period (1069–712 BC), a complex period of weak monarchies, civil wars and decentralized power. Egyptian culture continued to flourish in this period but Egypt would never recover its position as a great imperial power.

OPPOSITE **Ramesses II's mortuary chapel at Thebes.** *The archaeological wonders of ancient Egypt were first revealed to Europeans through the work of artists and lithographers such as the Scottish painter David Roberts (1796–1864) who painted this watercolour during his travels along the Nile in 1838–9.*

RIGHT **Shardan warrior.** *Bronze figurine of a warrior wearing a distinctive horned helmet from Sardinia's Nuraghic civilization (8th century BC). Warriors wearing similar gear, described as Shardana, appear in Egyptian friezes celebrating Ramesses III's victory over the Sea Peoples in 1180 BC.*

79

IMPERIAL RIVALS

1000–500 BC

Assyria led the recovery from the disasters of the late second millennium BC. An aggressive, militaristic state, Assyria built an empire that covered much of the Middle East. As the empire grew its demands for metals, timber, precious stones, dyes, textiles and other goods stimulated trade throughout the region.

Greeks and Phoenicians founded colonies all around the Mediterranean, helping to stimulate the growth of new civilizations in Italy and North Africa. Assyria eventually overreached itself and fell in spectacular fashion, to be briefly replaced by Babylon as the region's great power. By the end of the period, however, power had shifted decisively away from Mesopotamia and east to Persia, which, in little more than a decade, created the first world empire in the middle of the 6th century. Yet it was often the smaller states in this period that made the most important contributions to the development of civilization, such as the Israelite kingdom, the Greek city states and the rising Italian city of Rome.

c. 1000 BC

KING DAVID CAPTURES JERUSALEM ✦ The weakness of the great powers of Mesopotamia and Egypt in the late second millennium BC created a power vacuum in the Levant which local Canaanite, Phoenician, Philistine and Israelite rulers competed to fill. According to the Old Testament, the Israelites emerged as the leading power in the region under their second king, David (r. *c.* 1006–965 BC). David's predecessor, Saul (r. *c.* 1020–1006 BC), the founder of the Israelite monarchy, was killed in battle with the Philistines. David's first, and

PREVIOUS PAGES **Guardian spirit.** *Monumental statues of protective spirits called* lamassus *acted as gate guardians in Assyrian palaces and at the entrances to their cities. Lamassus were depicted as bulls or lions with eagle's wings and a human head. To protect houses, lamassus were engraved onto clay tablets which were then buried under the threshold of the door.*

RIGHT **Solomon's temple.** *The Bible's detailed description of the dimensions of Solomon's temple in Jerusalem still leaves much about its actual appearance to the imagination. This engraving of the temple by Matthias Merian was made around 1625 to illustrate a copy of Martin Luther's translation of the Bible into German. While the dimensions conform to the Biblical description, the architecture belongs to the 17th century.*

most important, achievement was to capture the Canaanite stronghold of Jerusalem *c.* 1000 BC, making it the capital of the Israelite kingdom. In the remainder of his reign David contained Philistine expansion and forced neighbouring Aramaean kingdoms to pay tribute. The Old Testament claims that David's kingdom eventually extended from the Gulf of Aqaba in the south to the Euphrates in the north. Archaeologists have so far failed to find any evidence to corroborate the biblical account, which many believe exaggerates the size of David's kingdom.

c. 958 BC

SOLOMON'S TEMPLE ✦ Jerusalem's place as one of the world's most important religious centres was sealed by when David's son and successor, King Solomon (r. *c.* 965–*c.* 928), built a temple there to house the sacred Ark of the Covenant, the chest which, according to the Bible, contained the tablets on which were inscribed the Ten Commandments. As described in the first book of Chronicles, the Temple was an impressive structure, about 27 metres (90 ft) long by 9 metres (30 ft) wide, with an entrance porch, an antechamber, and a sanctuary called the Holy of

Holies, where the Ark was kept. The interior was lavishly decorated with precious metals and rich textiles. The full height of the Temple is not given but two bronze pillars which flanked the entrance are described as being 15.5 metres (51 ft) tall. The Temple sat in an inner courtyard, which was for the use of the priests, which was in turn set within an outer courtyard. A bronze altar was set before the Temple's entrance and nearby was a huge bronze basin where the priests conducted their ritual washing. The exact location of Solomon's Temple is unknown. It is generally thought to have stood on the Temple Mount where the Dome of the Rock now stands. Because of the religious and political sensitivity of the site, archaeological excavations which might confirm or disprove this have not taken place.

It is thought that Solomon's Temple stood on the Temple Mount where the Dome of the Rock now stands. Because of the religious and political sensitivity of the site, archaeological excavations which might confirm or disprove this have not taken place.

BELOW **The Temple Mount** *and the Dome of the Rock at Jerusalem painted in 1862 by the German watercolourist Karl Friedrich Werner. Werner was one of the first non-Muslims to be given access to the Dome of the Rock, an Islamic shrine completed in AD 691, to mark the place where, according to Muslim tradition, Muhammad ascended to heaven with the angel Gabriel. In Jewish tradition this was also the place where Abraham prepared to sacrifice his son Isaac and the site of the Holy of Holies, the sanctuary of Solomon's Temple.*

LEFT **Jerusalem imagined.** *Until the first methodological archaeological excavations of the city began in the late 19th century, very little was known about the layout of Old Testament period Jerusalem. This did not deter generations of artists from producing imaginative portrayals of the city, including this one from 1846.*

934—912 BC

ASSYRIAN REVIVAL BEGINS ✦ Assyria began to recover from the disasters of the 11th century BC in the reign of King Ashur-dan II (r. 934–912 BC). Assyria at this time was reduced to its heartland in the far north of Mesopotamia and was constantly raided by Aramaean nomads. Ashur-dan successfully campaigned against the Aramaeans, securing the country's borders. He could now begin to resettle the many refugees who had been displaced by the raids in new towns and villages, and begin to rebuild Assyria's agriculture and government. Government offices were built in the provinces to improve administration and Ashur-dan established secure supply bases for the army. New irrigation canals were dug and, by providing ploughs throughout the land, he was able to boast that he had 'piled up more grain than ever before'. Ashur-dan's reforms created a strong base for his successors Adad-nirari II (r. 911–891 BC) and Tukulti-Ninurta II (r. 890–884 BC) to re-establish Assyrian rule in all of northern Mesopotamia and reduce the Aramaeans to vassalage.

> *New irrigation canals were dug and, by providing ploughs throughout the land, Ashur-dan was able to boast that he had 'piled up more grain than ever before'.*

c. 928 BC

A HOUSE DIVIDED ✦ The Temple at Jerusalem was only the most ambitious of King Solomon's building projects. These, and the lavish court he kept, became increasingly burdensome to his subjects. Solomon's use of Israelites as well as conquered Canaanites as forced labourers caused particular discontent, as did his favouritism towards his own tribe of Judah over the other Israelite tribes. Following Solomon's death in *c.* 928 BC, the ten northern tribes complained to his son and successor Rehoboam, hoping for reform. When Rehoboam arrogantly dismissed their complaints, promising more and worse oppression, the northern tribes rebelled and formed the separate kingdom of Israel under Jeroboam, who had been exiled by Solomon to Egypt for plotting against him. Rehoboam was left with the smaller kingdom of Judah, which he ruled from Jerusalem. With the region's great powers recovering from the 'dark age' of the late second millennium, this was a bad time for the Israelites to fall out with one another. A foretaste of what was to come arrived swiftly when, in 925 BC, the pharaoh Shoshenq, leading a brief Egyptian revival, ravaged both Judah and Israel, forcing Rehoboam to strip the Temple of its precious metals to buy him off, and making Jeroboam flee into temporary exile. Assyria was a more serious threat in the longer term, however, and for the next two centuries the Israelites faced a constant, ultimately unsuccessful, struggle to preserve their independence.

ABOVE **Phoenician merchant ship.** *Phoenician
navigators plied the entire length of the
Mediterranean Sea in search of metal ores and
other commodities to feed demand from the
growing Assyrian empire. By the 8th century BC
they had passed through the Straits of Gibraltar*

*and begun to explore the Atlantic coasts of Europe
and Africa. This carving from a sarcophagus from
Sidon (Lebanon) represents a Phoenician bulk
trader of the Roman period. The goose's head at
the stern is a symbol of the Egyptian goddess Isis
who was believed to protect seafarers.*

814 BC

PHOENICIANS FOUND CARTHAGE ✦

The Phoenicians were close relatives of the Canaanites and Israelites who lived along the coasts of what are now northern Israel, Lebanon and Syria. The Phoenicians were never a politically united people and their chief centres, Tyre, Sidon, Beirut, Byblos, Arvad and Ugarit, were all independent city states. The Phoenicians were, however, ideally situated to set themselves up as middlemen in trade between Egypt and Mesopotamia, and between Mesopotamia and the wider Mediterranean world. In their search for valuable metal ores, especially copper and tin (the ingredients of bronze), Phoenician seafarers pioneered a network of trade routes extending from Cyprus and Greece, to Italy, North Africa, Spain, and beyond into the Atlantic Ocean. They also possessed two sought-after commodities of their own – cedar wood from the Lebanon mountains (neither Egypt nor Mesopotamia possessed timber) and Tyrian purple, a dye made from the murex sea snail that was more valuable than gold.

In the course of their voyages, the Phoenicians founded colonies and trading posts in Sicily, Sardinia, Spain and North Africa. These colonies enjoyed friendly relations with the native peoples, who welcomed them for the new trading opportunities that they brought. The most successful of the colonies was Carthage. Founded by Tyre, Carthage was built on an easily defended site with a sheltered anchorage on a peninsula in northern Tunisia. Carthage's position allowed it to dominate trade routes into the western Mediterranean and it prospered, soon founding its own colonies and offering its protection to other Phoenician colonies in the region. Carthaginians

ABOVE **Terracotta funerary mask.** *Phoenicians placed masks, such as this example from Carthage, in tombs. The masks, which commonly have grotesque expressions, represent protective spirits who guard the dead.*

OPPOSITE **Greek discus thrower.** *The consciously homoerotic custom of men exercising naked began in Sparta and spread from there to the rest of Greece. In Sparta women also exercised naked but in other ancient Greek states they were not even allowed to participate in sports.*

later believed that their city was founded in 814 BC by Queen Elissa (also known in Greek and Roman tradition as Dido), who had fled Tyre after her husband, King Pygmalion, was murdered. Archaeological evidence, however, suggests that Carthage may really have been founded as much as a century later.

776 BC

THE EARLIEST OLYMPIC GAMES ARE HELD IN GREECE ✦ In the 8th century BC Greece finally emerged from the dark age that had followed the fall of the Mycenaean civilization. Increased trade with the empires of the Middle East fuelled the growth of hundreds of towns and cities, each of which was an independent state or *polis* (from which our word 'politics' comes), each ruled by a hereditary king or an aristocratic oligarchy. Trade also led to the readoption of writing, using a modified version of the Phoenician alphabet. To cope with their fast-rising populations, many Greek cities began founding colonies overseas, in Sicily and Italy, Libya, on the Mediterranean coasts of Spain and France, and all around the coast of the Black Sea. Greek cities were fiercely competitive and frequently at war with one another. Despite this, Greeks recognized that they shared a common cultural identity, using the name *Hellenes* to describe themselves collectively, and worshipping the same gods. Leagues of neighbouring cities were set up to protect shrines of pan-Hellenic importance, such as the prophetic Oracle of Apollo at Delphi, so that they would not be violated in wartime. Sacred truces were declared to allow people to travel safely to celebrate important pan-Hellenic religious festivals, the most famous of which were the games held every four years at Olympia to honour Zeus, the supreme god of the Greek pantheon.

The origins of the Olympic Games are shrouded in myth. The Greeks believed that the games had been founded in ancient times by the mighty hero Heracles

THE ALPHABET

Early writing systems such as Mesopotamian cuneiform and Egyptian hieroglyphic were difficult to learn and, as a result, literacy in those societies was largely confined to a small elite of professional scribes and bureaucrats.

The invention of the alphabet by the Canaanites around 1600 BC turned writing into a skill that was easily learned. Instead of the hundreds of signs of the cuneiform or hieroglyphic scripts, the Proto-Canaanite alphabet used only 19. Canaanite letters were adapted from Egyptian hieroglyphs but instead of complete words, they stood for consonants, allowing all words to be spelled out phonetically.

By *c.* 1000 BC the alphabet had been adopted, and adapted, by the Canaanites' neighbours, the Hebrews, Phoenicians and Aramaeans, and in Arabia by the Nabataeans and Sabaeans. The Aramaic alphabet became the most widely used in the Middle East. Adopted by the Mesopotamians and Persians, cuneiform died out in everyday use by *c.* 400 BC but survived in formal and religious inscriptions until around the time of Christ. Knowledge of the Aramaic alphabet spread from the Middle East to the Indian subcontinent where it became the basis of the Brahmic script, the ancestor of modern Indian and

Southeast Asian scripts, and the Mongol and Tibetan scripts. During the course of their mercantile voyages, the seafaring Phoenicians had carried knowledge of their alphabet to Greece, North Africa, Italy and Iberia by the 8th century BC.

The Greeks did far more than simply adapt the Phoenician alphabet to their language – they improved it by introducing signs for vowels as well as consonants. This created a more flexible alphabet which represented spoken language even more accurately. The Greek alphabet was itself the basis of the Etruscan and Latin alphabets, now the world's most widely used, and the Cyrillic alphabet.

92

OPPOSITE **Phoenician inscription.** *This inscription from the sarcophagus of Eshmunzar, a native of the Phoenician trading city of Sidon (now in Lebanon), recounts how he and his mother, the priestess Amashtarte, had built temples to the city gods.*

(Hercules) in honour of his father Zeus. These games were discontinued until they were revived in 776 BC by King Lycurgus of Sparta and other local kings at the behest of the Oracle of Delphi in an effort to abate a plague that was sweeping Greece. The first competitors came only from the local region but the games were soon attracting people from across Greece and from Greek colonies overseas. At first the games lasted only one day and comprised only a footrace, a sprint of between 180 and 240 metres (200 and 260 yards). As they became more popular more events were added. By 632 BC there were four footraces – including a race in armour – horse racing, chariot racing, boxing, wrestling and the pentathlon (running, jumping, discus, javelin and wrestling), spread over five days. A ritual feast to honour Zeus closed the games. Only Greek-speaking men who had trained for at least ten months were allowed to take part. Official prizes were only olive wreaths but winners were treated as heroes by their home cities and could expect to be lavishly rewarded.

753 BC

LEGENDARY FOUNDATION OF ROME ✦ Romans of the historical period dated all events in years since the foundation of the city by the twin brothers Romulus and Remus, which they believed had taken place in 753 BC. According to Roman tradition, Romulus and Remus were illegitimate descendants of the Trojan prince Aeneas who, escaping the sack of Troy, had settled with his followers in Latium (modern Lazio) in central Italy, married a local Latin princess and founded a dynasty. The unwanted twins were abandoned in infancy on the banks of the Tiber river but their lives were saved when they were suckled by a she-wolf. Rescued and brought up by shepherds, the brothers later decided to found a city on the spot where they had been abandoned. Romulus killed Remus in an argument over who should rule the city and decided to name the city Rome, after himself.

Romulus and Remus are, most likely, legendary characters, and historians today regard Numa Pompilius (r. *c.* 715–673 BC) as the first historical king of Rome. Rome at this time was essentially a farming community scattered across a number of low hills overlooking the lowest ford across the Tiber. Thanks to this ford, Rome became the natural focus of several overland trade routes, while the Tiber gave easy access to the Mediterranean. Within a century of Numa's death Rome had become the most prosperous and important market town in Latium, controlling a territory of around 30 square miles (48 km²). Rome was, however, still overshadowed by the powerful Etruscans to the north and showed no sign yet of its future greatness.

Later Romans recognized the importance of geography in their city's rise to power:

> *It seems to me that Romulus must at the very beginning have had a divine intimation that Rome would one day be the seat and hearthstone of a mighty empire, for scarcely could a city placed upon any other site in Italy have more easily maintained our present widespread domination.*
>
> CICERO (106–43 BC), *DE REPUBLICA* (TRANS. C.W. KEYES, 1928)

94

RIGHT **Romulus and Remus.** *This bronze sculpture, known as the Capitoline Wolf, shows Rome's legendary founders, the twin brothers Romulus and Remus, suckling from a she-wolf. The same scene was often portrayed on Roman coins, and the Roman writer* Cicero described a similar statue on the Capitoline Hill at Rome in 65 BC. This sculpture was long thought to be the same one that Cicero described but recent scientific analysis has shown that it is probably a medieval forgery, made in the 13th century.

729 BC

ASSYRIA ANNEXES BABYLON ✦ In 911 BC Assyria and Babylon became allies. In military terms Babylon was very much the junior partner in this alliance, often needing assistance against the Chaldaean nomads, but the Assyrians' respect for Babylonian culture was such that its kings were treated officially as equals. When a Chaldaean tribal chief called Ukin-zer captured Babylon and seized the throne in 734 BC, the Assyrian king Tiglath-pileser III marched south and overthrew him. Tiglath-pileser did not restore Babylonian self-rule after defeating the Chaldaeans. In 729 BC he 'took the hand' of Babylon's patron god Marduk and escorted his idol in the city's New Year festival, the most important religious event of the Babylonian year. The priesthood formally recognized Tiglath-pileser as king of Babylon and as Marduk's representative on earth by offering him a share of the sacramental meal of the gods. There was no opposition to this: to Babylonians, Assyria represented order and security.

714 BC

THE END OF A MOUNTAIN KINGDOM ✦ In the 9th century BC Assyria's northern frontiers came under threat from Urartu, a proto-Armenian kingdom which has given its name to Mount Ararat, well known from the Bible as the landing place of Noah's Ark after the Flood. Urartu's mountainous terrain and many natural strongholds made it difficult campaigning country and successive Assyrian campaigns achieved little. Assyria's Urartian problem was finally solved by Sargon II (r. 721–705 BC). Shortly after Sargon's accession the Urartians imposed a vassal king on Mannea, a horse-breeding area of critical importance to the Assyrian army. In 716 BC , Sargon invaded Mannea, captured the Urartian vassal king and flayed him alive. Urartu retaliated by invading and occupying Mannea. However, the Assyrians maintained a network of spies in Urartu and their reports told of preparations for further advances at Assyrian expense.

95

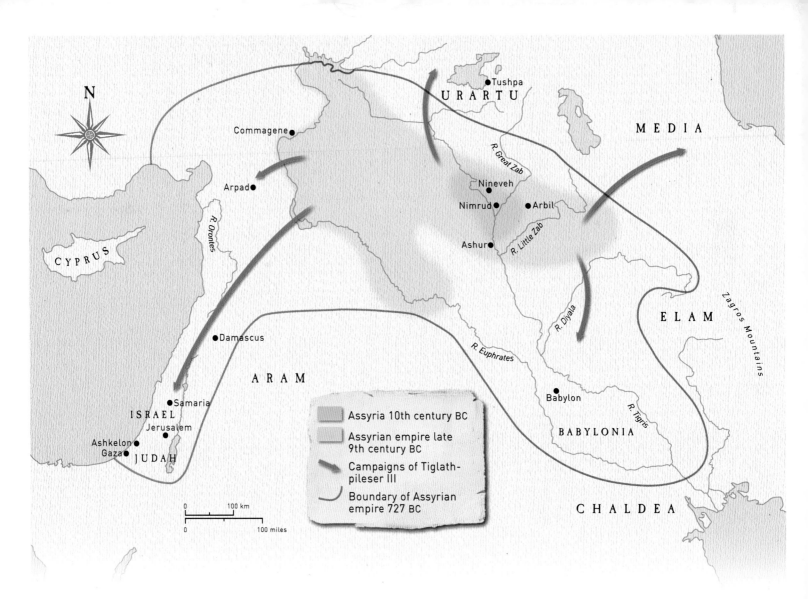

ABOVE **Growth of the Assyrian Empire.**

Map legend:

- Assyria 10th century BC
- Assyrian empire late 9th century BC
- Campaigns of Tiglath-pileser III
- Boundary of Assyrian empire 727 BC

Sargon decided to go on the offensive, invading Urartu in the summer of 714 BC. Sargon's plan was to strike right at the heart of Urartu and he made a long detour through the Zagros to outflank the kingdom's border defences, a bold move which meant that his army had no easy way to withdraw in case of defeat. The difficult mountain country took its toll on the Assyrians and, at times, engineers with the army constructed roads across cliff faces and other obstacles. By the time Sargon met the main Urartian army under its king Ursa at a pass guarding access to the capital at Turushpa, the Assyrian troops were tired, hungry and mutinous. Sargon rallied his troops, personally leading a charge of his elite household cavalry that broke the enemy line. Ursa withdrew to Turushpa in good order but, demoralized by this

ABOVE **Growth of the Assyrian Empire.**
In the 10th century BC Assyria was a minor state controlling a stretch of the Tigris river flood plain in northern Mesopotamia. A succession of able warrior kings made Assyria the dominant power of the Middle East by the 8th century BC.

OPPOSITE **Sargon II.** *Low relief sculpture of Sargon II giving instructions to his vizier, from his palace at Dur-Sharrukin ('Sargon's Fortress'), present-day Khorsabad, near Mosul in northern Iraq. The heavily fortified city, which covered roughly three square kilometres, was built in just ten years as a new capital for the Assyrian empire. After Sargon's death in battle in 705 BC the capital was moved north to Nineveh.*

Sargon completed his destruction of Urartu by sacking and plundering its religious capital, Musasir: the loot included over a ton of gold and more than 4 tons of silver, 6,170 captives and over 100,000 head of livestock.

unexpected defeat on home territory, his allies began to abandon him. As Sargon advanced on Turushpa, Ursa panicked and fled into the mountains, where he later committed suicide, stabbing himself in the heart. Sargon completed his destruction of Urartu by sacking and plundering its religious capital, Musasir, the home of the national god Haldi: the loot included over a ton of gold and more than 4 tons of silver, 6,170 captives, over 100,000 head of livestock, and large quantities of lead, bronze, iron, textiles and precious stones. Sargon's campaign left the Urartu in smouldering ruins – even natural woodlands were set on fire – and it never recovered.

712 BC

BLACK PHARAOH ✦ After the brief revival of Shoshenq's reign, Egypt's fortunes declined steadily. Civil wars and dynastic disputes tore the state apart and by the end of the 9th century BC Egypt was divided into several independent kingdoms and princedoms. Military government became the norm and most cities were heavily fortified. Egypt's weakness favoured the re-emergence of a Nubian kingdom in Kush, based at Napata, between the Third and Fourth Cataracts of the Nile. By this time, the Nubians had been exposed to Egyptian cultural influence for over a thousand years and they had adopted many Egyptian gods, including the royal cult of Amun, and funerary practices, including royal burials under small pyramids. Nubian art, architecture and statecraft were thoroughly Egyptian in character. Around 770 BC King Kashta of Kush became ruler of Upper Egypt as far north as Thebes. Kashta's son Piye continued to consolidate Kushite power in Upper Egypt, bringing the powerful Theban priesthood of Amun under his control by appointing his sister Amenirdis to the influential office of the God's Wife of Amun. Around 730 BC, Piye campaigned as far north as Memphis, bringing all of Upper Egypt under his control. Tefnakht, the king of the Delta city of Sais, raised a coalition of rulers from Lower Egypt to oppose Piye but it was crushed and, one by one, the rulers of Lower Egypt recognized Piye as their overlord. Piye seems to have been content with this formal submission and he made no attempt to impose direct Kushite rule in the

A COWARD FLEES

Ursa I shut up in his crowded camp and cut down from under him his draught horses with arrow and javelin. To save his life he abandoned his chariot, mounted a mare and fled in front of his army [kings only rode stallions].

LETTER OF SARGON TO THE GOD ASSUR DESCRIBING HIS CAMPAIGN TO HIM (TRANS. D.D. LUCKENBILL, 1926)

OPPOSITE **Assyrian gold necklace.** *This gold necklace, made c. 800 BC, is part of the 'Treasure of Nimrud', a hoard of over 600 pieces of gold jewellery and precious stones discovered at the* Assyrian city of Nimrud in 1988. The treasure was probably buried for safekeeping before the city was destroyed by the Babylonians in 612 BC, and was never recovered.*

area. It was left to Piye's brother Shabaka (r. 712–698) to complete the Kushite conquest of Egypt. Around 717 BC Sais came under the rule of a vigorous king called Bakenranef. Following Piye's death in *c.* 712 BC, Bakenranef quickly established his rule throughout Lower Egypt. Faced with a potential rival for control of Upper Egypt, Shabaka moved swiftly, invading Lower Egypt and deposing Bakenranef, who was executed by being burned alive. With the last obstacle to Kushite rule removed, Shabaka became pharaoh of all Egypt.

701 BC

JERUSALEM BESIEGED ✦ By *c.* 840 BC Israel was a vassal of Assyria, smaller but more distant from Assyria, Judah held out another century before it too accepted vassal status. So long as tribute was paid on time, the Assyrians did not interfere overmuch in the day-to-day affairs of their vassal states. In *c.* 737 BC Israel joined an Assyrian coalition with the Syrian kingdoms of Damascus and Aram. The Assyrian king Tiglath-pileser III easily put down the coalition and between 733 and 722 BC all three kingdoms were annexed and turned into provinces of the Assyrian empire under Assyrian governors. Hoshea, the last king of Israel, was imprisoned, and much of the population was deported and resettled in Mesopotamia, so beginning the worldwide diaspora of the Jews. In 701 BC Hezekiah, the king of Judah, joined an Egyptian-backed rebellion by Philistine and Phoenician cities against Assyria. The Assyrian king Sennacherib (r. 704–681 BC) suppressed the rebellion, defeated the Egyptians at the Battle of Eltekeh, ravaged Judah, taking many cities and deporting over 200,000 people to Mesopotamia and, finally, besieged Hezekiah in Jerusalem, 'like a bird in a cage'. In an interview with Hezekiah, recorded in the Bible, Sennacherib's ambassador delivered a message mocking him for trusting in the 'broken reed' that Egypt had become. Hezekiah emptied the royal treasury and stripped the Temple of its treasures to buy Sennacherib off with tribute

RIGHT **African pharaoh.** *Statue of the Nubian pharaoh of Egypt, Taharka (r. 690–664 BC). Taharka tried to restore Egypt's traditional influence in the Levant by supporting rebellions against its Assyrian overlords. This succeeded only in provoking an Assyrian invasion that ended Nubian rule in Egypt. The Nubian kingdom (roughly equivalent to present-day Sudan) remained a powerful presence on Egypt's southern border until the Arab conquest in the Middle Ages.*

and was allowed to keep his throne. Biblical writers attributed Judah's survival to the miraculous intervention of Yahweh who struck the Assyrians with a plague. Modern historians believe that Sennacherib did not press the siege because he needed to preserve his forces to deal with the troublesome Chaldaeans, who had once again seized Babylon.

689 BC

BABYLON SACKED ✦ In 721 BC another Chaldaean chief, Merodach-baladan, seized control of Babylon with the support of the Elamites. The Assyrians expelled Merodach-baladan in 710 BC but he escaped and seized Babylon for a second time in 703 BC, once again with Elamite support, but was again quickly expelled. To forestall any further Elamite interventions in Babylonia, Sennacherib invaded Elam in 694 BC, boldly taking a fleet down the Tigris into the Persian Gulf and attacking unexpectedly from the sea. The Elamite response was equally bold: instead of engaging Sennacherib directly, they sent their main army to invade Babylonia, cutting his lines of communication back to Assyria and capturing and killing the son he had left in charge of Babylon. Sennacherib's returning army quickly drove the Elamites out but while he was conducting a second invasion of Elam in 693 BC yet another Chaldaean, Mushezib-marduk, seized control of Babylon. In summer 691 BC Sennacherib fought a bloody but indecisive battle with the Chaldaeans and their Elamite allies on the Diyala river. Regrouping his forces, Sennacherib marched on Babylon the next summer and laid siege to the city. Fifteen months later, and devastated by famine, Babylon fell to Sennacherib's army. Frustrated by the long struggle and the death of his son, Sennacherib did not show the customary Assyrian respect for Babylon: the Assyrian troops were allowed to loot the city and its houses, temples and the city walls were burned or levelled to the ground. Sennacherib ordered canals to be dug to divert water from the Euphrates into the city to flood it and wash away its foundations. Mushezib-marduk and his family were captured and imprisoned in Assyria. Sennacherib's brutality alienated the previously sympathetic Babylonians. Many Assyrians were also horrified and it may have contributed to his murder in a family dispute in 681 BC. Although Sennacherib's son and successor Esarhaddon (r. 680–669 BC) lavished resources on rebuilding Babylon and restored its monarchy, placing his son Shamash-sum-ukin on the throne, the damage had been done.

671 BC

ASSYRIA INVADES EGYPT ✦ Defeat by Assyria in 701 BC did not stop Egypt's Kushite pharaohs continuing to support anti-Assyrian rebels in the Levant. This was partly motivated by a desire to restore Egyptian influence in the area and partly to keep expansionist Assyria as far from Egypt's borders as possible. However, it was a provocative policy. When the pharaoh Taharka supported another rebellion in the

THE DESTRUCTION OF BABYLON

Like the oncoming storm I [Sennacherib] *broke loose and I overwhelmed Babylon like a hurricane. ... The city and houses, from their foundations to their crenellations, I destroyed, I devastated, I burned with fire. The wall and outer wall, temples, gods, the ziggurat of brick and earth, as much as there was I razed and dumped them into the Arahtu canal. Through the middle of the city I dug canals, I flooded its ground with water, the structure of its foundations I destroyed. I made its destruction more complete than that by a flood. That in days to come, the site of that city, and its temples and gods might not be remembered, I completely wiped it out with water and made it like a meadow.*

INSCRIPTION OF SENNACHERIB AT BAVIAN NEAR NINEVEH (NORTHERN IRAQ) (TRANS. LUCKENBILL, 1924)

LEFT **The oldest world map.** *This clay tablet from Sippar shows the world as it was known to the Babylonians around 600 BC: north is at the top of the map. The earth is represented as a flat disc, surrounded by a circular ocean. Babylon is located in the eastern third of the rectangular box just above the centre of the map.*

Levant in 674 BC, Esarhaddon retaliated with an invasion of Egypt. He did not get far: Taharka met him in battle close to the Egyptian border and defeated him. Undeterred, Esarhaddon returned in 671 BC. Taharka again attempted to stop the Assyrians at the border but this time was defeated. Esarhaddon swept on and captured Memphis: most of the royal family were captured but Taharka escaped to Thebes. Esarhaddon left Lower Egypt under the control of local chiefs and provincial governors who were compelled to swear oaths of allegiance to Assyria.

664 BC

AMUN DESPOILED ✦ No sooner had Esarhaddon withdrawn than Taharka returned and reoccupied Lower Egypt. In 669 BC Esarhaddon set out to expel him but he died on the way and the expedition was aborted. Two years passed before his successor, his son Ashurbanipal (r. 668–627 BC), sent an army to Egypt to deal with Taharka. Memphis was retaken and Taharka retreated to Nubia, where he died a few years later. Led by Necho, the governor of Sais, the chiefs of Lower Egypt had opportunistically switched their allegiance to Taharka so they were now arrested and most were executed. The ringleader, Necho, was spared, showered with gifts and, after swearing a new oath of loyalty, was sent to Memphis as a native figurehead for the Assyrian administration.

Taharka's successor, his cousin Tantamani, attempted to regain control of Lower Egypt, besieging the Assyrians unsuccessfully in Memphis in 664 BC. Necho stayed loyal to the Assyrians but was killed fighting against the Kushites in the Delta. Ashurbanipal reacted quickly, sending another army to Egypt. After relieving Memphis, the Assyrian army pursued Tantamani as far south as the First Cataract, the border between Egypt and Nubia, ending Kushite influence in Egypt. On the way the Assyrians sacked the vast temple of the royal god Amun at Thebes and plundered its enormous treasury.

651 BC

EGYPTIAN INDEPENDENCE ✦ The conquest of Egypt marked the high-water mark of Assyrian imperial expansion. When Necho died in 664 BC, Ashurbanipal appointed his son Psamtek as his chief administrator in Lower Egypt. Psamtek was already in Assyrian service and was thought to be a loyal vassal. Upper Egypt was left in the care of Montuemhat, the governor of Thebes. The Assyrian empire was now seriously overextended and, while Ashurbanipal was preoccupied with other problems, Psamtek quietly began to build an independent power base, winning the personal loyalty of the chiefs of Lower Egypt and in 656 BC being acknowledged as overlord of Thebes by Montuemhat. In 652 BC Shamash-sum-ukin, the king of Babylon, rebelled against his brother Ashurbanipal, so starting a civil war. Psamtek was now free to raise his own army, reinforced by Greek mercenaries, and begin to expel the Assyrian garrisons from Egypt. By 651 BC Egypt was free and united under a native ruler for the first time in nearly 300 years.

By 651 BC Egypt was free and united under a native ruler for the first time in nearly 300 years.

c. 650 BC

THE HOPLITE STATE ✦ Thanks to the bitter rivalries between the city states, Greeks got plenty of practice at war. During the 'dark ages' war was the preserve of the military aristocracy and royalty. Battles were an opportunity for warriors to increase their status through individual acts of personal bravery. Sometimes, battles were settled by set-piece duels between aristocratic champion warriors, such as that between Achilles and Hector, described by Homer in the *Iliad*. The prosperous city states of the 7th and 8th centuries could afford to raise larger and better equipped armies than the petty dark age kings.

103

This led to the emergence of a new kind of Greek warrior, the hoplite. Hoplites were armoured infantry whose main weapon was a long thrusting spear. For protection the hoplite wore a bronze helmet, breastplate and greaves, and carried a large round wooden shield, known as a *hoplon*, from which he got his name. All able-bodied male citizens had the responsibility of fighting for their cities and were expected to provide their own weapons and armour. Citizens who could not afford to equip themselves as hoplites usually enjoyed lower status and fewer rights than those who could. Hoplites fought in a phalanx, a tight formation several ranks deep, which presented a wall of shields and a dense hedge of spear points to the enemy. There was no place in the phalanx for individual heroics. A hoplite could not fight effectively as an individual so any action which threatened the integrity of the shield wall was frowned upon. Consequently, this style of fighting created a strong sense of solidarity among the hoplite class.

The acknowledged masters of hoplite warfare were the Spartans, whose whole society was dedicated, to the exclusion of almost everything else, to producing good soldiers. Sparta was the dominant city of Laconia in the southern Peloponnesus. In the late eighth century, Sparta conquered the neighbouring region of Messenia. The conquered land was divided equally between all the Spartan citizens while the Messenians themselves were retained on the land as serfs called helots, who paid half their produce to their Spartan masters. After Sparta was defeated in a war with Argos in 669 BC the oppressed Messenians rebelled: the Spartans suppressed the revolt only after 17 years of bitter warfare.

The rebellion shook the Spartans: the Messenians outnumbered them seven to one and it convinced the Spartans that their future security could only

104

LEFT **Spartan warrior.** *This bronze figurine of a Spartan hoplite in breastplate and helmet from the sanctuary of Zeus at Dodona seems to radiate Sparta's confidence in its military superiority. The figure probably originally held a shield and spear, long since lost.*

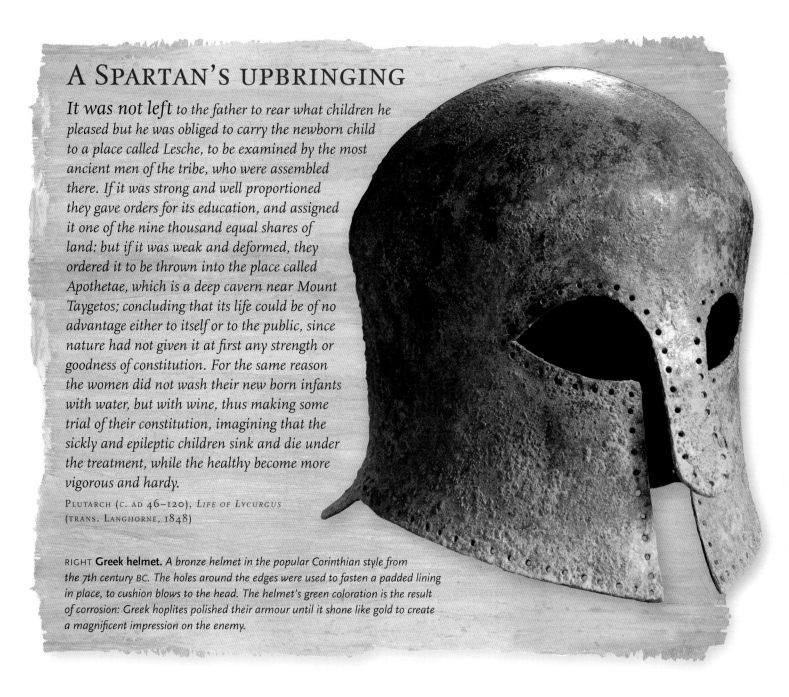

A SPARTAN'S UPBRINGING

It was not left to the father to rear what children he pleased but he was obliged to carry the newborn child to a place called Lesche, to be examined by the most ancient men of the tribe, who were assembled there. If it was strong and well proportioned they gave orders for its education, and assigned it one of the nine thousand equal shares of land: but if it was weak and deformed, they ordered it to be thrown into the place called Apothetae, which is a deep cavern near Mount Taygetos; concluding that its life could be of no advantage either to itself or to the public, since nature had not given it at first any strength or goodness of constitution. For the same reason the women did not wash their new born infants with water, but with wine, thus making some trial of their constitution, imagining that the sickly and epileptic children sink and die under the treatment, while the healthy become more vigorous and hardy.

PLUTARCH (C. AD 46–120), *LIFE OF LYCURGUS*
(TRANS. LANGHORNE, 1848)

RIGHT **Greek helmet.** *A bronze helmet in the popular Corinthian style from the 7th century BC. The holes around the edges were used to fasten a padded lining in place, to cushion blows to the head. The helmet's green coloration is the result of corrosion: Greek hoplites polished their armour until it shone like gold to create a magnificent impression on the enemy.*

be guaranteed by maintaining a constant state of readiness for war. To this end, Sparta developed a unique constitution that turned it into a hoplite state. Spartan tradition attributed the constitution to a single lawgiver called Lycurgus, but most modern historians regard him as a legendary figure. The most radical feature of the Spartan constitution was the *agoge* or state-organized upbringing. Male children were separated from their families at the age of seven and brought up communally. Education was almost entirely physical, consisting of gymnastics and training for war, lightened only by singing and dancing. The *agoge* was deliberately harsh, with few comforts (even underclothes and shoes were banned) and inadequate meals to encourage boys to use their initiative to get extra rations by fair means or foul. In the final stage of the *agoge* boys were sent to murder helots to prove their manhood. Boys who dropped out, the 'tremblers', lived with the shame for life and could never become full citizens. At the age of 20, those who completed the *agoge* became full citizens and joined a military training unit called a *syssitia*. A man could now legally marry but he had to live in the *syssitia* until he was 30 when he could finally live in his own household. This state upbringing created a tough, cohesive, disciplined and conformist society in which a man's birth counted for little. Spartans proudly described themselves as the *homoioi*, 'the men who are equal'. To keep things that way, money was not used in Sparta and trade was discouraged. While Spartan citizens may have been equal, they were superior to their non-citizen and helot subjects who performed all productive activities while the Spartans concentrated on military training.

BELOW **A gruesome triumph.** *Low relief frieze from the Assyrian royal palace at Nineveh showing king Ashurbanipal and his wife feasting in a shady garden to celebrate the conquest of Elam in 653 BC. The head of the defeated Elamite king Teumann hangs in a tree to the left. Scenes showing the harsh treatment of Assyria's enemies were placed prominently in palaces as a warning to potential rebels.*

646 BC

ASHURBANIPAL'S REVENGE ✦ Ashurbanipal did not regain control of Babylon until 648 BC, following a long and terrible siege in which Shamash-sum-ukin died. Ashurbanipal was enraged not only by his brother's treachery but by the assistance the Elamites had given to Babylon during its rebellion. At the beginning of his reign, Ashurbanipal did his best to cultivate good relations with Elam. When drought caused a famine in Elam, Ashurbanipal sent food aid to the Elamite king Urtaki and supported Elamite refugees who fled to Mesopotamia until the famine ended. Urtaki proved conspicuously ungrateful for Ashurbanipal's help, raiding Babylonia while Assyria's forces were fighting Taharka in Egypt in 665 BC. Urtaki died shortly after this incident and the throne was seized by his cousin Teumann. In summer 653 BC, Ashurbanipal received news that Teumann was planning to invade Assyria and so he launched a pre-emptive strike at Elam. Defeated in battle, Teumann was captured after his chariot overturned and was beheaded. Teumann's successor Attameti wisely kept a low profile but when he died in 648 BC, his son Humban-haltash got involved with an anti-Assyrian rebellion in Babylon. This sealed Elam's fate. After Ashurbanipal suppressed the Babylonian rebellion, he unleashed his full fury on Elam, ravaging the entire country in two devastating campaigns in 647 BC and 646 BC. The capital Susa was taken and sacked: its temples and their idols were destroyed, its royal tombs were desecrated and the bones of Elam's kings were carried off, with the rest of the spoil, to be 'imprisoned' at Nineveh, and its entire population was deported. Humban-haltash fled to the mountains of Luristan. There he was captured by a hostile tribe and handed over to Ashurbanipal, probably in 644 BC. Imprisoned at Nineveh, he and other captive kings were forced to draw Ashurbanipal's chariot at important religious festivals.

626 BC

BABYLON REBELS AGAINST ASSYRIAN RULE ✦ When Ashurbanipal died in 627 BC the Assyrian empire was in serious trouble. Ashurbanipal's campaigns against Egypt and Elam had strained the empire's resources and overextended its borders while his increasingly tyrannical rule spread fear and discontent. The last years of Ashurbanipal's reign were marked by increasing internal disorder. A mark of Assyrian weakness was the fact that a rebellion by King Josiah of Judah in 629 BC went unpunished. Ashurbanipal's appointed successor was his son Ashur-etil-ilani but he was opposed by his brother Sin-shar-ishkun and by a royal official Sin-shum-lishir, who also claimed the throne. Sin-shar-ishkun was the victor in the struggle but in the meantime a Chaldaean noble called Nabopolassar claimed the Babylonian throne and rebelled against Assyrian rule.

c. 621 BC

Draco's laws prescribed the death penalty for so many offences – apparently, even idleness was punished by death – that they have given us the word 'draconian' for describing any harsh measures.

DRACONIAN LAWS ✦ The development of hoplite warfare had profound political consequences for Greece. Greek hoplite armies were citizen armies and citizens believed that, as they were expected to fight for the state, they should have a greater say in its government. Between the mid-7th and the 5th centuries BC, popular leaders called tyrants, supported by the hoplite armies, overthrew the old aristocratic and monarchical order in many Greek states. In many others, fear of tyranny alone was enough to persuade the ruling classes to extend political rights. As used originally, the term tyrant (*tyrannos*) described a ruler who had achieved power by his own efforts rather than by inheritance. Tyrants courted popular support by cancelling debts and redistributing land from the aristocracy to the poor. However, tyrants were unwilling to give up the power they had won and, as the people gained political confidence, they came to be seen more and more as autocratic and oppressive rulers.

In most cities, the common citizens and the aristocracy eventually overcame their differences and united to overthrow the tyrant. Few tyrannies lasted more than three generations.

In 632 BC an aristocratic rebel called Cylon attempted to establish a tyranny in Athens. Athens was at this time ruled by an aristocratic oligarchy. Religious, military and judicial authority was in the hands of nine magistrates known as archons. When their term of office expired, former archons automatically became members for life of the council of elders, which met on the Areopagus hill below the Acropolis, and made all the important political decisions. Archons were elected annually by the citizen assembly but, as only those of aristocratic birth had the right to stand for office, this effectively excluded the majority of citizens from directly participating in their city's government. Cylon's coup failed but it shook the aristocracy, not into reform but into repression by commissioning the archon Draco to compile a harshly repressive law code in *c.* 621 BC. So that no one could claim ignorance of the law as an excuse, the code was inscribed on wooden tablets, which were publicly displayed on rotating pyramidal steles. Draco's laws prescribed the death penalty for so many offences – apparently, even idleness was punished by death – that they have given us the word 'draconian' for describing any harsh measures. When Draco was asked why he specified the death penalty for most offences he replied that small offences deserved death and he knew of no severer penalty for great ones. A later Greek writer remarked that Draco wrote his laws in blood instead of ink.

612 BC

FALL OF THE ASSYRIAN EMPIRE ✦ By 616 BC Nabopolassar had expelled all the Assyrian garrisons from Babylonian territory and was ready to take the offensive. Nabopolassar found an ally in the Medes, a powerful Iranian people closely related to the Persians, who could threaten Assyria from the north. In 615 BC Nabopolassar advanced into Assyria as far as the old capital Ashur before he was forced to retreat. The Assyrians besieged Nabopolassar at Takrit but were themselves forced to retreat when news came that the Medes had attacked eastern Assyria. In 614 BC the Babylonians and Medes together captured and sacked Ashur. Tribal rebellions, probably fomented by the Assyrians, forced the Babylonians and Medes to withdraw in 613 BC but they returned in strength the following year and laid siege to Nineveh, the Assyrian capital. Despite its strong defences, the city fell after just three months. It was as if the gods had deserted the Assyrians: an unseasonal flood washed away a section of the city wall, letting the besiegers storm in and sack the city. Sin-shar-ishkun was killed during the fighting.

NABOPOLASSAR'S TRIUMPH

I slaughtered the land of Assyria, I turned the hostile land into heaps of ruins. The Assyrians, who since distant days had ruled over all the peoples, and with his heavy yoke, and brought injury to the people of the land, I turned his feet away from Babylonia, I threw off his yoke.

BABYLONIAN CHRONICLE (TRANS. LUCKENBILL, 1926)

109

After 300 years of seeming invincibility, the Assyrian empire had collapsed in little more than a dozen years. The Assyrian heartland was systematically ravaged by the victorious Babylonian forces. None of Assyria's major cities survived the fall of the empire: their people were massacred or deported to Babylonia, and Assyria itself ceased to have any political importance.

609—605 BC

BABYLON AND EGYPT CLASH ✦ The fall of Nineveh was not quite the end for Assyria. A junior member of the Assyrian royal family, Ashur-uballit, escaped the destruction of Nineveh and, with other survivors, fled to Harran in Syria, where, with Egyptian support, he was proclaimed king. Two years later Ashur-uballit was driven out of Harran by Nabopolassar and retreated still further west to Carchemish on the Euphrates, where he waited for reinforcements from Egypt. The following year Ashur-uballit attempted to recapture Harran with the support of a large Egyptian army. The Babylonian garrison set to guard the road to Harran was defeated but after besieging Harran for over two months the Assyrian–Egyptian army was forced to withdraw. After this failure, Ashur-uballit disappeared from history and, with him, the last trace of the Assyrian state. The Egyptians did not withdraw from Carchemish, however. Egypt had benefited from Assyria's decline to reclaim its traditional sphere of influence in the Levant and the new pharaoh Necho II (r. 610–595 BC) would not allow this to be threatened by Babylon. In 608 BC Necho brought a new army to Carchemish, becoming the first pharaoh for nearly 900 years to stand on the Euphrates. On the way Necho defeated and killed King Josiah of Judah who had been harassing his army in alliance with the Babylonians. Nabopolassar's failing health forced him to return to Babylon in 606 BC and hand command of his armies over to his son Nebuchadnezzar (r. 605–562 BC), who was a far better soldier than his father. In 605 BC Nebuchadnezzar took an army to Carchemish and inflicted a bloody defeat on Necho. Nebuchadnezzar pursued the defeated Egyptians, defeating them again at Hama in southern Syria, and following this by occupying the whole of the Levant up to the borders of Egypt. Egypt was saved from a Babylonian invasion only because news reached Nebuchadnezzar that his father had died and he immediately returned to Babylon to take the throne of the Middle East's new dominant power.

OPPOSITE **Solon debating law.** *Ancient Greek philosophy and science were significant influences on the development of early Islamic civilization. This miniature, from a 13th-century Turkish copy of* The Book of Selections of Wisdom and Wonderful Sayings, *depicts the Athenian lawmaker Solon, seated on cushions in Islamic style, debating with his critics.*

OVERLEAF **Lions of Babylon.** *Dedicated to the Ishtar, Babylonian goddess of love and war, Nebuchadnezzar's new north gate for Babylon was entirely faced with brightly coloured glazed bricks with low relief figures of lions, wild bulls and mythical mushussus (part serpent, part lion and part eagle). The blue glaze was derived from semi-precious lapis lazuli brought from the mountains of Afghanistan.*

594–593 BC

SOLON REFORMS THE ATHENIAN CONSTITUTION ✦ Draco's laws did nothing to end social tensions in Athens, which were soon exacerbated by an economic crisis which forced many citizens to mortgage their lands in return for food and loans of seed corn. Debts were secured against the person and Draco's code allowed defaulters to be enslaved: many did so and lost their liberty and citizenship. Amid rising popular discontent, the aristocracy panicked: fearing that the people might support a tyrant, they gave the archon Solon (*c.* 639–*c.* 559 BC) absolute authority to draw up a new constitution in 594–593 BC. The aristocracy soon regretted their decision.

Solon believed that social justice was essential to *eunomia*, a well-ordered society. He abolished all Draco's laws, except those relating to homicide. Debt slavery was abolished and those who had been enslaved were freed and regained their citizenship. All outstanding debts were cancelled. Solon ended the aristocratic

111

SOLON GOES INTO VOLUNTARY EXILE

When his laws were published, Solon had visitors every day, finding fault with some of them, commending others, or advising him to make certain additions or deletions. But the greater part came to demand a justification for this or that article, or a clear and precise explanation of the meaning and intention. Aware that he could not well excuse himself from complying with their wishes, and that if he indulged their demands for changes, the doing it might cause controversy, he determined to withdraw from the difficulty and to get away at once from their cavils and exceptions. For as he himself observed 'not all the greatest enterprises can please'. Under pretence, therefore, of going on business he set sail for another country, having obtained permission from the Athenians for ten years' absence. In that time he hoped his laws would become familiar to them.

PLUTARCH, *THE LIFE OF SOLON* (ADAPTED FROM 1848 TRANSLATION)

monopoly of power by making wealth rather than birth the qualification for public office. He divided the population into four classes whose political rights were graduated according to their wealth. The richest class was the *pentakosiomedimnoi*, 'the 500-measure men', whose income exceeded 500 measures of corn a year (one measure or *medimnos* was approximately 9 litres, or 19 pints) or its equivalent in value. Next were the *hippeis*, men with an income between 300 and 500 measures, who were rich enough to equip themselves as cavalry. The third class were the *zeugites*, the hoplite class, which was mainly made up of small farmers and urban craftsmen who had an income of between 200 and 300 measures. The fourth, the poorest and largest class, were the *thetes*, who were hired labourers with an income of less than 200 measures. Men of this class fought as lightly armed skirmishers or archers and as oarsmen in Athens' fleet of galleys. Archons could only be elected from the two richest classes. To balance the aristocracy's control of the Areopagus, Solon introduced a popular legislative assembly of 400 elected members.

Solon's constitution went too far for the aristocracy – who could no longer use the threat of debt slavery to force peasant farmers into dependent relationships – and not far enough for most citizens – who had hoped that he would redistribute property from rich to poor. Unpopular with everyone, Solon went into voluntary exile when his term of office expired.

587 BC

BY THE RIVERS OF BABYLON ✦ Nebuchadnezzar's fame rests on his lavish building works at Babylon and his deportation of the Jews of Jerusalem. Nebuchadnezzar's building works continued throughout his reign, turning Babylon into a truly spectacular imperial capital. Among his most important buildings were the Ishtar Gate, which was completely covered in costly glazed bricks, a vast palace whose riverside terraces gave rise to the legendary Hanging Gardens of Babylon, one of the Seven Wonders of the ancient world, and a complete rebuilding of the Etemenanki ziggurat, which was the prototype of the biblical Tower of Babel.

Nebuchadnezzar's problem with the Jews was part of a wider problem of consolidating Babylonian rule in the Levant. Despite his crushing defeat at Carchemish, Necho could not resist meddling in the Levant, stirring up anti-Babylonian rebellions. Necho's interference provoked Nebuchadnezzar to invade Egypt in 601 BC but he met with stiff resistance in battle and was forced to retreat. King Jehoiakim of Judah was encouraged by this to transfer his allegiance to Egypt but in 597 BC Nebuchadnezzar laid siege to Jerusalem, forcing its surrender. Jehoiakim died during the siege and his son, Jehoiachin, together with the Jewish nobility, craftsmen and soldiers, was deported to Babylonia.

When, in 589 BC, the pharaoh Apries invaded the Levant, Judah's new vassal King Zedekiah ignored the advice of the prophet Jeremiah and, with other local rulers, rebelled against Babylonian rule. Nebuchadnezzar quickly retaliated, drove the Egyptians out, and again laid siege to Jerusalem. Thirty months later, the city finally fell. Zedekiah and his family were captured while trying to escape. After being forced to watch the execution of his sons, Zedekiah was blinded and spent the remainder of his life in captivity at Babylon. The Babylonians razed Jerusalem to the ground, destroying Solomon's temple and deporting the majority of the population to Babylonia. Judah ceased to exist as a political entity.

Among Nebuchadnezzar's most important buildings were a vast palace whose riverside terraces gave rise to the legendary Hanging Gardens of Babylon and the Etemenanki ziggurat, which was the prototype of the biblical Tower of Babel.

550 BC

CYRUS THE GREAT FOUNDS THE PERSIAN EMPIRE ✦ Persia – present-day Iran – derives its name from the Parsa, an Iranian nomad people whose original homeland was in Central Asia. Sometime during the 9th century BC they began to migrate south into Iran in company with another Iranian nomad people, the Medes, Babylon's ally in its final war with Assyria. While the Medes settled on the Iranian plateau, the Parsa continued south, finally settling between the Zagros mountains and the sea. The area became known after them as Parsa or Persia (now the southern Iranian province of Fars). The first king of Persia was Achaemenes (r. *c.* 700 BC) from whom the Persian ruling dynasty became known as the Achaemenids. After it was destroyed by Ashurbanipal in 646 BC, the Persians took over the lands of the Elamite kingdom but for most of their early history they were vassals of the Medes.

In 553 BC the Persian king Cyrus II (r. 559–530 BC) rebelled against Astyages, his Median overlord. In 550 BC Astyages laid siege to the Persian capital at Pasargadae but, for unknown reasons, the Median army mutinied and handed him over to Cyrus.

LEFT **Tower of Babel.** *The biblical story of the Tower of Babel is often associated with one of Nebuchadnezzar's most ambitious building projects, the restoration of the 300-foot-tall Etemenanki ziggurat, dedicated to the city god Marduk. The Tower of Babel was intended to reach to heaven but God destroyed it and punished its builders' pride by scattering them over the face of the earth. The architecture of this painting of the tower by Pieter Bruegel the Elder (c.1563) is inspired by the Colosseum in Rome which the artist had visited some years previously. Nebuchadnezzar's tower was destroyed by Alexander the Great, a man who thought himself to be a god.*

Cyrus followed up his bloodless victory – even Astyages was spared – by seizing the Median capital and treasury at Hamadan, and the whole Median kingdom, which stretched from Anatolia to Afghanistan, submitted peacefully to his rule. Within the space of a few weeks, Persia had become a great power. Cyrus was certainly helped by the close cultural relationship between the Persians and Medes: they spoke similar languages and worshipped many of the same gods. Cyrus' mother was a Median princess, so he was related to the Median royal house, and he conciliated the Medes by making a Median his chief adviser and by making Hamadan the joint capital of his empire. This was more a dynastic takeover than a conquest.

546 BC

BETRAYED BY AN ORACLE ✦

The sudden rise of Persia alarmed Croesus, the ruler of the wealthy kingdom of Lydia in western Anatolia. Croesus sought the advice of the famous oracle of the sun god Apollo at Delphi, the holiest site in Greece. The oracle was an ordinary woman, known as the Pythea, who served for life. Consultations took place in the temple of Apollo at Delphi, the innermost sanctuary of which contained the Omphalos, an egg-shaped stone which the Greeks believed marked the centre of the world. During consultations, the Pythea entered a trance and was possessed by Apollo who spoke through her. The god's words were incomprehensible to ordinary mortals and had to be interpreted by priests called

LEFT **Croesus on his pyre.** *Red figure painted amphora showing the despairing king Croesus preparing to burn himself alive on a funeral pyre following his defeat by Cyrus the Great of Persia in 546 BC. Greek painted pottery was made as a substitute for vessels of silver and gold. The red painted figures represent gold inlay and the black paint stands for silver: ancient Greeks did not polish their silverware because it gradually wore the metal away, making the owner poorer. Greek painted pottery was widely exported: this amphora was made in Attica (the region of Athens) but was found in Italy.*

COINS

Defined as pieces of metal of standardized size, weight and value, stamped with a mark guaranteeing their standard, coins were first issued in western Anatolia in the 7th century BC. In later Greek historical traditions, the invention of coins is attributed to the kingdom of Lydia, a source of electrum (a natural alloy of gold and silver), which was the metal used to make the earliest known coins. By 500 BC the use of coins had spread to Greece, Cyprus, North Africa, Italy and Persia. As durable valuable items that were easily transported and widely distributed, the potential of coins as a medium for circulating propaganda was quickly realized by rulers, who could stamp them with idealized images of themselves, or with symbols of their states. Some of the earliest such coins were issued by Athens after its victory in the Persian Wars. These coins depict an owl, the sacred bird of Athens' patron goddess Athena, holding an olive branch, which was a symbol of peace.

ABOVE **Athenian silver tetradrachm.** *Issued in the mid-5th century BC, this four-drachma coin bears an image of an owl, symbol of Athens' protector Athena, the goddess of wisdom, and of the city itself. This design remained unchanged for 200 years.*

prophetai, who shaped them into coherent, but notoriously ambiguous, answers. When Croesus asked the oracle about the consequences of war between Lydia and Persia he was told that if he went to war with Cyrus he would destroy a great empire. Encouraged by this, Croesus asked the oracle if his reign would be a long one. The oracle replied that 'when a mule becomes king of the Medes, then, tender-footed Lydian, flee by the pebbled River Hermus and do not delay, nor feel shame at being a coward'. Feeling quite sure that the king of the Medes would always be a man, Croesus took this final reply as a clear guarantee of victory and he confidently began to prepare for war. What Croesus did not know was that Cyrus, being of mixed Persian and Median birth, was a 'mule'.

In summer 547 BC Croesus invaded Persia and fought a fierce but indecisive battle against Cyrus before withdrawing ahead of the onset of winter. On his return

119

to Sardis, his capital, he stood down his army, intending to campaign again in the spring. Cyrus, however, did not stand down his army and early in 546 BC he arrived unexpectedly outside the walls of Sardis. The city was completely unprepared for a siege and it fell after only 14 days. Too late, Croesus understood that the empire he would destroy by going to war with Cyrus was his own. According to legend, Croesus tried to commit suicide by throwing himself alive onto his funeral pyre but Apollo doused the flames with a rain shower and he and his family were captured. Showing his customary mercy to defeated enemies, Cyrus spared Croesus' life and later made him governor of Barene in Media. Cyrus immediately left to campaign in Central Asia, leaving his general Harpagus to consolidate Persian control of Anatolia by conquering the Greek cities along its Ionian coast.

539 BC

BABYLON IS FALLEN ✦ Nebuchadnezzar died in 562 BC and with him passed Babylon's moment of glory. Nebuchadnezzar's successor, his son Amel-marduk, lasted only two years before he was overthrown in a palace coup and replaced on the throne by his brother-in-law Nergal-shar-usur. Nergal-shar-usur died only four years later, shortly after a failed campaign against the Medes, and his son Labashi-marduk had barely ascended the throne when he too was overthrown by a palace official called Nabonidus (r. 555–539 BC). Nabonidus became unpopular because he favoured

ABOVE **The Cyrus Cylinder.** *This clay cylinder from Babylon carries a text in the name of Cyrus the Great, declaring him the legitimate ruler of the city, extolling his efforts for the welfare of its people and invoking the protection of its god Marduk for the royal family.*

OPPOSITE **The writing on the wall.** *According to the Book of Daniel, the miraculous writing which appeared on the wall while the prince Belshazzar was feasting foretold the fall of Babylon to the Medes and Persians.* Belshazzar's Feast, *by Rembrandt (c. 1635), is perhaps the most famous of many works of art, literature and music inspired by the story.*

the moon god Sin over Babylon's national god Marduk. To escape the controversy, Nabonidus spent ten years in self-imposed exile in Arabia, leaving Babylon under the control of his son Bel-shar-usur (the Belshazzar of the Bible). This only cemented his unpopularity because, in the king's absence, the important New Year festival could not be celebrated. By the time Nabonidus returned to Babylon around 543 BC the international situation had become very threatening because of the meteoric rise of Persia, which had been only a minor power when he left for Arabia.

Cyrus began a skilful propaganda campaign against Nabonidus, playing on the widespread religious discontent within Babylonia. In 539 BC, Cyrus invaded Babylonia and in September defeated Nabonidus at Opis near modern Baghdad. Nabonidus took flight and Babylonian resistance crumbled. Nabonidus had few supporters left and when a Persian army under Governor Ugbaru arrived outside the walls of Babylon the city surrendered without a fight. The Persian forces kept good order in the city until Cyrus arrived to a rapturous reception several weeks later: the Babylonians cheered and scattered palm leaves at his feet. Cyrus made no changes to Babylon's civil administration and religious institutions, only appointing a Persian governor. The exiled Jews welcomed Cyrus' victory even more than most: he gave them leave to return home and to rebuild the temple at Jerusalem. Cyrus' son Cambyses performed the New Year ceremony on his behalf, establishing his right to rule Babylon as Marduk's representative and not just as its conqueror. Nabonidus, the last king in the Mesopotamian tradition, surrendered and was spared and exiled to Kerman in southeast Iran. In only 11 years, and with remarkably little fighting, Cyrus had built the largest empire the world had yet seen.

530 BC

THE DEATH OF CYRUS THE GREAT ✦ By the 530s BC Cyrus' empire extended as far into Central Asia as the Syr Darya river in present-day Kazakhstan. The vast open steppes beyond the river were dominated by the Scythians, Iranian horse-mounted nomads who exploited their mobility to launch devastating raids on their settled neighbours. Cyrus tried to secure the frontier by building a chain of forts along the Syr Darya, by paying subsidies to friendly chieftains and by sending punitive expeditions against hostile ones. It was in the course of one of these expeditions, in December 530 BC, that Cyrus, now around 70 years old, was killed. Cyrus was interred in a relatively modest mausoleum at Pasargadae, which still stands substantially intact today. An inscription on the mausoleum, now lost to weathering or vandalism, proclaimed 'O man, I am Cyrus, the son of Cambyses, who founded the empire of Persia, and was king of Asia. Grudge me not, therefore, this monument.' Cyrus' achievements, gained by diplomacy as much as by force, and his reputation for moderation and tolerance, made him greatly admired even by Persia's enemies. In his *Cyropedia*, a fictionalized biography, the Greek author Xenophon (*c.* 420–350 BC) presented Cyrus as the epitome of all the virtues expected of an ideal ruler in the ancient world.

CHARISMATIC CONQUEROR

Cyrus did indeed eclipse all other monarchs, before or since, and I include not only those who have inherited their power, but those who have won empire by their own exertions. ... Cyrus was able to conquer his vast empire by the sheer terror of his personality that the inhabitants were prostrate before him: not one of them dared lift hand against him. And yet he was able, at the same time, to inspire them all with so deep a desire to please him and win his favour that all they asked was to be guided by his judgment and his alone. Thus he knit to himself a complex of nationalities so vast that it would have taxed a man's endurance merely to traverse his empire in any one direction, east or west, south or north, from the palace at its centre.

Xenophon, Cyropedia ('The education of Cyrus'), 1, 4–5 (trans. Henry Graham Dakyns)

BELOW **Cyrus' mausoleum.** *After his death in 530 BC, Cyrus was buried in this limestone mausoleum at Pasargadae, his capital city, in southern Iran. Though its commemorative inscriptions have been worn away,* *it still has its original appearance. However, the gardens which once surrounded it have long vanished, as have its contents, including Cyrus' golden coffin, which was looted on the fall of the Persian empire.*

525 BC

EGYPT CONQUERED – AGAIN ✦

Cyrus was succeeded by his son Cambyses (r. 529–522 BC), whose main achievement was the conquest of Egypt in 525 BC. Since throwing off Assyrian rule a century earlier, Egypt had enjoyed prosperity but had failed to reassert itself as an imperial power and remained militarily weak. When Cambyses invaded Egypt in 525 BC, its pharaoh Psamtek III (r. 526–525 BC) had only been on the throne six months and was young and inexperienced. Cambyses also benefited from the advice of Phanes, a Greek mercenary general who had defected from the Egyptian army. Cambyses crossed the Sinai desert with the aid of Bedouin guides and fought a fierce battle against Psamtek at Pelusium in the Delta. The Egyptians wrought a savage vengeance on Phanes. His sons, who he had left behind in Egypt, were paraded in front of the army in full view of their father. The Egyptians cut the boys' throats over a bowl, mixing their blood with wine and water to make a drink, which they all shared before joining battle. The Egyptians did not, however, show the same savagery in battle and the Persians routed them. Psamtek fled to Memphis, which surrendered after a siege of several months. Cambyses ordered the public execution of 2,000 leading Memphites, and Psamtek was sent to Persia in chains, and was later also executed: Cambyses was not as generous to his defeated foes as his father had been. Legend has it that

RIGHT **Greek tributaries.** *Using craftsmen and architectural styles drawn from all corners of the Persian empire, Darius I (r. 521–486 BC) built a spectacular palace at his new capital city of Persepolis. A low relief frieze at the entrance to its audience chamber shows a parade of Persia's subjects bringing tribute, like these Greeks from Iona bearing bundles of cloth.*

Cambyses hoped to legitimize his rule in Egypt by winning the endorsement of the Oracle of Amun at Siwa Oasis, deep in the Libyan desert. However, the expedition he sent, 50,000 strong, was engulfed in a sandstorm and disappeared.

522 BC

IMPOSTERS AND USURPERS ✦ While in Egypt, Cambyses campaigned in Nubia and contemplated an expedition to conquer the great Phoenician trading city of Carthage in modern-day Tunisia. Before he could do so, his brother Bardiya (also known as Smerdis) seized the throne, forcing Cambyses to hurry back to Persia. On the way, somewhere in Syria in summer 522 BC, Cambyses unexpectedly died, whether by natural causes, suicide or by murder is unclear. After Cambyses' death, Darius, a member of a junior branch of the Achaemenid family who was with the king, hurried on to Media. With the support of six Persian nobles, Darius murdered Bardiya and claimed the throne for himself. In an inscription he had made at Bisitun, Darius later claimed that before leaving for Egypt Cambyses had ordered Bardiya to be killed secretly for plotting treason and that the Bardiya who seized the throne was really a lookalike impostor called Gaumata. Most historians now believe that Darius invented this story so that he could claim to be restoring the legitimate Achaemenid line rather than usurping the throne. Many of Darius' subjects certainly did doubt his legitimacy, and he had to spend the first three years of his reign (522–486 BC) suppressing rebellions throughout the empire.

The Egyptians wrought a savage vengeance on Phanes. The Egyptians cut his sons' throats over a bowl, mixing their blood with wine and water to make a drink, which they all shared before joining battle.

513 BC

DARIUS INVADES EUROPE ✦ By 520 BC Darius had destroyed all opposition to his rule, freeing him to lead an army across the Hindu Kush mountains and conquer the Indus river valley. Darius then travelled the entire breadth of his empire and in 513 BC he invaded Thrace (roughly modern Bulgaria). The expedition, which brought the Persian empire to its greatest extent, was only a partial success. Thrace was conquered and the kingdom of Macedon was forced to become a vassal state but Darius failed in his main aim of seizing the Scythian-controlled gold mines in the foothills of the Carpathian mountains north of the Danube. Darius crossed the Danube on a bridge of boats built by Greek engineers but as the Persian army advanced into their territory the nomadic Scythians simply retreated north before it. Scythian cavalry constantly harassed the Persians but Darius was never able to bring them to battle. After two months Darius gave up and withdrew across the Danube. The European expedition was far from a disaster but, by showing their limitations, it would have serious consequences for the Persians.

ABOVE **Golden chariot:** *part of the Oxus Treasure, a hoard of 170 golden objects manufactured in different provinces of the Persian empire around the 5th and 4th centuries BC, discovered by travelling merchants near the Amu Darya (Oxus) river in Afghanistan in 1880. Robbed by bandits, the merchants appealed for help to the local British political officer, Captain F.C. Burton, who pursued the bandits and recovered the hoard. The merchants later sold the hoard to a British official in Rawalpindi (now in Pakistan) and it is today displayed in the British Museum in London. The hoard is believed to have been originally part of a temple treasury.*

509 BC

ROME BECOMES A REPUBLIC ✦ By the late 6th century BC Rome had become an impressive city. Earlier in the century the Forum, then a marsh, had been drained and laid out as a public square surrounded by monumental buildings and shops, while the newly completed temple of Jupiter on the Capitoline Hill was one of the largest temples in the Mediterranean world. Rome's population, at 20,000–40,000 already twice as large as any other city in Latium, was growing fast, in part as a result of immigration from the surrounding countryside. Rome's attitude to citizenship made it attractive to immigrants. Unlike most cities in the ancient Mediterranean, where birth was the basis of citizenship, in Rome any free male resident was eligible for citizenship. At least two Roman kings were immigrants and even freed slaves could become citizens. This ability to assimilate new populations would be a decisive factor in Rome's later rise as an imperial power.

The kings of Rome ruled in consultation with the Senate, an assembly made up of the male heads of a small group of patrician families who claimed to be

OPPOSITE **Darius enthroned.** *Low relief sculpture of the Persian king Darius I on his throne, from the royal palace at Persepolis. Darius brought the Persian empire to its greatest territorial extent but it was also during his reign that it suffered its first serious reverse, at the hands of the Athenians at Marathon in 490 BC.*

ABOVE **Scythian gold.** *A 6th-century BC Scythian neck ring and belt plate showing horse riders resting, discovered in Siberia. The Scythians, an Indo-Iranian nomad people, dominated the Eurasian steppes from Eastern Europe to the borders of China around the middle of the first millennium BC. Unusually for a nomad people, the Scythians were exceptionally skilful metalworkers and their decorative styles were a major influence on the early development of Celtic art.*

descended from senators appointed by Romulus after the founding of Rome. As a counterbalance to the aristocratic Senate, King Servius Tullius (r. *c.* 578–535 BC) created a new popular assembly, which came to be known as the *comitia centuriata*. This placed citizens in voting units called centuries and divided them into classes according to how much property they owned and what weapons and armour they could afford to equip themselves with. The assembly became the basis for raising Rome's citizen army of around 6,000 infantry and 600 cavalry. Only property owners were eligible to serve. Tarquin the Proud (r. *c.* 535–509 BC), the last king of Rome, alienated the patrician class when he decided to rule without consulting the Senate. When, in 509 BC, Tarquin's son Sextus raped Lucretia, a Roman noblewoman, a group of patricians led by Lucius Junius Brutus rose, overthrew the monarchy and established a republic (from Latin *res publica* meaning literally 'a public affair').

In later times, Romans regarded the overthrow of the monarchy as the pivotal moment in their history, the beginning of Rome's rise to dominance. Traditionally, the establishment of the republic was presented as liberation from oppression but in reality it was liberation only for the aristocracy. To maintain popular support, the Roman kings had often challenged aristocratic privilege. Now that the kings were gone, the patricians were determined to maintain the monopoly of power they had won as a class. In order to prevent any single person or family from gaining control of the state, the Senate created a unique collegiate magistracy in which two men, the consuls, shared regal powers. So that neither could achieve dominance, each consul had the power to veto the decisions of the other. So that they could not consolidate a hold on power, consuls were not allowed to stand for re-election to a second consecutive term of office. The first consuls to be elected were Lucius Junius Brutus, now known as 'the Liberator', and Lucius Tarquinius Collatinus, Lucretia's husband. It was recognized that divided leadership could be a disadvantage in a military emergency, so the constitution allowed that under these conditions one man could be appointed dictator with absolute powers for a term of one year.

Consuls were elected annually by the *comitia centuriata*, which had the right also to vote on, but not debate or make, policy: that remained the exclusive preserve of the Senate, which was dominated entirely by patricians who sat in it by hereditary

> *The Senate created a unique collegiate magistracy in which two men, the consuls, shared regal powers. So that neither could achieve dominance, each consul had the power to veto the decisions of the other.*

OPPOSITE **The Rape of Lucretia** *by the Italian Renaissance artist Titian (c. 1488–1576). According to Rome's historical traditions it was the rape of Lucretia by Sextus, the son of King Tarquin the Proud, that precipitated the fall of the Roman monarchy. Lucretia disclosed the rape to her father and husband and, after they had sworn to take vengeance, she committed suicide by stabbing herself in the heart, so, in Roman eyes, recovering her honour. Subsequently, Lucretia became a popular symbol of feminine virtue. The story was a popular theme for painters in early modern Europe because it provided an opportunity to portray female nudity in an edifyingly moral setting.*

THE FIRST ACT OF THE CONSULS

The first step towards political liberty *in Rome consisted in the fact that the consuls were annually elected magistrates — in the limitation, that is, not of their powers but of their period of office. The earliest consuls exercised the full powers of the kings, and carried all their insignia, with one exception — the most important of all — namely the fasces* [a bundle of birch rods often shown containing an axe]. *These were allowed to only one consul of the two, to avoid the duplication of this dreadful symbol of the power of life and death. Brutus by his colleague's consent was the first to have the fasces, and he proved as zealous in guarding liberty as he had been in demanding it. His first act was to make the people, while the taste of liberty was still fresh upon their tongues, swear a solemn oath never to allow any man to be king in Rome.*

LIVY, *THE HISTORY OF ROME*, BOOK 2 (TRANS. AUBREY DE SÉLINCOURT, *THE EARLY HISTORY OF ROME*, 1960)

right. Voting in the *comitia centuriata* was by class and was structured to ensure that the richer classes could always outvote the numerically larger poorer classes. It was essentially a massive exercise in gerrymandering to exclude the plebeians (citizens of non-noble birth) from political influence.

508 BC

THE FIRST DEMOCRACY ✦ In the long term, Solon's constitution of 594 BC laid the foundations for Athens' most important political legacy, the introduction of democracy, but in the short term it did nothing to alleviate the city's social tensions. The aristocracy refused to give any more ground and in 546 BC the tyrant Peisistratos seized power. Peisistratos won widespread popular support for his reforms, which included a property tax on wealthy landowners, a monumental building programme to provide work for labourers, craftsmen and artists, and the development of silver mines and marble quarries. Peisistratos died in 527 BC and was succeeded in turn by his sons Hipparchus (d. 514 BC) and Hippias. Their rule was harsher than their father's so their popularity gradually waned, and in 510 BC a Spartan invasion forced Hippias into exile in Persia.

The Spartan invasion was engineered by Cleisthenes, an exiled Athenian aristocrat who won popular support by introducing a democratic constitution in 508 BC. Cleisthenes placed the day-to-day government of the state in the hands of a council of 500 representatives elected by the demes (communities) of Athens. Any citizen belonging to the *zeugites* (the hoplite class) or above, who was aged 30 or over, was eligible to stand for the council. All citizens had the right to vote in elections and at the monthly meeting of the citizen assembly, where every major decision of state, including declarations of war, was decided by majority voting. Athenian democracy was narrowly based. Only freeborn

OPPOSITE **Banished.** *As a safeguard against tyranny, the Athenian constitution allowed citizens to vote to exile anyone they thought was becoming too powerful and influential. Votes were cast by scratching names onto potsherds, called* ostraka, *from which we get the word 'ostracism'. These ostraka name the general Themistocles, son of Neocles, who was banished from Athens in 470 BC. Themistocles had led the Athenian fleet to victory over the Persians at Salamis in 480 BC but this counted for nothing when he alienated the Athenians by his perceived arrogance. Themistocles entered the service of the Persian king Artaxerxes and became governor of Magnesia in Anatolia, dying there in 459 BC.*

ELIGIBILITY FOR ATHENIAN CITIZENSHIP

Men belong to the citizen body *if they are of citizen parentage on both sides, and if they are registered as members of their demes at the age of eighteen. When they are registered, the deme members take a vote about them on oath, first to decide whether they have reached the age prescribed by the law (if they decide they have not, the candidates return to the ranks of the boys), and secondly to decide whether they are free men and born as prescribed by the laws.*

Then, if they reject a man as unfree, he appeals to the jury court, and the deme members choose five of their number as prosecutors: if he is found to have been unjustly registered, the state sells him as a slave; if he wins the case, the deme members are obliged to register him.

ARISTOTLE, *THE ATHENIAN CONSTITUTION* 42, 1–11, TRANS. P.J. RHODES, *THE GREEK CITY STATES: A SOURCE BOOK* (1981)

Athenian men aged over 20 could become full citizens and vote. Women, foreign-born residents and slaves, who made up the majority of Athens' population of around 300,000, were excluded.

Cleisthenes left one bastion of aristocratic privilege. This was the Areopagus council of former archons, which was given the right to veto unconstitutional decisions of the citizen assembly. Aristocrats also retained the advantage in the new democratic politics in that, as they did not have to work for a living, they had the most time to spare for politics, and the wealth to advance their influence through patronage and networks of clients. Another of Cleisthenes' reforms recognized the danger this posed to democracy by allowing citizens to vote annually to exile overambitious politicians as a safeguard against tyranny. This became known as ostracism because votes were cast by scratching names on pieces of broken pottery called *ostraka*. Cleisthenes did not, however, get his reforms through without opposition. A diehard aristocratic clique called in a Spartan army to stop the reforms, but a popular uprising forced them to withdraw. By around 507 BC Athenian democracy was up and running.

THE
AGE OF
GREECE
500–323 BC

Mighty Persia's nemesis was Greece. The small but militarily proficient Greek city states united against a common enemy to defeat Persia's invasion in 480–479 BC and almost immediately went back to their interminable internecine wars. The balance of power swung from Athens, to Sparta, to Thebes but none was able to achieve a decisive advantage and unite Greece into a single state. Despite the constant conflict, this was an age of brilliant cultural achievement for the Greeks in art and architecture, philosophy, drama and science.

Unity was imposed from the outside, by the Balkan kingdom of Macedon, whose king, Philip II, conquered Greece in 336 BC. By conquering the Persian empire, Philip's charismatic son Alexander the Great brought an end to the ancient civilizations of the Middle East and made Greek civilization the dominant cultural force from the Mediterranean to the Indus.

499 BC

TROUBLE IN IONIA ✦ The rapid expansion of the Persian empire under Cyrus the Great and his successors was made much easier by the long traditions of imperial rule in the Middle East, which had made people accustomed to be ruled by foreigners. The Persians respected local beliefs and customs, and were careful not to overtax their subjects. For most people, therefore, Persian rule brought few changes and there was little spirit of popular resistance. The Ionian Greeks were an important exception to this general rule. Like all Greeks, the Ionians lived in city states and were not accustomed even to being ruled by other Greeks, let alone foreigners, who were all considered barbarians regardless of their accomplishments. Ionia was part of the satrapy of Sardis. The satraps (governors) ruled the Ionians indirectly by appointing compliant tyrants. This suited many among the Ionian aristocracy well enough but most Ionians wanted what the Athenians had got in 508 BC – democracy.

PREVIOUS PAGES **The last stand of King Leonidas** *and his 300 Spartan hoplites against the Persians at Thermopylae in 480 BC bought time for the Greeks to organize their defences at the cost of their own lives. Leonidas subsequently became the object of a hero cult which continued until the 2nd century AD. This modern statue of Leonidas was erected in Sparta in 1968.*

In 500 BC, Aristagoras, the tyrant of Miletos, hatched a plan to widen his power base by persuading Artaphernes, the satrap of Sardis, to send an expedition to conquer the Aegean island of Naxos and set him up as tyrant over it. A sympathetic Ionian warned the Naxians and by the time the Persians arrived they were well prepared behind their fortifications. After four months, the Persians ran out of supplies and withdrew. After this embarrassing failure against a very minor Greek state, Artaphernes decided that Aristagoras had to go. Having nothing now to lose, Aristagoras jumped first, abdicating his tyranny in 499 BC and calling for the establishment of democracy, not just in Miletos but throughout Ionia. Revolutions broke out across Ionia, the hated Persian-backed tyrants were overthrown and democracies were proclaimed in their place. By an audacious coup Aristagoras seized Persia's Aegean fleet and sailed it to Miletos. The Ionians formed a common council to pursue their war against Persia. Realizing that they needed allies if they were to defeat the superpower of the day, they appealed for help to their fellow Greeks across the Aegean. Sparta, the acknowledged leading military power of Greece, refused but Athens and Eretria sent ships and troops.

494 BC

THE REBELLION FAILS ✦ Rather than await Persian attack, the Ionians and their Athenian and Eretrian allies marched on Sardis in spring 498 BC, taking the city by a surprise attack and burning it. Artaphernes was trapped in his heavily fortified palace but the rebels had no siege engines and could not breach the walls. Dispirited, the Greeks retreated to the coast, harassed by Persian horse archers all the way. The main Persian army finally caught up with the Greeks near Ephesus and routed them. The surviving Athenians and Eretrians fled to their homes and refused to take any further part in the revolt. Despite this, the revolt spread to Greek cities in Cyprus and the Hellespont (the Dardanelles).

In 497 BC the Persians, now fully recovered from their initial surprise, gathered their forces and began to reconquer the rebel cities one by one. Realizing that the rebellion was doomed, Aristagoras abandoned the Ionians and fled to Thrace, where he was killed in a skirmish in 496 BC. In 494 BC the Persian general Datis captured Miletos by storm and, to make an example of the city, massacred its adult men and enslaved and deported its women and children. The remaining rebel cities quickly surrendered, and their exiled tyrants returned.

490 BC

BATTLE OF MARATHON ✦ On hearing of the sack of Sardis Darius swore to take vengeance against the interfering Athenians. In 492 BC he sent a punitive

Like all Greeks, the Ionians lived in city states and were not accustomed even to being ruled by other Greeks, let alone foreigners, who were all considered barbarians regardless of their accomplishments.

137

LEFT **Immortals.** *Glazed brick reliefs from the palace of the Persian king Darius I at Susa (Iran) showing soldiers from the elite royal lifeguards regiment, known as the Immortals. The regiment was maintained at a constant strength of 10,000 soldiers. The regiment's name is said to have originated from the custom of immediately replacing any guardsman who was killed or seriously injured. The name may really derive from the confusion by Greek writers of the Persian word* anûsiya *('companions') with* anausa *('immortals'). The Immortals' main weapons were the bow and the spear and they wore armour underneath their fine embroidered robes.*

ABOVE **Battle of Marathon.** *Painted in 1889 by the German artist Hermann Knackfuss, and now in the state museum, Kassel, Germany. Although historically accurate by the standards of the time, the painting has a propagandist and racist purpose. The artist,* *a favourite of the German kaiser, saw Asians as a threat to European civilization. Seen in this context, the painting of the Athenians' victory over the Persian invaders is a reminder to viewers of the ever-present threat from the east.*

THE BATTLE BEGINS

After the troops were in position and the sacrifices had proven favourable, when the Athenians were let loose and allowed to advance, they charged at a run towards the barbarians. The space between the two armies was about a mile, and the Persians, who saw the Athenians advancing towards them at the double, prepared to meet their attack; they assumed that the Athenians were seized by some utterly self-destructive madness, as they observed how few the Athenians were in number and how they were charging towards them with neither cavalry nor archers in support. So the barbarians suspected that the Athenians had gone mad, but when the Athenians closed with them in combat, they fought remarkably well. For they were the first of all Hellenes [i.e. Greeks] *we know of to use the running charge against their enemies, as well as the first to endure the sight of the Medes' [i.e. the Persians'] clothing and the men wearing it. In fact, until then, even the name 'Medes' spoken would strike terror into Hellenes.*

HERODOTUS, 6.112, TRANS. STRASSLER (2008)

expedition to Greece but it was recalled after its supporting fleet was wrecked in the Aegean. In 490 BC Darius prepared a second expedition. Persian envoys travelled through Greece demanding offerings of earth and water as tokens of submission. Most Greek cities complied but the Athenians and Spartans executed the envoys, a provocatively sacrilegious act which they knew made war with Persia inevitable. When the Persian envoys demanded earth and water from Sparta, the Spartans threw them down a well, telling them that would find plenty of both at the bottom. Artaphernes and Datis gathered a force of 300 ships and 40,000 men in Ionia before striking directly across the Aegean Sea, taking Naxos and Eretria before landing unopposed on the Greek mainland at Marathon, a day's march from Athens.

The Athenians immediately sent a runner to call for help from the Spartans but they were celebrating a religious festival and said that they could set out only once it was over, in two weeks' time. Meanwhile 9,000 Athenian hoplites, together with 1,000 hoplites from Plataea, faced the Persians alone at Marathon. This suited the Persian plan, which was to draw the Athenian troops away from their city, leaving it undefended. While half of the Persian troops were put ashore at Marathon, the other half remained on board their ships waiting for the right moment to sail around Attica and occupy Athens.

The Athenians were acutely aware of the weakness of their position. Though outnumbered on the ground by two to one, the Athenian hoplites were well armoured while most of the Persians were not. If they could come to close quarters they would have the advantage but the Persians had brought a strong force of cavalry archers. If caught in the open by the cavalry the Athenian

ABOVE **Father and son.** *Relief from Persepolis showing Darius I enthroned with his son and eventual successor Xerxes standing behind him. Xerxes was reluctant to take up his father's feud with the Greeks but was persuaded by advisers that it was necessary to maintain the prestige of the Persian empire.*

phalanx would be broken up by archery and then ridden down. Most of the Athenian commanders wanted to wait for the Spartans to arrive but the general Miltiades, who had served as a mercenary with the Persians, argued that, despite the risks, they needed to attack as soon as a suitable opportunity arose.

That opportunity arose at early dawn when scouts reported that the Persian cavalry had withdrawn in the night, probably to find water for their horses. Miltiades saw his chance and ordered an immediate attack. The best Persian troops were placed in the centre of the line and only they had the courage to stand their ground against the massed spears of the Athenian phalanx. As the Persian troops on the flanks broke ranks and fled back to their ships, those in the centre were surrounded and slaughtered. The Persians lost 6,400 men: the Athenians lost only 192 and their Plataean allies 11. However, all was not necessarily lost for the Persians, who set sail hoping to reach Athens before its hoplites could get back to defend it. Guessing the Persians' intentions, Miltiades force-marched his exhausted men back to Athens and they were waiting on the shore when the Persian fleet arrived later the same day. Seeing this, the Persians immediately turned for home. The next day 2,000 Spartan hoplites arrived in Athens. Finding that they were not needed, they went to Marathon to view the Persian dead, praised the Athenians for their achievement and went home.

483 BC

A WISE INVESTMENT ✦ Miners in the silver mines at Laurion, southeast of Athens, struck a spectacularly rich seam of ore. The mines were owned by the Athenian state and the excited citizens met to vote on what to do with the unexpected bounty. The most popular proposal was that every citizen should be given the sum of ten drachmas. The archon Themistocles, who expected a new attack by Persia at any time, eloquently persuaded the Athenians to reject this attractive course of action and invest their newfound wealth in building 200 triremes, fast war galleys equipped with rams, to make Athens the major sea power of Greece.

480 BC

THE 300 ✦ Darius was undeterred by the defeat at Marathon and he immediately began to plan another campaign. However, he was diverted by a rebellion in Egypt and preparations were still not complete when he died in 485 BC. Darius' successor, his son Xerxes (r. 485–465 BC), had no interest in Greece, but his advisers persuaded him that it was essential for the prestige of the empire that the Greeks be punished for their defiance. Determined not to be humiliated like his father, Xerxes spent four years planning an expedition of such enormous strength that he believed it would crush the Greeks once and for all. According to some reports, very probably exaggerated, the army which set out for Greece in 480 BC was half a million strong and was supported by a fleet of 1,000 ships. Two mile-long bridges of boats built across the Hellespont

LEONIDAS' LAST STAND

The Hellenes knew they were about to face death at the hands of the men who had come around the mountain, and so they exerted their utmost strength against the barbarians, with reckless desperation and no regard for their own lives. By this time most of their spears were broken, so they were slaying the Persians with their swords. And it was during this struggle that Leonidas fell, the man who proved himself the most valiant of all, and with those other famous Spartans who also proved themselves to be worthy men.

HERODOTUS (TRANS. STRASSLER)

ABOVE **The self-sacrifice of the Spartans** at the battle of Thermopylae had great appeal to early 19th-century Romantics, who saw the contemporary Greek struggle for independence against the Turks as a modern continuation of the Persian wars. This painting by the Italian Massimo Taparelli d'Azeglio was completed in 1823, the same year that the English poet Lord Byron joined the Greek rebels at Missolonghi, where he died in 1824.

allowed this massive army to cross from Asia to Europe without getting its feet wet.

Xerxes hoped that his huge army would so overawe the Greeks they would submit without resistance. Many Greek states did in fact do so when Persian ambassadors came calling and demanding offerings of earth and water. Pointedly, Xerxes sent no ambassadors to Athens and Sparta. They got the message and prepared to resist, rallying other anti-Persian states to support them. The odds against them were not, however, quite so hopeless as they at first appeared. The sheer size of the Persian army created huge problems of supply, and it would prove impossible to control it effectively on the battlefield. Most of the troops were unenthusiastic conscripts who had already spent months on the road travelling to join the army as it gathered at Sardis. Only around 10,000 of the elite troops were as well armed and armoured as the Greek hoplites, who were experienced, disciplined and highly motivated – citizens fighting to defend their states, their hard-won political privileges, and their homes and families.

The Greeks sent an army of 10,000 north to Thessaly but it was forced to retreat as soon as it became clear that the Persians could outflank the position. The narrow pass of Thermopylae, 160 km (100 miles) south, seemed a stronger position and it was here that the Spartan king Leonidas decided to make a stand. With craggy mountains on one side of the Greek position and the sea on the other, the Persians were unable to take advantage of their numerical superiority. The battle raged for three days. For two days the Greeks drove off the Persian attacks with ease but on the second night the Persians discovered a path through the mountains and outflanked the Greeks. With a force of 300 Spartans and 1,400 allies, Leonidas fought to the death to buy time for the rest of the Greek army to escape.

The Greeks drove off the Persian attacks but on the second night the Persians outflanked the Greeks. With 300 Spartans and 1,400 allies, Leonidas fought to the death to buy time for the rest of the Greek army to escape.

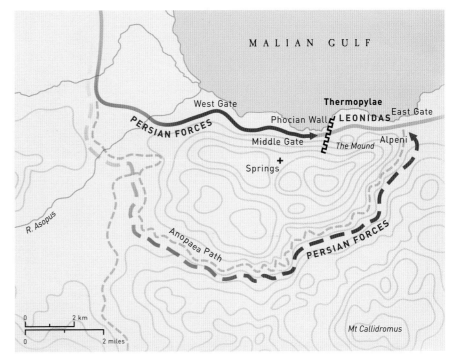

145

ABOVE **The battle of Thermopylae.** *Leonidas chose Thermopylae for his stand against the Persians because the narrow passage between the sea on one side and the mountains on the other prevented the Persians from exploiting their superior numbers. Leonidas held out easily for two days but on the second night a traitor, Ephialtes of Trachis, guided the Persians along a shepherd's track through the mountains to outflank the Greek position. Ephialtes expected to be well rewarded by Xerxes, but the defeat of the Persian army at Plataea in 479 BC left him a hunted man and he was eventually killed in 470 BC.*

RIGHT **Leonidas' departure from Sparta for Thermopylae** *by the French Neoclassical artist Jacques-Louis David. David conceived the painting around 1800 but was kept too busy with works glorifying his patron, the emperor Napoleon, to make a start until 1812. By this time, Napoleon's fortunes were waning and the painting has been seen as representing a premonition of his eventual defeat. By the time David completed the painting in October 1814 Napoleon was an exile on the Italian island of Elba.*

After the defeat at Thermopylae the Greeks retreated to the narrow, fortified Isthmus of Corinth. The Greek fleet, led by Athens, withdrew to the island of Salamis, taking most of the population of Athens with it. When the Persian army arrived at Athens, which they occupied and sacked, they found it deserted except for a small garrison on the Acropolis, who held out for two weeks. The whole of Greece now seemed to be within Xerxes' grasp. The Spartan defences on the Isthmus could easily be bypassed by sea but Themistocles, commanding the Greek fleet, lured the larger Persian fleet into an ambush off Salamis, sinking around a third of its ships. Xerxes watched the disaster unfold from the shore. It was now clear that Greece would not be conquered in a single campaign. Fearing a Greek attack on the Hellespont bridges, Xerxes returned to Asia with 60,000 men leaving his general Mardonius with the rest of the army to winter in Thessaly. The Athenians returned to find their city ruined.

ABOVE **Greek warriors fighting,** *from a painted vase dating to the middle of the 6th century BC. The warriors are depicted fighting naked but, although athletic nudity was normal, it is far from certain that Greek warriors really went into battle like this. One of the conventions of Greek art was 'heroic nudity' in which gods and heroized individuals, such as kings, great warriors, and successful athletes, were depicted naked with idealized physiques. Until about 330 BC only male nudes could be shown in respectable art (the Greeks also had a tradition of pornography); after that, female nudes were also acceptable but they were most commonly shown slightly draped to preserve some modesty.*

479 BC

BATTLE OF PLATAEA ✦ The victory at Salamis did not secure Greek independence from Persia. Despite Xerxes' withdrawal, Mardonius remained with a considerable force. During the winter of 480–479 BC the eternally quarrelsome Greeks began to fall out over what to do next. The important city of Thebes went over to the Persians while Sparta, ever fearful of its old rival Argos, refused to let its army fight north of the Peloponnesus. When Mardonius reoccupied Athens in the spring, the Athenians too threatened to abandon the alliance if Spartan support was not forthcoming. The prospect of the Athenian fleet falling under Persian control finally forced Sparta's hand. In summer 479 BC Sparta sent an army of 5,000 hoplites and 25,000 auxiliary troops north under the regent Pausanias. They were joined by 8,000 Athenian hoplites and 10,000 from other Greek states. Mardonius drew the Greeks onto the plain of Plataea, in Theban territory, where he could deploy his cavalry to better effect. According to Herodotus, Mardonius' force was about 300,000 strong, outnumbering the Greeks six to one: modern historians estimate that the army was more likely to have numbered between 80,000 and 120,000, including many Greeks from Thebes and other pro-Persian states.

The two armies faced each other for over a week, both waiting for a favourable moment to attack. Mardonius sent his cavalry out to range the countryside, attacking supply trains and fouling the springs on which the Greeks relied for water. This forced Pausanias to order a withdrawal under cover of night to a new position with secure water supplies. In the darkness the Spartans, Athenians and the allied Greeks lost touch with one another and when dawn broke they were spread out in three disconnected groups. Mardonius saw his chance and ordered an attack, leading his best forces against the Spartans in person. The Spartans held their formation under a hail of arrows and then unexpectedly charged the advancing Persians, throwing them into confusion. The battle became a desperate melee but, after Mardonius was killed fighting with the Spartans, the Persians began to lose heart and then broke into flight. Tens of thousands were killed by the pursuing Greeks. The Thebans fought hard and after the battle the victors executed their leaders as traitors to the Greek cause. It was a decisive victory. The Greeks followed up their success by destroying the Persian fleet at the Battle of Mycale. The Ionians rebelled and a Spartan-led fleet liberated the Greek cities on the Hellespont and Bosphorus straits, opening the Black Sea to Greek shipping.

477 BC

THE DELIAN LEAGUE ✦ With the Persians expelled from Greece, Sparta considered the war to be over and in 478 BC it withdrew from the alliance. Most other mainland Greek states followed Sparta's lead. The Ionians, who still feared a revival of Persian power, called upon Athens to take up leadership of those states that were still willing to continue the war. Athens, which had strong historical links with Ionia – many of the Ionian cities had originally been Athenian colonies – was happy to oblige. Delegates from Athens, the Aegean islands and the newly liberated cities of Ionia, the Hellespont and the Bosphorus met on Delos, the sacred island of the sun god Apollo, to form a new alliance, the Delian League. The express purpose of the league was attack Persian territory to gain recompense for the damage its members had suffered at its hands. Formal arrangements were made to divide the spoils of war. Each member of the league was given one equal vote but Athens, its main naval and military power, dominated from the start. The league's treasurers were all Athenians and it was Athens that decided whether members should contribute military forces or taxes: most, however, were happy to pay taxes and leave the fighting to the Athenians. The league's first major victory came in 466 BC when the Athenian general Cimon defeated a Persian attempt to reconquer Ionia at the Battle of Eurymedon river (now the Köprüçay) on the southern coast of Anatolia.

465 BC

XERXES IS MURDERED ✦ The failure of his expedition to Greece in 480–479 BC left Xerxes feeling demoralized and he gradually withdrew from active government into his harem. Harems were hotbeds of intrigue and faction as the women plotted with the palace eunuchs to advance the interests of their children, only one of whom could hope to succeed as king. It was as a result of one of these feuds that Xerxes was murdered in 465 BC by his uncle Artabanus and one of the harem eunuchs. Artabanus successfully framed the crown prince Darius for the crime. The prince's brother Artaxerxes I (r. 465–424 BC) killed him to avenge their father and succeeded to the throne himself. Artabanus then hatched a plot to murder Artaxerxes and seize the throne for himself. The plot was betrayed by a Greek mercenary and, in a fight, Artaxerxes was wounded but Artabanus was killed. Artaxerxes finally secured his throne after defeating another brother, Hystaspes, in a battle in a sandstorm.

461 BC

DEMOCRATIC REVOLUTION ✦ Athens' growth as a naval power had important political consequences. Only comfortably off citizens could afford to equip themselves as hoplites but no equipment was needed to be an oarsmen in a trireme. It was, therefore, from the landless *thetes*, the largest and poorest class of citizens, that the crews of the Athenian fleet were recruited. The need for manpower was enormous. Each trireme needed around 170 oarsmen and they had to be well trained and highly motivated. Athenian power depended more on its fleet than its army and the *thetes* were quick to realize how important their role was to the defence of the state and press for further democratic reforms. In 461 BC the democratic politicians Ephialtes and Pericles forced through a raft of reforms which abolished the last bastions of aristocratic privilege. The Areopagus council was demoted to hearing cases of murder and sacrilege; its right of veto was abolished and its other powers were transferred to the council of 500, the citizen assembly and the law courts, giving them full control of the Athenian state. To break the aristocratic dominance of the judiciary, pay for jurors was introduced so that the less well-off could serve. The right to stand for election as an archon was extended to the hoplite class in *c.* 457 BC.

OPPOSITE **The ruins of Xerxes' winter palace,** *the Tachara, at Persepolis. Begun by Darius I, it was one of the few buildings at Persepolis that was not burned after Alexander the Great captured the city in 330 BC. The mud brick walls of the palace have weathered away completely, leaving the door frames, each one carved from a single block of stone, standing alone.*

ABOVE **Marble bust of Pericles (495–429 BC)** *by the Athenian sculptor Cresilas. The helmet is a symbol of Pericles' position of strategos (general-in-chief), a rank to which he was re-elected for an unprecedented 15 years in succession. Pericles was Athens' most influential politician from the beginning of the First Peloponnesian War until his death. A champion of democracy, his hostility to Sparta ultimately brought disaster on Athens.*

460 BC

THE FIRST PELOPONNESIAN WAR BEGINS ✦ Athens' increasing influence rankled with the Spartans, who felt that their traditional leadership of Greece was being undermined. Spartan power took a severe blow in 463 BC when the Messenian helots rebelled and overran Laconia, forcing Sparta to appeal for help from other Greek states. The Athenians divided into pro- and anti-Spartan factions. The pro-Spartan faction won the day but was discredited when the Spartans refused Athens' help out of fear that Athenian soldiers might sympathize with the oppressed helots and spread democratic ideas. Angered, Athens allied with Sparta's old rival Argos in 461 BC. Then, in 460 BC, Athens went to war with Corinth and Aegina in support of Megara, a former Spartan ally which had switched allegiance.

This extension of Athenian influence into the Peloponnesus was intolerable to Sparta. After Athens destroyed the combined navies of Corinth and Aegina in 458 BC, Sparta allied with Thebes and declared war. Sparta still had the best army in Greece and it defeated a larger Athenian army at Tanagra in 457 BC but failed to follow up its victory. The following year Athens defeated Thebes and imposed a democratic constitution on the city. In 456 BC Aegina was conquered and forced to join the Delian League. This was as close as Athens was ever going to come to dominating Greece. All the while Athens was fighting in the Peloponnesus it was also fighting Persia, and the strain was beginning to show.

449 BC

ROMAN LAW ✦ The aristocratic patricians who overthrew the Roman monarchy in 509 BC set up the republican constitution in such a way as to exclude the plebeian majority from any real political influence. The plebs were not a monolithic class – it included urban wage labourers, small farmers, craftsmen, and wealthy merchants and landowners – but it was united by a common interest in ending the patricians' monopoly of power. In 494 BC the plebs formed their own assembly, the *consilium plebis* (popular assembly) and elected their own officers, the tribunes. To protect the tribunes from attack by the patricians' hired thugs, the plebs declared the tribunes to be sacrosanct and invoked curses on anyone who harmed them. Their personal inviolability made the tribunes powerful and influential figures who could act as effective advocates for the victims of arbitrary decisions by magistrates. Gradually the popular assembly won greater political rights for the plebs. Plebs could become consuls from 342 BC (and so be eligible to become senators); the hated debt-bondage was abolished in 326 BC; and in 287 BC decisions of the popular assembly, known as plebiscites, were recognized as having the force of law.

The laws, known as the 'Twelve Tables', became the foundation of the Roman law tradition. They were inscribed on 12 bronze tablets and posted in the Forum where all Roman citizens could read them.

152

ABOVE **Triumphant Centaur.** *Marble sculptures on the south side of the Parthenon depict a legendary battle between the human Lapiths and the half-human, half-horse Centaurs, which broke out after the Centaurs got drunk at a wedding feast. For the Athenians the legend symbolized the struggle between the civilized Greeks and the barbarian Persians. Most Parthenon Marbles were removed in 1798 by Lord Elgin (after whom they are also known as the Elgin Marbles) and were later purchased by the British Museum. Early conservators at the museum failed to recognize that the sculptures had originally been painted and cleaned them to their present polished white.*

The plebs' most effective weapon was 'secession', a form of mass civil disobedience that was first used successfully in 449 BC. A frequent complaint of the plebs was that the laws were kept secret by the patrician priesthood; consequently, citizens could find themselves being prosecuted for offences they did not know existed. In 462 BC the tribune Terentilius called for the law to be codified. The patricians opposed the request but in 451 BC finally appointed a board of ten men who drew up ten law codes. A second board completed two further codes in 449 BC. The Senate had no intention of publishing these codes but their hand was forced by a secession of the plebs which brought all commerce in Rome to a grinding halt. The laws, known as the 'Twelve Tables', became the foundation of the Roman law tradition. They were inscribed on 12 bronze tablets and posted in the Forum where all Roman citizens could read them. As the tables were destroyed when the Gauls sacked Rome in 390 BC, their full text is not known.

ABOVE **The ruins of the Parthenon,** *painted before its modern restoration, by the American landscape artist Frederic Edwin Church in 1871. Church travelled extensively in Europe and the Middle East in 1871–2. On his return to the USA, Church built an eclectically styled mansion at Olana, New York state, incorporating elements from the architecture of many of the places he had visited.*

448 BC

TREATY OF CALLIAS ✦ Despite the Athenian victory at the Eurymedon river in 466 BC, Persia refused to accept the loss of Ionia and the war dragged on. Athens tried to put pressure on Persia by supporting a rebellion in Egypt but this was defeated in 454 BC. The stalemate was finally broken when the Athenians won a decisive double victory on land and sea against the Persians at Salamis in Cyprus in 450 BC. This disaster persuaded the Persian king Artaxerxes I (r. 465–425 BC) to negotiate peace terms in 448 BC, finally bringing the Greek–Persian Wars to an end. By the Treaty of Callias (named after the chief Athenian negotiator) Persia recognized Ionia's independence in return for Athenian recognition of its rule in Cyprus and Egypt. Persia remained a great power, however, and still had a great power's hegemonic ambitions. Persian kings continued to intervene in Greece but from now on did so only by diplomatic means.

THE STATUE OF ATHENA

As you enter the temple that they name the Parthenon, all the sculptures you see on what is called the pediment refer to the birth of Athena, those on the rear pediment represent the contest for the land between Athena and Poseidon. The statue itself is made of ivory and gold. On the middle of her helmet is placed a likeness of the Sphinx and on either side of the helmet are griffins in relief. ... The statue of Athena is upright, with a tunic reaching to the feet, and on her breast the head of Medusa is worked in ivory. She holds a statue of Victory about four cubits high, and in the other hand a spear; at her feet lies a shield and near the spear is a serpent.

PAUSANIAS, *GUIDE TO GREECE*, C. AD 150
(TRANS. W.H.S. JONES, LOEB, 1918)

447 BC

CONSTRUCTION OF THE PARTHENON BEGINS ✦ In the aftermath of the democratic reforms in 461 BC, Pericles emerged as Athens' dominant political figure. A brilliant orator, Pericles secured re-election as Athens' general-in-chief for an unprecedented 15 years in succession. For years after Xerxes' invasion, the Athenians had left their city in ruins as a monument to their sufferings. Following the final victory over Persia, Pericles won support for his plan to rebuild Athens in a truly imperial style. The centrepiece of Pericles' plan was the Parthenon, the temple of the city's patron goddess Athena on the Acropolis. Built in the Doric style, it displays the restraint and proportion of classical Greek architecture at its finest. The elegant naturalism of the Parthenon's sculptural friezes, by the Athenian sculptor Phidias, are widely regarded as the high point of classical Greek art but it was another of Phidias' works, a giant statue of Athena, that the temple was most famous for in ancient times. The statue, which stood in the sanctuary, was made of silver, ivory and around a ton of gold. Thought to have been destroyed by Christians in the 5th century AD, several copies of the statue have survived from Roman times. The architects Iktinos and Kallikrates began work on the temple in 447 BC and it was substantially complete by 432 BC. The funds to pay for the temple were taken from

155

THE ORIGIN OF THE PELOPONNESIAN WAR ACCORDING TO PLUTARCH

It is not, indeed, easy to discover what was the real origin of the war: but at the same time all agree that it was the fault of Pericles that the decree against Megara was not annulled. Some say his firmness in that case was the result of prudence and magnanimity, as he considered that demand only as a test, and thought that the least concession would be understood as an acknowledgement of weakness: but others will have it that his treating of the Spartans with so little ceremony was owing to his obstinacy, and an ambition to display his power.

PLUTARCH, *THE LIFE OF PERICLES*

the treasury of the Delian League. Converted into a church in the 5th century AD, and then into a mosque in the 15th century, the Parthenon survived substantially intact until 1687 when Turkish gunpowder stored in the building exploded during a Venetian bombardment. The pure white marble of the Parthenon's sculptures as they survive today gives a misleading impression: they were originally brightly painted.

445 BC

THE THIRTY YEARS' PEACE ✦ Ironically, the Treaty of Callias weakened rather than strengthened Athens' position. When it was founded in 477 BC, the Delian League had been conceived as a free alliance of equal partners under Athenian leadership. As the dominant partner, Athens soon began to see the league in very different terms. When Naxos tried to leave the league in 469 BC, the Athenian fleet was sent to enforce its obedience. Four years later the Athenians seized a gold mine on Thasos, provoking a rebellion which was quickly crushed. Members were not free and equal as they had thought. After the league's treasury was moved from Delos to Athens in 454 BC – ostensibly for greater security – it became clear that Athens regarded the league as nothing less than its empire. Despite this, most league members remained loyal. Many smaller members gained great commercial advantages from the close link with Athens while all feared the possibility of Persian invasion. When the Treaty of Callias lifted that threat, league members became more confident in expressing their discontent. Sparta actively encouraged league members to rebel while attacking Athenian possessions on the mainland. After several reverses, Pericles concluded that Athens simply did not have the manpower it needed to be both a great naval power and a match for Sparta as a military power on land. On his initiative, Athens agreed the Thirty Years' Peace, which recognized the Peloponnesus as Sparta's sphere of influence.

OPPOSITE **The main campaigns** *of the Second Peloponnesian War (431–404 BC), showing the contrasting strategies of Athens and Sparta. Athens relied on its naval power effectively to neutralize Sparta's superiority on land. Safe behind their city walls, the Athenians used their fleet to bring supplies into their city and to raid the territory of Sparta's allies. The turning point of the war came in 412 BC when the Persians helped the Spartans build a large navy. Athens lacked the resources to fight Sparta on land and at sea and was forced to surrender in 404 BC.*

Byzantium

Chalcedon

MACEDONIA

422
Amphipolis

THRACE

CHALCIDICE

Aegospotami
405

429

Abydos
411

Cyzicus
410

422

Scione

A E G E A N   S E A

Cynossema
411

429

EPIRUS

PERSIAN
EMPIRE

Argos

406

THESSALY

406

Chios

EUBOEA

Delion
424

Chalcis

Thebes

Decelea

Notium
407

Cephalonia

Patrai

Megara

Ephesus

ACHAEA

Corinth

■Athens

Samos

Zante

PELOPONNESE

431–425

Piraeüs

406

Argos

Serifos

To Sicily
427–424
415–413

Mantinea
418

415

Paros

Naxos

Sphacteria
425

■Sparta

410

Cos

424

Melos

RHODES

425

431–404 BC

THE SECOND PELOPONNESIAN WAR ✦
The Thirty Years' Peace did nothing the dampen
the bitter rivalry of Athens and Sparta and actually
lasted less than 14 years. In 435 BC Corcyra (now
Corfu) defeated Corinth, a Spartan ally in a war
over the city of Epidamnos (now Durrës, Albania).
Fully expecting Corinthian retribution, the Corcyrans allied with Athens, reigniting
Sparta's fear of Athenian encroachment on the Peloponnesus. A further provocation
came in 432 BC when Athens mounted an economic blockade against Megara, a
commercial rival but also an ally of Sparta. At a conference of its allies, Corinth and
Megara condemned Sparta for not confronting Athenian aggression. Sparta sent an
embassy to Athens to demand that the embargo against Megara be lifted but Pericles
brusquely dismissed the request, leaving Sparta little choice but to declare war if it
was to maintain its leadership of the Peloponnesian states.

Sparta had no fleet, nor did any of its allies except Corinth, so its war plan was
to starve Athens into surrender by repeatedly ravaging its agricultural hinterland in
Attica. Pericles had anticipated this and Athens was well prepared. During the First

Athens + members of
Delian League c. 431 BC

Athens' allies

Athenian campaign

Athenian victory

Sparta + allies c. 431 BC

Spartan campaign

Spartan victory

Persian empire

Neutral states

N

0   50 km

0   50 miles

157

Peloponnesian War, the Athenians had built the 'Long Walls', a protected corridor linking their city with its port at Piraeus. Pericles brought the entire population of Attica within the walls, abandoning it to the Spartans, while using Athens' wealth and command of the seas to import all the supplies it needed and raid at will around the Peloponnesian coast. Athens suffered an early setback, in 429 BC, when Pericles died in a plague that was introduced into the crowded city by a supply ship. His successor as general-in-chief, Cleon, conducted the war with less skill. Brilliant victories by the Athenian general Demosthenes at Olpae, in 425 BC, and Pylos, in 425 BC, led Sparta to sue for peace. Cleon foolishly refused and in 424 BC Athens suffered a heavy defeat by Sparta's ally Thebes at Delium. Reinvigorated, Sparta sent an army under Brasidas, its best general, north to Thrace to attack Athens' allies there and threaten its crucial supply route from the Black Sea. The army Cleon took to Thrace to counter this threat was crushingly defeated in 422 BC at Amphipolis: both Brasidas and Cleon were killed in the battle.

With the two main war leaders of each side dead, Athens and Sparta concluded the 50-year Peace of Nicias, which simply restored the pre-war territorial status quo. The peace caused great dissatisfaction with Sparta's allies, who felt it sidelined their interests. Three Peloponnesian states, Argos, Mantinea and Elis, went to war with Sparta but, after early successes, they were defeated at Mantinea in 418 BC. Athens aided the rebels but Sparta refrained from widening the war. Athens did not. After Cleon's death Alcibiades emerged as one of the most influential figures in Athenian politics. A charismatic orator and an able general, Alcibiades also had the knack of making enemies and his career was a controversial one. In 415 BC Alcibiades persuaded the Athenians to send an expedition to Sicily to capture Syracuse, the greatest Greek city on the island, which was at war with the Athenian colony of Segesta. Capturing Syracuse would, Alcibiades argued, allow Athens to deprive its enemies of Sicilian grain supplies and establish it firmly as the leader of the Greek world. Shortly after the expedition left, Alcibiades was charged with sacrilege by his political enemies.

LEFT **Alcibiades (c. 450–404 BC)** *was the controversial figure of the Second Peloponnesian War, changing allegiance between his native Athens and Sparta several times. Though both benefited from his advice when he served them, he was trusted by neither. After Athens' decisive defeat at Aegospotami in 405 BC, Alcibiades prepared to set out on a mission to persuade Sparta's ally, the Persian king Artaxerxes, to change sides, but he was cornered in his house by Spartan agents and killed.*

HERODOTUS AND THUCYDIDES

Classical Greece saw the birth of modern history writing. Most ancient civilizations, such as those of Mesopotamia and Egypt, recorded history in the form of annals, which simply listed and described events.

If events were explained it was usually in terms of divine intervention. What happened on earth depended on the will of the gods: success was a sign of divine favour, failure of divine displeasure. The first historian to go further was Herodotus of Halicarnassus (*c.* 484–420 BC) who wrote a monumental narrative history of the Persian Wars. Herodotus is the first historian whose works have survived who is known to have systematically researched his material, cited his sources and assessed their reliability. Herodotus described his work as ἱστορίαι ('istoriai'), literally meaning 'inquiries' or 'researches', from which we get our word 'history'. Because of his achievements, Herodotus is often known as 'the father of history' but his younger contemporary, the Athenian Thucydides

(*c.* 460–395 BC), has an even better claim to the title. While Herodotus often invoked supernatural explanations for events, in his *History of the Peloponnesian War* between Athens and Sparta Thucydides drew his conclusions only from eyewitness and written accounts and an understanding of human psychology and motives. An important difference between Thucydides' history writing and that of modern historians is his inclusion of formal speeches. As Thucydides himself admitted, these are not based on actual records of speeches but are literary reconstructions of what the author judged a person would have said under the circumstances. As such they are powerful devices for examining character and motivation: adopted by generations of Greek and Roman writers such speeches are a characteristic feature of classical history writing.

Knowing that the penalty if convicted was death, Alcibiades defected to the Spartans and persuaded them to send an expedition to support Syracuse. The Athenians suffered a devastating defeat, losing the entire expeditionary force of 12,000 men and 200 ships. Demosthenes was among the casualties. Meanwhile, Sparta established a permanent garrison in Attica, forcing the closure of Athens' silver mines.

Worse was to come for Athens in 412 BC when Alcibiades negotiated a treaty between Sparta and Persia, giving Persia a free hand in Ionia in return for funds to build a Spartan fleet to cut off Athens' food supplies. After it was discovered that aristocrats were secretly negotiating peace with Sparta, the Athenian assembly called Alcibiades back from exile and put him in command of the fleet. In 410 BC Alcibiades destroyed the new Spartan fleet at Cyzicus on the Sea of Marmora and secured Athens' supply route from the Black Sea. In 408 BC the Spartan general Lysander and Cyrus the Younger, the Persian satrap of Sardis, began to work closely together on rebuilding the Spartan fleet. Finally, in 405 BC, Lysander trapped and destroyed the Athenian fleet at Aegospotami on the Hellespont while Cyrus' forces

RIGHT **One of the casualties**
of Athens' defeat in the Second
Peloponnesian War was the philosopher
Socrates. Socrates had always been
contemptuous of democracy, believing
that most people were incapable of
making rational choices. His praise
of Sparta, and his ability to make
people engaging in argument with him
contradict themselves and look foolish,
alienated the Athenians who made him
a scapegoat for their city's misfortunes.
In 399 BC Socrates was accused
of corrupting the youth of Athens.
According to the account of his trial by
his pupil Plato, Socrates went out of his
way to antagonize the jury. He made
no attempt to disguise his intellectual
elitism, provoking them to impose the
death penalty rather than the lesser
sentence of exile. In his painting The
Death of Socrates (1787) Jacques Louis
David shows Socrates, surrounded by
his friends and pupils, preparing to
drink the poison hemlock.

reoccupied Ionia. Lysander put Piraeus under close naval blockade, while a Spartan army besieged Athens from the land. Completely cut off from supplies, Athens surrendered in 404 BC. The Delian League was disbanded, Athens' walls were demolished, democracy was abolished and the city was placed under the rule of the 'Thirty Tyrants', a Spartan-appointed aristocratic junta (which was overthrown within a year, however). Sparta was now clearly the strongest state in Greece, but was it strong enough to achieve permanent dominance and unite Greece into a single state?

404 BC

THE PHARAOHS RETURN ✦ Egyptians hated Persian rule and they rebelled unsuccessfully several times in the 5th century. Dynastic troubles in the Persian empire finally gave them the opportunity to reclaim their independence. In 405 BC Darius II (r. 423–405 BC) died. He was a weak character who always struggled to assert himself against his ambitious wife – his half-sister Parysatis – and the palace eunuchs. Parysatis schemed tirelessly to secure the succession of her favourite son Cyrus the Younger, the satrap of Sardis. However, Darius appointed their elder son Artaxerxes II (r. 404–359 BC) as his heir and it was he who succeeded him as king. Cyrus was denounced by the general Tissaphernes for plotting to kill Artaxerxes and seize the throne for himself but, through the influence of his mother, he escaped punishment and was allowed to keep his satrapy. While Artaxerxes was distracted by this affair, Amyrtaeus (r. 404–399 BC), the prince of Sais, who had been fighting a guerrilla war against the Persians in the Delta for six years, declared himself pharaoh and by 401 BC was ruler of all Egypt.

PERSIA'S WEAKNESS REVEALED

Whereas the king's empire was strong in that it covered a vast territory with large numbers of people, it was also weak because of the need to travel great distances and the wide distribution of its forces, making it vulnerable to a swift attack.

XENOPHON, *THE MARCH OF THE TEN THOUSAND*

401 BC

EXPEDITION OF THE 10,000 ✦ When Cyrus the Younger returned to Lydia he began to recruit an army of 10,000 Greek hoplites and 3,000 other Greek mercenaries. Officially these were to campaign against the Pisidians, a rebellious mountain tribe in southwest Anatolia. Their real purpose was to support Cyrus in a bid for the Persian throne. In spring 401 BC Cyrus gathered his forces and advanced from Sardis, through Syria into Mesopotamia where he met Artaxerxes in battle at Cunaxa, on the Euphrates river about 40 miles (64 km) north of Babylon, in August. Fighting in a phalanx, the Greeks swept Artaxerxes' army from the field at the cost of one man wounded, but in a cavalry skirmish Cyrus received a fatal head wound. Though victorious, the Greeks were unpaid, short of supplies and stranded in the heart of the Persian empire. Despite this, the Greeks refused to surrender while the Persians, having seen how well the hoplites fought, were unwilling to attack them. The Persians therefore invited the Greeks' commander Clearchus and his senior officers to a conference and treacherously executed them. However, the Greeks still refused to surrender: instead they elected new commanders and set out an epic march across Anatolia to the Black Sea where the 6,000 survivors took ship back to Greece. Throughout their march, the Greeks were opposed only by local forces, revealing Persia's underlying military weakness. The Greeks were too busy with their own interminable quarrels to take advantage, however.

ABOVE **The Chigi Vase** has the earliest representation of Greek hoplites fighting in a phalanx formation, dating to c. 650–640 BC. The phalanx was the normal Greek battle formation for foot soldiers from this time until Greece was annexed by the Roman Empire in the mid-2nd century BC. The hoplites have typical arms and armour. Their main weapon is the spear and for protection they are wearing bronze helmets, breastplates and greaves (shin protectors), and carrying the large round shield or hoplon from which the hoplite got his name. The phalanx proved to be formidable when used against lightly armoured troops, such as the Persians, but was less successful against the Roman legions, which used more flexible tactics.

396 BC

ROME'S FIRST CONQUEST ✦ The Roman republic's first military victory came in 499 BC when it defeated a coalition of its Latin neighbours at the Battle of Lake Regillus. After the war, colonies of Roman citizens were founded on land seized from the Latins. This policy of colonizing newly won lands continued into imperial territory and served both to consolidate Roman control of conquered territory and to defuse social tensions in Rome by offering land and opportunities to poorer citizens. Soon after the end of the war, Latium came under threat by hill tribes from the Apennine mountains: the Volsci, Aequi and the Sabines. In 493 BC the Latin cities united with Rome to form a defensive league against the common enemy. The Latins accepted Roman military leadership in return for arrangements to share any loot and land won in campaigns. The league was successful and by the end of the century Latium was secure, leaving Rome free to deal with the Etruscan city of Veii, a walled hill town about ten miles north of Rome. Veii was a natural rival for control of the Tiber valley trade route and there had already been a number of wars between the two cities when Rome declared war in 406 BC. The Romans besieged Veii for ten years until it finally fell after the general Camillus tunnelled into its sewer system. The entire male population of Veii was massacred and all the women and children were sold into slavery. Camillus paraded through Rome in a four-horse chariot and popular celebrations continued for four days. The victory nearly doubled the size of Rome's small territory and set it on the road to empire.

> *The Romans besieged Veii for ten years. The entire male population of Veii was massacred and all the women and children were sold into slavery.*

396–386 BC

SPARTA STUMBLES ✦ Other Greeks always thought the Spartans to be rather arrogant and this was to be their downfall. Sparta's willingness to abandon the Ionians to Persian rule did not make it a convincing champion of Greek liberty. The behaviour of their chief general Lysander after Sparta's victory in the Peloponnesian Wars did nothing to reassure the doubters. Lysander cultivated a personality cult, becoming the first Greek to receive cultic honours as a god or hero in his lifetime and, it was discovered after his death in 395 BC, he secretly planned to overthrow the Spartan monarchy and install himself as tyrant. Lysander was eager for Sparta to replace Athens as the ruler of the Aegean but his arrogant approach destroyed what little pro-Spartan sentiment there was. Democracies were abolished and ten-man juntas, called dekarchies, were imposed on the Aegean states, who were forced to pay a heavy annual tribute to maintain the Spartan fleet. This was even worse than Athenian rule. However, it was Lysander's close relationship with Cyrus the Younger that was the immediate cause of the unravelling of Spartan ambitions.

Lysander helped Cyrus recruit the Greek mercenaries he used to support his unsuccessful bid for the Persian throne. The Ionians had also supported Cyrus so

Artaxerxes sent an army to punish them for their disloyalty. These events soured relations between Sparta and Persia. Belated Spartan support for the Ionians finally led to the outbreak of war when King Agesilaos invaded Anatolia in 396 BC. Artaxerxes retaliated by funding an alliance of Athens, Thebes, Corinth and Argos to attack Sparta in 395 BC, forcing Agesilaos to withdraw. At the Battle of Coroneia in 394 BC Agesilaos defeated the alliance but the Persian fleet, commanded by the Athenian general Conon, destroyed the Spartan fleet at Cnidos. With its Persian subsidies, Athens rebuilt its walls and its fleet, and set about recovering its Aegean empire. This alarmed Artaxerxes, who withdrew support from Athens in 388 BC and then allied with Sparta in 387 BC. Sparta quickly recovered its dominance on land and at sea and in 386 BC Artaxerxes was able to dictate his own peace terms, known as the King's Peace. Sparta remained the strongest Greek state but Persia was the biggest winner of the war. By his skilful manipulation of the balance of power, Artaxerxes had ended the Spartan threat without raising up any of its rivals. Persia had become the arbiter of Greece.

390 BC

THE GAULS SACK ROME ✦

In 391 BC the Romans sent three ambassadors to mediate in a territorial dispute between the Etruscan city of Clusium (modern Chiusi) and the Senones, one of a group of Gaulish tribes who had settled in northern Italy

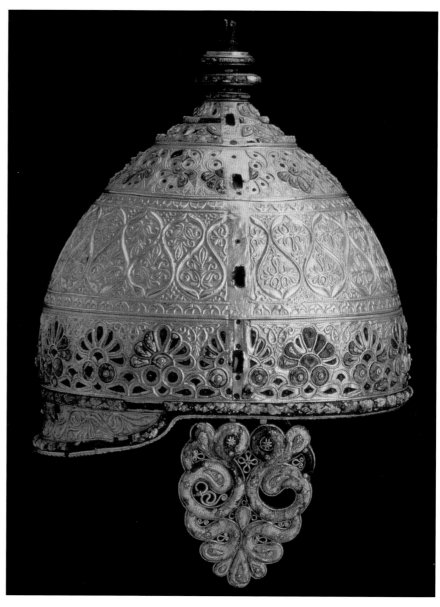

ABOVE **This 5th-century BC gold-covered iron and bronze helmet** *from Agris in western France belonged to a wealthy Gaulish chieftain. The Gauls were a group of Celtic-speaking peoples who inhabited a large area of western Europe including most of modern France, Belgium, Luxembourg, western Germany, the Czech Republic, Austria and Switzerland. Around 400 BC*

Gaulish tribes crossed the Alps and occupied most of northern Italy, threatening Rome. The helmet typifies the Celtic warrior's love of display: its elaborate vegetal-style decorations are typical of the early Celtic Hallstatt art style, which flourished from the 7th to the 5th centuries BC.

According to Roman tradition a token garrison of diehards who held out on the Capitoline Hill were saved from a surprise night attack only when alerted at the last minute by the cackling of the sacred geese in Juno's temple.

during the previous century. When negotiations failed and fighting broke out, the Roman envoys breached the rules of diplomacy by joining in on the side of the Etruscans and killing one of the Gauls' chieftains. Such an offence demanded retaliation and, after the Romans stubbornly refused to hand over the guilty men for punishment, an army of Gauls crossed the Apennines in July 390 BC and headed with terrifying speed down the valley of the river Tiber towards Rome. Brennus, the leader of the Gauls, was an able general and he easily routed the Roman army sent to stop him at the river Allia a few miles from Rome.

Undefended and abandoned by all except those who were too old or sick to flee, Rome fell the next day and was comprehensively sacked. According to Roman tradition a token garrison of diehards who held out on the Capitoline Hill were saved from a surprise night attack only when alerted at the last minute by the cackling of the sacred geese in Juno's temple. Fortunately the hungry soldiers had not dared to eat the geese for fear of incurring the wrath of the notoriously short-tempered queen of the gods. After the Gauls had besieged the Capitoline Hill for seven months, hunger forced the Romans to pay them the huge ransom of a thousand pounds of gold in return for their agreement to leave the city. The experience of defeat was highly traumatic for the republic, coming so soon after its victory over Veii, and it left a deep-seated fear of the northern barbarians. However, the defeat proved nothing more than a temporary setback for Rome. The Romans' Etruscan neighbours suffered far more from Gaulish raiding: by weakening them the Gauls may unintentionally have helped Rome on its road to achieve dominance in Italy.

371 BC

SPARTA'S DOWNFALL ✦ In 382 BC an aristocratic clique seized power in Thebes and abolished democracy. The new oligarchy appealed to Sparta for support against their own people. Sparta responded by garrisoning the city and ending Theban independence. The Spartans also occupied all the cities of the Theban-dominated Boeotian League (Boeotia was the region of Thebes). In 379 BC the Thebans rebelled, with Athenian support, and by 374 the Spartan garrisons had been expelled and democracy restored to the Thebes and the Boeotian cities. At the same time, the Athenians rebuilt a more loosely organized successor to the Delian League to pursue the war with Sparta. In 376 BC the Athenians decisively defeated the Spartan fleet at Naxos. Intoxicated by success, the Athenians believed that the leadership of Greece was once more within their grasp but their pretensions merely caused a split with Thebes and the war became a three-way stalemate. Artaxerxes II now intervened and proposed a new King's Peace. However, negotiations failed because both Sparta and Athens, wishing to prevent Thebes becoming a major power, called for the Boeotian League to be disbanded.

These terms were unacceptable to Epaminondas, the brilliant general who had emerged as the leader of Thebes. The Spartans invaded Boeotia but at the Battle of Leuctra in 371 BC their army was destroyed by Epaminondas' unconventional tactics. Sparta's king Cleombrotus fell in the battle with over 2,000 of his hoplites; Theban casualties were negligible. The defeat struck a fatal blow to Sparta's military prestige. As news of the disaster spread, democratic revolutions broke out in Corinth and other Peloponnesian cities where Sparta had imposed aristocratic juntas. The following year Epaminondas went on the offensive, invading the Peloponnesus, liberating the Messenian helots and reducing Sparta, now deprived of its captive labour force, to the rank of a second-class power. The Theban victory did not bring freedom to the Peloponnesus, however. Corinth and Megara on the strategically important Isthmus became Theban client states and the other Peloponnesian states were enrolled in the Theban-controlled Arcadian League to prevent any recovery of Spartan power.

362 BC

THEBES CUT DOWN TO SIZE ✦ Thebes proved no more able to achieve permanent domination of Greece than Sparta or Athens. In 362 BC Mantinea left the Arcadian League and appealed to Athens for help. Athens, which had still not given up hope of recovering the leadership of Greece, allied with Sparta, Elis and Mantinea against Thebes. Epaminondas invaded the Peloponnesus and defeated the allied army near Mantinea but was fatally wounded. Deprived of Epaminondas' leadership, Theban power quickly faded but Sparta and Athens were so exhausted by decades of ultimately futile warfare that they were in no position to fill the power vacuum. The Greek world was as fragmented as it had ever been.

343 BC

THE LAST OF THE PHARAOHS ✦ Artaxerxes II never accepted the loss of Egypt but his problems with the Greeks prevented any attempt at reconquest until after the King's Peace in 386 BC. The pharaoh Achoris (r. 393–

'WOE TO THE VANQUISHED'

Day after day, the garrison looked to see if help was near; but at last when hope as well as food began to fail ... they admitted that they must either surrender, or buy the enemy off on the best terms they could get. ... The Gallic chieftain Brennus agreed upon the price of one thousand pounds' weight of gold – the price of a nation soon to rule the world. Insult was added to what was already sufficiently disgraceful, for the weights which the Gauls brought for weighing the metal were heavier than standard, and when the Roman commander objected the insolent barbarian flung his sword into the scale, saying 'Woe to the vanquished!' – words intolerable to Roman ears.

LIVY, *THE HISTORY OF ROME*, BOOK 5 (TRANS. AUBREY DE SÉLINCOURT, *THE EARLY HISTORY OF ROME*, 1960)

167

380 BC) used the breathing space to strengthen his army and navy with Greek mercenaries, and he and his successors defeated a succession of Persian invasions. Egypt was finally brought back into the Persian empire by Artaxerxes II's son and successor Artaxerxes III (r. 358–338 BC) in 343 BC. The pharaoh Nectanebo II (r. 360–343 BC) prepared to stand against Artaxerxes, who led the Persian army in person, in strong defences near the fortress city of Pelusium in the eastern Delta. Artaxerxes had recruited large numbers of Greeks into his army, many of whom had previously served in Egyptian armies and knew their way around the Delta. In an amphibious operation, the Greeks outflanked the Egyptian position,

causing Nectanebo to withdraw to Memphis. The Persians quickly took Pelusium and mopped up the garrisons in the Delta. Nectanebo gave up hope, abandoned Memphis to the Persians and fled to Upper Egypt, where he may have held out for a year or two before going into exile in Nubia. Nectanebo, the last of the pharaohs, disappears from history after this but, according to a later Greek legend, he found his way to Macedon, where he attracted the attentions of Philip II's wife Olympias and became, unknown to Philip, the true father of Alexander the Great, who ended Persian rule in Egypt for good in 332 BC.

341–338 BC

THE LATIN WAR ✦ In 343 BC Rome went to war with the Samnites, a powerful tribe of the southern Apennine mountains, without consulting their allies in the Latin League. The war lasted two years: the Samnites were defeated and Rome acquired valuable new territory in Campania. The Latins resented the high-handed way the Romans had involved them in the war and in 341 BC they asked for the formation of a single republic in which all members had equal rights. When the Romans refused, the Latins rebelled, so the Romans allied with their former enemies, the Samnites, and defeated the Latins in 338 BC. The treatment of the defeated Latins provided the blueprint for future Roman expansion in Italy. Some of the conquered Latin cities were fully incorporated into the Roman state and their inhabitants were given Roman citizenship. Other Latin cities kept local self-government and became half-citizens. This gave them most of the rights and responsibilities of a Roman citizen, including military service, but not that of voting in the assemblies. As they became more Romanized, it was expected that in time half-citizens would become full citizens and be fully assimilated into the Roman state. In addition, colonies of Roman citizens were founded as strategic outposts in the newly conquered territories.

OPPOSITE **The death bed of Epaminondas** *by Isaak Walraven (c. 1735). The Theban general Epaminondas was the most important of the casualties at Mantinea. Epaminondas was struck in the chest by a Spartan spear, which broke leaving its iron tip in his body. The Thebans carried Epaminondas back to camp alive but he died soon after the spear point was removed from the wound. Deprived of Epaminondas' brilliant military leadership, Theban power collapsed.*

NECTANEBO FORESEES THE END OF THE KINGDOM OF EGYPT

Nectanebo ... gazed into the bowl [he used for divination]. *There he saw the gods of Egypt steering the ships of the barbarians and the armies under the command of the same gods. Nectanebo, being a man experienced in magic and accustomed to talk with his gods, realised that the end of the Egyptian kingdom was at hand. He filled his garments with gold and shaved his hair and beard. Thus transformed in appearance, he fled to Pelusium. From there he sailed away to Pella in Macedonia, and settled there as an Egyptian prophet and foretold to many people events that were hidden in the stars.*

THE GREEK ALEXANDER ROMANCE, 3RD OR 2ND CENTURY BC
TRANS RICHARD STONEMAN (1991)

169

BATTLE OF CHAERONEA
2 August 338 BC

The victory of Philip II of Macedon over the allied Athenians and Thebans at Chaeronea was one of the decisive battles of the ancient world, bringing an end to the age of the Greek city states. Philip had advanced to within a few miles of Thebes and the allies hoped to block his further progress by making a stand near Chaeronea on the only easy route south through the mountains. Both armies were roughly equal in size, probably around 30,000 strong, but while the allied army consisted entirely of hoplites, the Macedonian army included 2,000 cavalry, led by his son Alexander (the Great), who was eager to prove himself in battle. The Macedonians were also more battle hardened and fitter than the allied troops. The exact course of the battle is uncertain. Philip commanded the Macedonian left wing, facing the Athenians, and Alexander the Macedonian right, facing the Thebans, who had stationed their finest regiment, the Sacred Band, on their right flank. After the battle had been raging for some time, Philip began to pivot the Macedonian phalanx: his wing slowly withdrawing in front of the Athenians, while Alexander advanced against the Thebans. Philip's manoeuvre gradually extended the Athenian phalanx, drawing it away from the Thebans. Alexander exploited the gap that opened up, breaking apart and routing the Theban phalanx. The Sacred Band stood their ground and were wiped out. Now completely exposed, the Athenians withdrew in disorder, bringing the battle to an end.

338 BC

MACEDON CONQUERS GREECE ✦ Following the end of the Theban War in 362 BC the Greek city states expended the last of their strength in minor wars, making them easy meat for a new power rising in the north, the kingdom of Macedon. Founded *c.* 640 BC, Macedon, with its mixed population of Greeks, Illyrians and Thracians and weak monarchy, was regarded as a cultural and political backwater by the rest of the Greeks. That changed with the accession of Philip II (r. 359–336 BC), a brilliant soldier and diplomat whose military reforms and innovative tactics turned Macedon into a great power capable of imposing unity on the city states. For the Greeks cavalry had always played an auxiliary role; the hoplite phalanx was always the battle-winning arm. Philip saw the phalanx differently: its role was simply to hold the enemy infantry until the cavalry could manoeuvre to deliver the decisive blow. The main Macedonian weapon was the *sarissa*, a 5.5-metre (18-ft) long spear, double the length of the Greek spear, which was used by both cavalry and infantry. Because they fought at long range, Macedonian soldiers largely dispensed with the heavy armour worn by Greek hoplites, making them much more mobile. Macedon

ABOVE **Philip II's iron breastplate** *from his tomb in the Macedonian royal cemetery at Vergina, northern Greece. In the undisturbed tomb was a golden larnax, or 'ash chest', containing the king's ashes, a golden funerary wreath, fine quality weapons and armour, and luxury tableware. The tomb itself was constructed of marble and was buried under a huge earth mound which protected it from looters.*

RIGHT **The School of Athens**
(1510–11) fresco in the Papal
Palace in the Vatican by the Italian
Renaissance artist Raphael. The
paintings include representations,
many of them based on surviving
ancient sculptures, of almost
all significant ancient Greek
philosophers: the two central figures
are Plato, on the left, and his pupil
Aristotle. The architectural setting
owes nothing to ancient Greece:
it was inspired by the plans drawn
up by the architect Bramante for
St Peter's Basilica which was begun
in 1506. Most teaching in ancient
Greece was actually conducted
outdoors, under the shade of a
convenient tree.

ABOVE **Illustration from a 13th-century copy of the**
***Shahnama* ('*The Book of Kings*'),** *a semi-legendary history
of the kings of Persia by the poet Firdawsi (d. 1020), showing
Alexander the Great building an iron wall to keep two giants
out of his kingdom. In the Middle East Alexander was known
as Iskander and in India as Sikander.*

controlled rich mineral resources, allowing Philip to rely solely on professional mercenary soldiers. The city states relied on citizen soldiers and after a century and a half of near continuous warfare their numbers were in steep decline due to war casualties, emigration and the natural extinction of family lines. Sparta, for example, which could field 8,000 citizen hoplites in 479 BC, could field a mere 800 after the Battle of Leuctra. The losses were not made good by immigration because citizenship was a jealously guarded privilege restricted to those whose parents were also native-born citizens. Nor could the city states afford to fill the ranks of their armies with mercenaries.

Philip made his first move in 352 BC with the conquest of Thessaly. The Chalkidike peninsula followed in 349–348 BC. The rapid growth of Macedonian power caused despair and panic in Athens. The orator Demosthenes tried to rally the Athenians, telling them that 'it was unworthy of you and the history of Athens and the achievements of your forefathers to let all the rest of Greece fall into slavery'. Despite many hostile acts open war did not break out until 340 BC when Philip laid siege to Byzantium (modern Istanbul) on the Bosphorus and captured 230 Athenian merchant ships, thus threatening to cut off Athens' food supplies. Demosthenes managed to cobble together an alliance with Thebes and the Boeotian League in time to face Philip when he invaded Greece in spring 338 BC.

Philip crushed the Greek alliance in a hard-fought battle at Chaeronea near Thebes on 2 August 338 BC. The two armies were approximately equal in numbers but the professionalism of Philip's troops and his superior cavalry told in his favour. As the two armies manoeuvred, a gap opened up in the Greek phalanx and Philip sent in his elite Companion cavalry, commanded by his teenage son Alexander, and broke up the Greek army. Thebes surrendered to Philip immediately after the battle and was given harsh terms. At Athens there was defiant talk of fighting to the last man but when Philip offered generous terms it too surrendered. The relieved Athenians granted citizenship to Philip and erected a statue of him in the marketplace, hailing him as the saviour of Greece. Philip now dictated terms to the Greeks. The Greek states were enrolled in a federal union, the Corinthian League, which was allied to Macedon. Philip was elected the league's leader with full power to command all Greek military forces. Sparta alone refused to join: Philip deprived it of most of its territory but left it its independence.

Alexander the Great was supposedly descended from Heracles (Hercules) on his father's side, and Achilles, the hero of the Trojan War, on his mother's.

175

336–323 BC

THE CONQUESTS OF ALEXANDER THE GREAT ✦ Philip's plan, after his conquest of Greece, was to invade the Persian empire. He got as far as sending an advance guard into northwest Anatolia before he was murdered at his daughter's wedding in autumn 336 BC, just days before he was to set out to join his army. It is possible that Philip's killing was instigated by one of his six wives, Olympias,

ALEXANDER'S DIVINITY

It is my belief that there was in those days, no nation, no city, no single individual beyond the reach of Alexander's name; never in all the world was there another like him, and therefore I cannot but feel that some power more than human was concerned in his birth.

ARRIAN, *THE CAMPAIGNS OF ALEXANDER* (TRANS. AUBREY DE SÉLINCOURT)

to ensure the succession of their son Alexander (r. 336–323 BC), then aged 20. Alexander was one of the most charismatic figures of the ancient world: highly educated – his tutor was the philosopher Aristotle – imaginative, bold to the point of recklessness and violent. Alexander was supposedly descended from Heracles (Hercules) on his father's side, and Achilles, the hero of the Trojan War, on his mother's. From childhood he burned with the desire to emulate his mythological ancestors and become a great hero and achieve divinity. Alexander had already proven himself as a soldier on the battlefield of Chaeronea: Philip had left him a fine army and Alexander soon showed that he knew how to use it.

News of Philip's death sparked rebellions across Greece. The Athenians, who only two years before had showered Philip with honours, now voted to give a crown to his murderer. Thebes called for the dissolution of the Corinthian League. Alexander destroyed Thebes, cowing the Greeks back into submission. With his home base secure, Alexander was free to carry out his father's planned invasion of the Persian empire. Leaving a garrison behind in case the Persians tried to stir up more rebellions in Greece, Alexander launched his invasion in April 334 BC, landing in northwest Anatolia, not far from Troy, which he visited to pay homage to his legendary ancestors. Alexander brought with him about 37,000 men consisting of 5,000 cavalry, 24,000 Greek and Macedonian infantry, and 8,000 auxiliary troops, including archers, slingers, javelin throwers, surveyors, siege engineers, a secretariat and a medical corps. Waiting for him in Anatolia were the 10,000 men Philip had sent in the advance party the year before. Though not a large army by Persian standards, its troops were of a uniformly high quality. Four days after leaving Troy, Alexander met and defeated his first Persian army on the Granicus river (now called the Kocabas). Alexander marched triumphantly down the Ionian coast, liberating one Greek city after another. By the year's end Alexander had won control of all of western Anatolia. Determined to earn a reputation as a lenient conqueror, he did not allow his army to plunder and made no demands for tribute above what was already being paid to the Persians.

The threat of Persian intervention in Greece was a constant concern for Alexander during this time and he planned to prevent this by conquering the Levant and Egypt, so cutting Persia off from the Mediterranean. By this time the Persian king Darius III (r. 336–330 BC) had raised a large army, estimated at 100,000 strong, and was marching west. The two kings met in battle in early November 333 BC near Issus, on the Gulf of Iskenderun in southern Turkey. Alexander led his Companion cavalry in a charge through the Persian lines. Fearing capture, Darius took to his chariot and fled for his life. Seeing their king in flight, the rest of the Persian army broke and ran too. Alexander's loot included Darius' baggage train and his wife and mother, who had been left behind when he fled. To mark his victory, Alexander founded the first of many cities he would name Alexandria after himself. Darius now desperately sued for peace, offering Alexander all of the Persian territories west of the Euphrates river, a ransom for his family and his daughter's hand in marriage in return for an alliance.

ABOVE **The Battle of Arbela (Gaugamela)** *by the Spanish artist José del Castillo (1737–93). At Gaugamela, a charge led by Alexander once again forced Darius to flee the battlefield, leaving his authority and prestige in tatters. The similarity of this scene with the Roman mosaic of Alexander at the Battle of Issus is striking but coincidental: the mosaic was not*

OVERLEAF **Roman mosaic** *from the House of the Faun in Pompeii showing the incident during the battle of Issus (333 BC) when Alexander led his cavalry on a charge through the Persian lines, forcing King Darius III to flee in his chariot to*

Alexander contemptuously rejected Darius' offer: those territories were no longer his to give.

Alexander began 332 BC by laying siege to the Phoenician port of Tyre, which provided the bulk of Persia's naval forces. Tyre refused to submit while the outcome of the war was still in doubt and Alexander took the strongly fortified city only after an eight-month siege. After this, he faced little resistance as he marched south down the Mediterranean coast until he reached Gaza. At the end of 332 BC Alexander entered Egypt. The Persian satrap surrendered immediately and the Egyptian people greeted Alexander as a liberator. While in Egypt, Alexander visited the Oracle of Amun at Siwa Oasis. The oracle told him that his true father was not Philip but the supreme god Zeus, confirming Alexander's belief, and that of many of his contemporaries, that his amazing achievements showed him to be a living god. While in Egypt too, he founded the most successful of his Alexandria's, on a good harbour close to the western mouth of the Nile.

In 331 BC Alexander invaded Mesopotamia and defeated Darius for a second time at the Battle of Gaugamela near Nineveh on 1 October. Just as at Issus, Alexander led a direct charge on Darius' position, forcing him to flee the battlefield, and once again the Persian army broke up in panic. Demoralized by this second humiliating defeat, Darius fled to Hamadan, abandoning Babylon and the Persian treasury at Susa to Alexander. The following year, Alexander destroyed another Persian army in the Battle of the Persian Gate – a narrow mountain pass – and captured Persepolis, the empire's ceremonial capital, which was sacked and burned.

When Alexander left Persepolis and advanced on Hamadan, Darius fled again, hoping to find a refuge somewhere in the eastern satrapies. Alexander pursued him. Near the Caspian Gates pass, Darius, full of the apathy of despair, refused to go any further. Seeing the dust of Alexander's pursuing army darkening the horizon, the nobles murdered Darius and proclaimed his kinsman Bessos king and continued their flight. Alexander arrived on the scene a few hours later and ordered that Darius be given a royal burial at Persepolis. Bessos, the last of the Achaemenids, remained a fugitive for 18 months until he was finally captured by Alexander and executed.

VERDICT ON DARIUS III

Though in other respects his conduct appears to have been moderate and decent, in military matters Darius III was the feeblest and most incompetent of men. ... His life was an unbroken series of disasters from the moment of his accession to the Persian throne.

ARRIAN, *THE CAMPAIGNS OF ALEXANDER*

181

LEFT **A procession of Immortals,** *the royal lifeguard regiment, from Persepolis. The title of 'Immortals' has been revived several times, first by the Sassanian dynasty who ruled Persia from the 3rd to 7th centuries AD and then by the medieval Byzantine empire, which used the title to describe two of its elite regiments. The French referred to Napoleon's Imperial Guard as the 'Immortals' and the last Shah of Iran's elite Javidan Guard also bore that title.*

HELLENISTIC CIVILIZATION

Alexander's conquests led to profound cultural changes. Alexander and the Diadochi who followed him were enthusiastic founders of cities, which they populated with Macedonian and Greek veteran soldiers and with immigrants from Greece attracted by new opportunities.

These widely scattered cities became agents for the expansion of Greek cultural influence across western Asia and into central Asia and northern India. In this vast melting pot, aspects of Greek civilization were adopted and adapted by Egyptian, Persian, Indian and other cultures to create a new Hellenistic civilization. Compared to the governments of the Greek city states, the rulers of the Hellenistic kingdoms which emerged from the break-up of Alexander's empire had vast wealth, which they displayed with lavish entertainments and magnificent art and architecture. The restraint that characterized Greek art and architecture gave way to flamboyance, extravagance, complexity and size.

BELOW **The sculptural friezes** of the monumental altar dedicated to Zeus and Athena at Pergamon (now in Turkey), carved c. 170 BC, display the flamboyance of Hellenistic art at its finest. This section shows one of the Morai (Fates) battling the monstrous children of the primordial goddess Gaia. The temple-sized altar was erected to celebrate Pergamon's victories over the Galatians.

ALEXANDER ATTEMPTS SUICIDE

When he knew that his death was imminent, he went out with the intention of throwing himself into the Euphrates, in order to disappear without trace and make it easier for posterity to believe that one of the gods was his father and he had gone away to join them. His wife Roxana ... happened to see him as he left the building, and stopped him, whereupon he gave a great cry and bitterly reproached her for grudging him the eternal fame of divine birth.

ARRIAN, *THE CAMPAIGNS OF ALEXANDER*

Now that Darius was dead, Alexander's men considered the war to be over and asked to be sent home so that they could enjoy the fruits of their victory. Alexander persuaded them reluctantly to fight on and complete the conquest of the Persian empire. Despite this, the original unity of purpose was gone and relations between Alexander and his Macedonian followers began to deteriorate. Alexander increasingly relied on Persian mercenaries to fill the depleted ranks of his army; he used Persian administrators, adopted Persian customs and married a Persian bride.

It took Alexander three more years of campaigning to bring the Persian empire's eastern satrapies under his control. In 327 BC Alexander crossed the Indus river and invaded the Punjab. There, in May 326 BC, Alexander defeated the Indian king Porus at the Battle of the Hydaspes river (now the Jhelum river, Pakistan): it was his last major victory. When Alexander prepared to advance further into India, the Macedonians in his army mutinied: they had marched nearly 17,000 miles since the start of the campaign and were war-weary and homesick. Alexander marched south down the Indus to the sea and turned west. After a gruelling march through the deserts of southern Iran, Alexander arrived at Susa in spring 324 BC. The following year, Alexander died at Babylon, probably from malaria, aged 33.

Alexander's heirs were a posthumous son and a mentally retarded brother, neither of whom was capable of ruling. The regent Perdiccas tried to hold the empire together but, after he was murdered in 321 BC, Alexander's generals fought one another for power in a complex succession of conflicts known as the Wars of the Diadochi ('successors'). By 301 BC Alexander's empire had been divided into five kingdoms under Macedonian dynasties. Macedonia itself fell to Cassander, who murdered both of Alexander's legitimate heirs. Lysimachos took Thrace; Antigonus Anatolia, Greece, Syria and the Levant; Ptolemy Egypt; and Seleucus Mesopotamia, Persia and the east.

> *When Alexander prepared to advance further into India, the Macedonians in his army mutinied: they had marched nearly 17,000 miles since the start of the campaign and were war-weary and homesick.*

183

THE RISE
OF ROME

323–30 BC

Alexander the Great's empire did not long survive his death in 323 BC. In the Wars of the Diadochi ('successors'), Alexander's generals fought one another for 20 years, carving his empire up into five kingdoms, which in their turn soon began to fragment. Meanwhile, events in the western Mediterranean were dominated by the rivalry between Rome and the North African city of Carthage. Rome's eventual triumph in 201 BC turned it into the Mediterranean's greatest power.

There followed two centuries of inexorable Roman expansion, into Spain, Gaul, Greece, Anatolia, Syria and the Levant. The annexation of Egypt in 30 BC completed Rome's domination of the Mediterranean world. Rome's explosive growth from city state to world empire strained its republican constitution to breaking point and it ended in civil war and the dictatorship of Julius Caesar. Caesar's murder in 44 BC provoked another civil war, won eventually by his nephew Octavian.

321 BC

ROMANS UNDER THE YOKE ✦ In 326 BC war broke out between the Romans and the Samnites after the Greek colony of Neapolis (Naples) appealed to Rome for help against Samnite aggression. The Romans won a succession of victories, leading the Samnites to sue for peace in 321 BC. Roman terms were unacceptably harsh so the war continued. Later in the same year the Samnite commander Gaius Pontius used false intelligence to trap a Roman army in the Caudine Forks, a narrow mountain pass near Capua. Lacking supplies or any chance of breaking out the Romans gave in to despair and sent envoys to negotiate a surrender.

The Samnites could not decide how to exploit their advantage. Pontius' father Herennius advised that the Romans must either be slaughtered to the last man, leaving Rome powerless for years, or be released without harming or humiliating them, so winning Rome's friendship. Reluctant either to massacre defenceless men or to let his enemies escape scot-free, Pontius disarmed the Roman soldiers and humiliated them by forcing to pass under a yoke in a traditional ritual of subjugation.

PREVIOUS PAGES **Relief portraying Cleopatra VII** *wearing the traditional clothing of an ancient Egyptian queen. Cleopatra became notorious for her affairs with two of the most powerful men of the late Roman Republic, Julius Caesar and Mark Antony, both of whom she tried to manipulate in an ultimately unsuccessful attempt to preserve her kingdom's independence from Rome.*

OPPOSITE *Romans under the Yoke by the Swiss artist Marc-Charles-Gabriel Gleyre (1806–74) depicts the humiliation of captured Roman soldiers by forcing to them to bow under a yoke like oxen. Gleyre's painting was actually inspired by an incident in 107 BC when the Helvetii, a Celtic tribe from whom Switzerland gets its French name, Helvetia, forced captured Romans under the yoke. The Romans captured by the Samnites at the Caudine Forks in 321 BC were probably treated in a very similar way, however.*

ABOVE **Painted plate showing a war elephant,** *probably made in Greece* c. *250* BC. *Elephants were introduced into Mediterranean warfare by Seleucus who was given 400 in exchange for the Indus valley by the Indian king Chandragupta Maurya. Elephants were powerful if sometimes dangerously unpredictable. Archers and spearmen stationed in fighting platforms on the* *elephants' backs could shoot down on enemy soldiers, the elephants' size and smell terrified horses, and their sheer bulk allowed them to smash through infantry formations. However, when wounded, the animals were likely to turn and flee causing chaos in the ranks of their side. The Romans became particularly adept at countering elephant attacks.*

This succeeded only in antagonizing the Romans without in any way weakening them. Fighting broke out again in 316 BC and in 311 BC the Etruscans joined in on the Samnite side. The Romans made short work of the Etruscans, who sued for peace in 308 BC. The Samnites followed suit and made peace in 304 BC. The war left the Samnites hemmed in on three sides by Roman territory. It was also during this war that the Romans built the first of their famous all-weather roads, the Via Appia (begun 312 BC), and the Via Valeria (begun 306 BC), to speed troop movements.

301 BC

THE BATTLE OF IPSUS ✦ The Wars of the Diadochi were dominated by the struggle between Antigonus and Seleucus for control of Alexander's Asian conquests. At first Antigonus, aided by his able son Demetrius (a former commander in the Companion cavalry), seemed to have the upper hand and it appeared possible that he might reunite Alexander's empire under his own rule. Antigonus' success led Cassander of Macedon and Lysimachus of Thrace to ally against him and invade his territory in Anatolia. Antigonus' forces greatly outnumbered those of the allies but he was unable to bring them to battle before they linked up with his rival Seleucus. Fielding around 75,000 men each the two armies were equal in size but the allies were superior in cavalry and also had around 400 war elephants which Seleucus had obtained from the Indian king Chandragupta Maurya in exchange for the Indus valley. It was Seleucus' elephants that proved decisive when the two armies met in battle at Ipsus in Anatolia in 301 BC, blocking an outflanking manoeuvre by Antigonus' cavalry while allied archers broke his infantry. Antigonus was killed in the battle and his territory was shared between Lysimachus and Seleucus. The last chance of maintaining the unity of Alexander's empire had passed. Over the next 250 years, the kingdoms created by the surviving Diadochi gradually fragmented, making them easy prey for the new rising powers of Rome and Parthia.

Pyrrhus defeated the Romans at Heraclea (280 BC) and Ausculum (279 BC) but at such heavy cost that it broke the back of his army and gave us the expression 'Pyrrhic victory' for any success gained at too high a price.

272 BC

ROME BECOMES MASTER OF ITALY ✦ In 272 BC Tarentum (modern Taranto), a Greek colony on the 'heel' of Italy, became the last city in peninsular Italy to fall to the Romans. The final phase of Rome's conquest of the peninsula had begun with its decisive victory in the Third Samnite War in 298–290 BC. With their toughest adversary eliminated, the Romans easily conquered the Etruscans and Umbrians, bringing all of central Italy under their control.

AN EXPENSIVE VICTORY

We are told *that Pyrrhus said to one who was congratulating him on his victory [at Asculum], 'If we are victorious in one more battle with the Romans, we shall be utterly ruined.' For he had lost a great part of the forces with which he came, and all his friends and generals except a few; moreover, he had no others whom he could summon from home, and he saw that his allies in Italy were becoming indifferent, while the army of the Romans, as if from a fountain gushing forth indoors, was easily and speedily filled up again, and they did not lose courage in defeat, nay, their wrath gave them all the more vigour and determination for the war.*

PLUTARCH, *THE LIFE OF PYRRHUS*

Around 282 BC Rome began to bring southern Italy under its control also by offering protection to Greek colonies on the coast against the fierce hill tribes of the interior. Most of the Greek colonies welcomed Roman protection but Tarentum, the leading naval power in Italy, saw this as a threat to what it regarded as its sphere of influence. War broke out in 281 BC and the Romans occupied Tarentum, only to driven out by troops sent by the city's ally, King Pyrrhus of Epirus in eastern Greece. Pyrrhus was an able soldier with pretensions to be the new Alexander. In 280 BC he brought an army of around 25,000 men and 20 war elephants to Italy to support Tarentum. Pyrrhus defeated the Romans at Heraclea (280 BC) and Asculum (279 BC) but at such heavy cost that it broke the back of his army and gave us the expression 'Pyrrhic victory' for any success gained at too high a price. After he was defeated by Rome at Beneventum in 275 BC, Pyrrhus withdrew from Italy, leaving a garrison behind to protect Tarentum. Discontented soldiers from this garrison betrayed the city to the Romans in 272 BC. The city was looted, its walls were destroyed and around 30,000 of its inhabitants were sold into slavery. In the same year that Pyrrhus was killed in street fighting in Argos, by an old woman who threw a tile onto him from a rooftop. By this time, Rome had grown wealthy on spoil and tribute from its Italian wars. With a population of around 150,000 it was one of the largest cities in the Mediterranean world and, with the manpower of Italy at its command, Rome was a power to be reckoned with.

OPPOSITE **Bronze ram from Athlit,** *near Haifa in Israel, c. 200 BC. A ram mounted on the bows was the main offensive weapon of war galleys in the ancient world. The head of the ram was designed to break the timbers of an enemy ship's hull just below the waterline without penetrating it, so as to avoid it getting stuck. Rams were cast in a single piece, requiring great skill on the part of the metalworkers: the large quantities of bronze required made them expensive weapons.*

OVERLEAF **Roman war galleys** *of the 1st century AD are shown in this wall painting preserved on the wall of a house at Pompeii that was buried by ash during the eruption of Vesuvius in AD 79. The projecting rams on the bows are very prominent, as are soldiers massed on the decks ready to board and capture enemy ships.*

264–241 BC

THE FIRST PUNIC WAR ✦ One of the first acts of the Roman republic after its foundation in 509 BC was signing a treaty of friendship with the Phoenician of Carthage. Carthage had not long been independent of its parent city of Tyre but it was already the dominant mercantile and naval power of the western Mediterranean, with an empire that included western Sicily, Sardinia, Corsica, Malta, the Balearic Islands and colonies, such as Gades (Cadiz), controlling the Pillars of Hercules (Straits of Gibraltar) and access to the ore-rich lands of Europe's Atlantic coast. The treaty was renewed in 348 BC and 306 BC but, as Roman power spread through Italy, a conflict of interests became increasingly likely. When Pyrrhus withdrew from Italy in 275 BC, he predicted that Rome and Carthage would very soon go to war over Sicily. He was right. In 264 BC the city of Messana (Messina) appealed to Rome for protection against the Greek king Hiero of Syracuse. Fearful of allowing the Romans to get a foothold in Sicily, Carthage allied with Syracuse, so starting the First Punic War (from *Poeni*, the Latin word for Phoenician). The war lasted over 20 years and was remembered by the Romans as the hardest and most costly of all their wars.

The Romans enjoyed an early success when they laid siege to Syracuse in 263 BC, forcing Hiero to change sides. However, the Romans soon realized that they would not be able to win complete control of Sicily while Carthage could use its unchallenged control of the sea to supply and reinforce its colonies. The Romans had no traditions of shipbuilding or naval warfare but they captured a beached Carthaginian galley and copied it. In just a few months the Romans had built and manned a fleet of 100 galleys. They even added their own innovation, the raven (*corvus*), a boarding bridge with an iron spike on the end

which could be dropped onto the deck of an enemy ship to hold it fast while Roman marines stormed across to attack its crew. Using their new weapon, the Romans won a decisive victory over the Carthaginian fleet at Mylae in 260 BC. The Romans followed this up by seizing the Carthaginian colonies in Corsica and Sardinia.

In 256 BC, the Roman general Regulus gathered a force of 330 ships and 150,000 men for an invasion of Africa. A Carthaginian fleet of 350 ships intercepted the Romans off Cape Ecnomus on the south coast of Sicily but it was defeated, again largely due the Romans' use of the raven. After a brief delay for repairs, the Roman fleet crossed unhindered to Africa, landing near Carthage. Regulus won an easy victory at the Battle of Adys later that year, prompting the Carthaginians to sue for peace. However, Regulus' terms were so severe that the Carthaginians resolved to fight on, hiring the Spartan mercenary Xanthippus to reform their army. In 255 BC Xanthippus led the revived Carthaginian army to a stunning victory at Tunes (Tunis), killing or capturing around 15,000 Roman soldiers. Regulus was one of the prisoners. The survivors were evacuated by sea but the fleet was hit by a storm and two-thirds of the Roman ships, made top-heavy by their ravens, capsized and sank. The raven was not used again.

The disaster allowed the Carthaginians to return to Sicily in 254 BC and reoccupy their lost colonies. The war now became one of dogged attrition. In 251 BC, the Carthaginians again sued for peace, giving the captured general Regulus parole to negotiate terms. When he got to Rome, Regulus advised the Senate not to make peace and then, honouring his parole, returned to Carthage. The angry Carthaginians tortured him to death. The war swung in Carthage's favour in 249 BC when they defeated a Roman fleet under Claudius Pulcher off Lilybaeum (Marsala). Pulcher was blamed for the defeat. Before joining battle, he had released sacred chickens onto the deck of his galley, expecting them to peck at grain and provide a favourable omen. When the seasick chickens refused to eat, Pulcher threw them overboard saying 'If they won't eat, then let them drink.' Later the same year, the Carthaginian general Hamilcar Barca defeated a Roman attack on Eryx (Erice), and soon after what remained of their fleet was destroyed in a storm.

Taking these setbacks as a warning from the gods, the Romans ceased large-scale naval activity for several years. Hamilcar defeated all efforts by the Romans to make headway in Sicily, while Carthaginian ships raided the Italian coast. However, in 242 BC the Romans rebuilt their fleet and in a major land and sea operation captured Lilybaeum, the main Carthaginian naval base on Sicily. Carthage sent a fleet to recapture Lilybaeum in 241 BC, but the Romans defeated it off the Aegates Islands. Carthage's capacity to wage war was now exhausted and when Rome offered generous peace terms – reparations and the evacuation of Sicily – it accepted. Rome had gained its first overseas province. In the end, Rome had won because it had the manpower to raise large armies and man a large fleet at the same time, while the Carthaginians did not. Because of the heavy burden of reparations, Carthage neglected to pay its soldiers in Sardinia. In 238 BC they mutinied and the Romans opportunistically occupied the island, together with Corsica. This act, in breach of the peace treaty, created more bitterness in Carthage than the war had done.

225—222 BC

ROME COMPLETES THE CONQUEST OF ITALY ✦ After the First Punic War, the Gauls of northern Italy concluded that it was only a matter of time before the Romans turned their attentions to them. Deciding to strike first, the Gauls invaded Roman territory in 225 BC with an army of 50,000 infantry and 20,000 cavalry and charioteers. The invasion initially went well for the Gauls: they defeated one Roman army at Fiesole, near Florence, and captured an enormous quantity of plunder, prisoners and cattle. When only three days' march from Rome the Gauls learned that a second Roman army was approaching from the south and began an orderly withdrawal north along the Mediterranean coast. Unknown to the Gauls a third Roman army, which had been hurriedly withdrawn from Sardinia, had landed at Pisa to their north and cut off their line of retreat. At Telamon, near the coast of Etruria 100 miles (161 km) north of Rome, the Celtic army was trapped between these two Roman armies and annihilated after heavy fighting. Though the Romans fielded only around the same number of men as the Gauls, their superior discipline, weapons and armour told heavily in their favour. The Romans immediately seized the initiative and began the complete subjection and annexation of the Po valley. The conquest took only three years and was completed with the capture of Mediolanum (Milan), the main settlement of the Insubres, in 222 BC. All of present-day Italy was now under Roman control.

218—202 BC

THE SECOND PUNIC WAR ✦
Carthage was reluctant to accept its defeat by Rome. In 237 BC Hamilcar Barca began establishing a new overseas empire in southern Spain, where he founded a new capital, Carthago Nova (Cartagena). The Romans watched suspiciously as Carthaginian power spread north, and in

RIGHT **Bronze statuette of a Gaulish warrior** or god from Saint-Maur in northern France, 1st century BC. The long drooping moustache and swept-back hair are typical of the Celts, who used lime to stiffen their hair so it would keep its style.

OVERLEAF **Romans battle Gauls** in this high relief from a finely sculpted Roman sarcophagus of the 2nd century AD. The Gauls were long pacified by the time the sarcophagus was made but the sculptor probably used older monuments celebrating Roman victories as a source for their shields and armour.

Hannibal's route
Carthaginian territory
Roman territory

226 BC they demanded that the Carthaginians confine their activities to the south of the Ebro river. Hamilcar died in 228 BC and in 221 BC Carthage's military leadership passed to his son Hannibal. Hamilcar had brought Hannibal up to be an implacable enemy of Rome and he believed that further conflict was inevitable. When the city of Saguntum (Sagunto) accepted Roman protection, Hannibal saw this as a threat to Carthage's Spanish empire and he laid siege to the city, knowing full well that this would lead to war. Hannibal realized that Carthage did not have the manpower to win a war of attrition with Rome so he planned to invade Italy and, by posing as a liberator, hoped to persuade Rome's Italian subjects to rebel and fight on his side, so neutralizing Rome's main advantage over Carthage.

The Romans were confident that their hard-won control of the sea would prevent a Carthaginian attack on Italy. They were, therefore, taken completely by surprise when Hannibal set out from Cartagena in May 218 BC to march his army overland, across the Pyrenees, through southern Gaul and across the Alps to attack Italy from the north. Hannibal's army included around 50,000 infantry, 9,000 cavalry and 37 war elephants. Hannibal evaded the army Rome sent to intercept him by striking north up the Rhône river valley and crossing the Alps by the difficult Col de Clapier. Resistance from local tribes had slowed Hannibal's progress: it was late October when he began the final ascent of the pass and it was already snowbound. Hannibal's men were unprepared for the Alpine cold and thousands died of exposure. On the descent thousands more men and animals fell to their deaths from the narrow icy path. By the time Hannibal's army completed the descent into the Po river valley in northern Italy it numbered only 20,000 infantry and 6,000 cavalry but, amazingly, all his elephants survived.

ABOVE **Hannibal's campaigns 221–202 BC.** *Hannibal's decision to invade Italy by marching from Spain overland and crossing the Alps took the Romans by surprise, but despite winning spectacular victories he was unable to strike a knockout blow. Effectively isolated in Italy, Hannibal was unable to prevent the Romans conquering Spain and invading North Africa.*

OPPOSITE **The Battle of Zama** *by an unknown artist of the Roman School (1521). At Zama, Hannibal was relying on an elephant charge to break up the Roman legions. The Romans countered the charge by opening lanes in their ranks for the elephants to pass through and then attacked them with javelins. The panicked animals turned and fled, causing chaos in the Carthaginian army.*

If his plan was to work, Hannibal needed a quick victory to establish his credibility. Hannibal's opportunity came within weeks, when he defeated a strong Roman scouting force under the consul Publius Scipio near the Ticino river, near Turin. Following this success 15,000 Gauls, still resentful after their defeat at Telamon, joined Hannibal's army. With these reinforcements Hannibal easily defeated another Roman army on the Trebia river at the end of December. In spring 217 BC Hannibal marched south into Etruria, pursued by a new Roman army. On 21 June Hannibal drew his pursuers into an ambush on the northeast shore of Lake Trasimene where the road passed through a narrow defile between steep hills on one

By the time Hannibal's army completed the descent into the Po river valley in northern Italy it numbered only 20,000 infantry and 6,000 cavalry but, amazingly, all his elephants survived.

side and the lake on the other. Aided by thick morning fog, Hannibal concealed his forces above the defile. As the Romans passed below in a long stretched-out column, Hannibal sprung the trap and won another stunning victory. Despite his unbroken run of victories, Hannibal was painfully aware by the end of 217 BC that his strategy was not working. Many Gauls had come over to his side but Rome's Latin allies remained stubbornly loyal and he had failed to capture a single important town. If Hannibal was to succeed, he had to achieve something spectacular. After Lake Trasimene the Romans appointed Fabius, an experienced soldier, as dictator, to deal with Hannibal. Fabius recognized Hannibal's genius as a tactician and decided to avoid battle and let fatigue, disease, hunger and desertion wear down his army. Many Romans found this strategy humiliating: it earned Fabius the derisive nickname 'the Delayer'. When Fabius' term expired, the new consuls Varro and Paullus decided to go on the offensive.

In June 216 Hannibal moved his army to the small town of Cannae in Apulia. Varro and Paullus left Rome to confront Hannibal with the largest army the Romans had ever fielded, around 86,000 strong. Hannibal was outnumbered nearly two to one but, crucially, he fielded more and better cavalry than the Romans and, once again, fought on ground of his own choosing. It was also to his advantage that Paullus and Varro disagreed with one another over what tactics to use. The battle, fought

LEFT **Hannibal after his victory at the battle of Cannae.** *Statue by the 17th-century French sculptor Sebastien Slodtz, portraying Hannibal with a Roman eagle standard in one hand and by his side an urn filled with three bushels of gold signet rings said to have been taken from the Roman dead.*

R. Anfidius

Paullus' cavalry

ROMAN FORCES

Hasdrubal's cavalry

Geminus

Hannibal and Mago

Varro's cavalry

CARTHAGINIAN FORCES

Maharbal's cavalry

CANNAE

R. Anfidius

Hasdrubal's cavalry

Geminus and Paullus

Varro's cavalry

Hannibal and Mago

Maharbal's cavalry

CANNAE

Hasdrubal's cavalry

Geminus and Paullus

Hannibal and Mago

CANNAE

THE BATTLE OF CANNAE

One of the greatest battles of the ancient world, Cannae displayed Hannibal's tactical genius at its finest. Hannibal all but annihilated a Roman army twice the size of his own, suffering relatively light casualties himself, but despite the spectacular scale of the victory, it barely dented Rome's capacity to wage war.

Hannibal chose to base himself at Cannae in the uplands of Apulia because it was surrounded by open rolling countryside where he would be able to deploy his superior cavalry to advantage. The Romans were confident of victory. Their army of around 80,000 infantry and 6,000 cavalry was nearly twice the size of Hannibal's army of around 40,000 infantry and 10,000 cavalry. Hannibal's army included many lightly armed Iberian and Celtic mercenaries and only his Carthaginian heavy infantry were as well armed as the Romans.

Hannibal planned to use the Romans' weight of numbers against them. Hannibal formed his infantry up in an arc, its centre facing outwards towards the Romans, with lighter armed troops at the centre and heavy infantry towards the flanks. Hannibal stationed his cavalry on both flanks. When the fighting began, the lightly armed troops at the centre of Hannibal's line gradually gave ground, encouraging the Romans to press ahead strongly. Meanwhile, the Carthaginian cavalry chased the inferior Roman cavalry off the field. As the Roman infantry continued to advance, it was gradually outflanked by the Carthaginian heavy infantry and when the Carthaginian cavalry returned from its pursuit and attacked from the rear, the Romans found themselves completely surrounded.

As the Carthaginians pressed their attack, the Romans became so crowded together that they could scarcely lift their weapons to fight back and the battle turned into a massacre. Barely 15,000 of the Roman infantry were able to break out of Hannibal's trap: by the day's end around 50,000 Romans were dead and 15,000 had been taken prisoner. Hannibal's casualties were around 5,700.

201

on 2 August, was Hannibal's masterpiece and it is still taught at military academies as the classic envelopment. Hannibal's battle plan used the Romans' weight of numbers against them. When the Romans attacked, the centre of Hannibal's line fell back, drawing the overconfident Romans on into a perfect trap. Once surrounded, Roman numbers counted for nothing; they were too tightly packed to fight effectively. It was the most serious defeat ever suffered by a Roman army. Roman losses amounted to 50,000 killed and 15,000 captured. Hannibal lost around 5,700 men.

After Cannae, Hannibal's commanders urged him to march on Rome at once. Hannibal refused, perhaps missing his best chance to end the war. He did not have enough men to besiege the city and he mistakenly believed that, after suffering such a disaster, even the Romans would be willing to talk peace. Capua, Campania and many of the Greek cities of southern Italy did now defect to Hannibal but even the intervention on Hannibal's side of Syracuse and Philip V (r. 221–179 BC) of Macedon in 215 BC did not shake the loyalty of most of Rome's Italian allies. Rome, therefore, had the manpower to recover even from this defeat and it showed no interest in making peace. When the Romans reverted to Fabius' strategy of avoiding battle, the true weakness of Hannibal's position was exposed. Hannibal was isolated in southern Italy and unable to influence the wider course of the war, which was not going in Carthage's favour.

In 218 BC the Romans sent an army to invade Spain under Gnaeus Scipio: his brother Publius Scipio joined him with a second army in 217 BC. While Hannibal rampaged through Italy, the Scipios won a series of victories over his brother Hasdrubal. In 215 BC Rome invaded Macedon and in 211 BC captured Syracuse after a two-year siege. In the same year the Romans also captured Capua, Hannibal's most powerful Italian ally, but suffered a setback when both Scipios were killed in battle in Spain. Publius Scipio, later nicknamed Africanus, the son and namesake of Publius Scipio, was sent to replace them. A veteran of Cannae, Scipio had made a careful study of Hannibal's

LEFT **Marble bust of Publius Scipio 'Africanus' (236–183 BC)**, *the Roman general whose decisive victory over Hannibal at Zama in 202 BC effectively ended the Second Punic War. Scipio first showed his military abilities when he defeated Hannibal's brother Hasdrubal at the battle of Baecula in Spain in 209 BC.*

HANNIBAL HESITATES AFTER CANNAE

When the Carthaginians, flocking round *Hannibal, congratulated him on the victory [at Cannae], ... Maharbal, the commander of the cavalry, who was of the opinion that no time should be lost, said to him, 'that if you want to know how much has been accomplished by this engagement, in five days you shall be feasting, victorious, in the Capitol. Follow me: I will advance with the cavalry, so that the enemy may see me at the gates of Rome, before they know that we are on the way.' To Hannibal these hopes appeared too* sanguine, *and the prospect too vast for his mind to comprehend at first view. He therefore replied, that 'he applauded Maharbal's zeal; but the affair required time for consideration'. On which Maharbal observed, 'I perceive that the gods do not bestow on the same person all kinds of talents. You, Hannibal, know how to acquire victory, but you do not know how to use it.' There is good reason to believe that the delay of that day proved the preservation of Rome, and of the empire.*

LIVY, HISTORY OF ROME (ADAPTED FROM TRANSLATION BY GEORGE BAKER)

tactics. He quickly regained the initiative for Rome and in 209 BC captured Carthago Nova, and defeated Hasdrubal at Baecula. Hasdrubal escaped, taking his army overland to Italy hoping to reinforce Hannibal, but was killed at the Battle of the Metaurus in 207 BC before he could join his brother. The following year Scipio destroyed the last Carthaginian army in Spain at Ilipa.

After Scipio invaded Africa in 204 BC, the Carthaginian senate recalled Hannibal from Italy while at the same time opening peace negotiations. When Hannibal arrived, bringing around 18,000 veterans with him, he put new heart into the Carthaginians and the senate broke off negotiations while Hannibal raised a new army. Hannibal met Scipio in battle on the plain of Zama in October 202 BC and was crushingly defeated. It was Hannibal's lack of cavalry that proved decisive. The Numidians (a Berber people), who supplied Carthage's best cavalry, had gone over to the Romans. After Zama, Scipio dictated peace terms to Carthage. Carthage would lose its empire, pay Rome a huge indemnity, destroy its fleet and never wage war again without Roman permission. Realizing that further resistance would only invite harsher terms, Hannibal persuaded the Carthaginian senate to accept, ending the war in 201 BC. Rome now dominated the western Mediterranean.

203

197 BC

ROME TURNS EAST ✦ Philip V's intervention in the Second Punic War achieved nothing beyond antagonizing the Romans. When Pergamum (in Anatolia) and Rhodes appealed for protection against Philip in 200 BC, Rome seized the opportunity to punish him for his unprovoked aggression. In 197 BC at the Battle of Cynoscephelae, brought on when Roman and Macedonian armies stumbled upon

THE LEGION

The word legion (from *legio*, the levy) originally referred to whole Roman army. As Rome's manpower increased, and larger forces could be fielded, the word became used to describe the army's major fighting units.

The Roman army of the early republic was a part-time citizen militia that served only for a few weeks or months. Only property owners could be conscripted to serve as the Romans believed that only people with a stake in the survival of the state could be relied upon to defend it. The Roman army originally fought in a phalanx but experience fighting the Gauls and Samnites taught them to adopt a more flexible tactical organization based on the *maniple* ('handful'), made up of two centuries of 60–80 men. By the time of the Second Punic War a full strength Roman legion comprised 3,000 heavy infantry, 1,200 lightly armed *velites* (skirmishers) and 300 cavalry. The heavy infantry formed up in three lines, the youngest, the *hastati*, at the front, the more experienced *principes* in the second line, and the old veterans, the *triarii*, at the rear. Soldiers were supposed to provide their own armour and weapons but by the time of the Punic Wars, the state was beginning to take over this responsibility. Pay was also introduced because soldiers could now be absent from their homes for years at a time.

As Rome's commitments increased, its military system came under increasing strain. Around 102 BC, the consul Marius began to professionalize the Roman army by ending the connection between service and property ownership and opening recruitment to the landless proletarians. Marius'

reforms set the pattern of the Roman legion for the next 400 years. Marius abandoned the maniple as the basic tactical unit in favour of the larger cohort of 480 men, subdivided into six units of 80 men called centuries. Centuries were subdivided into ten 'tents' of eight men each. A legion was made up of ten cohorts, one of which was double strength, and a small cavalry unit was attached to each legion for scouting. Legion commanders were usually senators and staff officers, who came from the higher social classes whilecenturions (century commanders) were promoted from the ranks on merit. Equipment was standardized. All soldiers were issued an oblong shield, a chain-mail coat, iron helmet, javelin and *gladius*, a short thrusting sword ideally suited to close order fighting. Arms drill and weapons training, adapted from the gladiatorial schools, was introduced and soldiers had to carry emergency supplies, cooking equipment and tools to build a fortified camp every night when on campaign. Fierce discipline was imposed. Units which mutinied or showed cowardice in the face of the enemy were subject to decimation, the execution of one in ten of their numbers, chosen at random by lot. Only Roman citizens could join the legions but auxiliary units, often of specialist troops such as archers and cavalry, were recruited from the provinces and allied states.

RIGHT **Military insignia.** *This page from the Notitia Dignitatum, a unique document setting out the battle order of the Roman army at the beginning of the 5th century, shows the insignia of the legions and auxiliary regiments stationed on the Rhine frontier to protect Gaul from Germanic invaders.*

OPPOSITE TOP **Bronze legionary helmet.** *The Romans adopted the design of their legionary helmet from the Celts. This example is incomplete, missing its protective cheek guards. Stamped inscriptions inside the helmet show that it had been issued to four different soldiers before it was lost in London around the time of Boudicca's revolt (AD 60).*

OPPOSITE BOTTOM **Shield boss.** *The main purpose of the iron boss on a legionary's shield was to protect the hand, but it could also be used as a weapon, for smashing against an opponent during close-quarters fighting.*

Hannibal took poison, remarking 'it is now time to end the anxiety of the Romans. Clearly, they are no longer able to wait for the death of an old man who has caused them so much concern.'

one another in fog, the Roman legions formed up for battle more quickly than the inflexible Macedonian phalanx and won a devastating victory for little loss. Macedon was forced to become an ally of Rome and the Greek city states were freed from Macedonian rule under Roman protection. The Romans had no territorial ambitions in Greece and they then withdrew their forces. However, the Romans soon found that it was not that easy to disengage from the complex conflicts and rivalries of the Hellenistic kingdoms.

189 BC

THE BATTLE OF MAGNESIA ✦ The expansion of Roman influence into Greece alarmed Antiochus III (r. 222–187 BC), the ruler of the Seleucid kingdom, which at that time was the largest of the Hellenistic kingdoms, extending from Anatolia east to Afghanistan. The Romans became equally alarmed when Antiochus took Hannibal into his retinue in 195 BC. Antiochus confirmed his hostile intention by invading Greece in 192 BC but a Roman army arrived quickly and drove him out the next year. Shortly afterwards, the Roman fleet defeated the Seleucid fleet, commanded by Hannibal, near the Eurymedon river, opening the way for an invasion of Anatolia in alliance with Pergamon. In January 189 BC the Romans brought Antiochus to battle at Magnesia. Antiochus formed his army up behind a screen of war elephants; unfortunately, these played an unintended part in his defeat when they charged the Roman infantry. The Romans had learned how to deal with elephants when fighting Carthage, and they sent the wounded beasts crashing back through Seleucid lines. Before the Seleucids could recover, the Roman cavalry took them in the flank, while the infantry made a vigorous frontal assault. The Romans followed up their victory by occupying most of western Anatolia. Antiochus made peace in 188 BC, losing all his territories west of the Taurus mountains. The Romans divided most of this territory between its allies Pergamon and Rhodes, keeping only a few islands as naval bases.

ANTIOCHUS ABOLISHES JUDAISM

And king Antiochus wrote to his whole kingdom, that all should be one people, and that each should forsake his own laws. And all the nations agreed according to the word of the king; and many of Israel consented to his worship, and sacrificed to the idols, and profaned the sabbath.

I MACCABEES (1894 TRANSLATION)

183 BC

THE DEATH OF HANNIBAL ✦ After the Romans defeated Antiochus at Magnesia in 189 BC, Hannibal secretly fled to Crete. When the Romans began to take an interest in the island, he took refuge with King Prusias of Bithynia on

Anatolia's Black Sea coast. In 183 BC the Romans sent a force to capture him. When he realized Roman soldiers had surrounded his house, Hannibal took poison, which he had long carried with him in a ring, remarking 'it is now time to end the anxiety of the Romans. Clearly, they are no longer able to wait for the death of an old man who has caused them so much concern.'

172—148 BC

THE END OF MACEDON ✦ In 172 BC war broke out between Macedon and Pergamon. Both were Roman allies and after some hesitation Rome sided with its older ally Pergamon and sent an army to invade Macedon. It was promptly thrashed by the Macedonian king Perseus (r. 179–168 BC), as were the two armies Rome sent after it. The Romans finally enjoyed a decisive victory at the Battle of Pydna on 22 June 168 BC. At first the Macedonian phalanx swept the Romans before it but the gaps began to open in the line when it reached rough ground. The Romans counterattacked, taking advantage of the gaps in the phalanx. Once the Romans had penetrated the phalanx it broke apart completely and the battle turned into a one-sided massacre. Perseus escaped but was captured the next year and paraded in a triumphal procession in Rome. He died in captivity. Macedon was divided into four separate states and then, after a rebellion in 150–148 BC, formally annexed, becoming a province of the Roman empire.

ABOVE **Gold coin of the Seleucid king** *Antiochus III 'the Great' minted at Antioch (Antakya, Turkey). Ambitious and expansionist, Antiochus styled himself the champion of Greek freedom against the Romans when he invaded Greece in 192 BC. However, he found few allies in Greece and was quickly driven out by the Romans, who pursued him to Anatolia. Antiochus' crushing defeat by Rome at Magnesia in 189 BC sent the Seleucid kingdom into a rapid decline.*

207

ABOVE **Grave steles in the Tophet of Salammbó at Carthage.** *The term 'tophet' is derived from a site at Jerusalem described in the Bible where the Canaanites are said to have sacrificed children. The Tophet of Salammbó was close to the temple of Carthage's patron deity, the Moon goddess Tanit, and held around 20,000 urns containing the cremated bones of newborn children. Historians disagree about the true purpose of the tophet. Following Roman accounts that the Carthaginians practised child sacrifice, some believe that the tophet was a sacred site where newborns were sacrificed to Tanit for the welfare of the city. Others argue that the Roman accounts are black propaganda against their enemies, and that the tophet was simply a necropolis for children who died in early infancy and were being placed under the protection of Tanit.*

168–142 BC

THE WARS OF THE MACCABEES ✦ A decision in 175 BC by the Seleucid king Antiochus IV (r. 175–163 BC) to turn Jerusalem into a Hellenized city caused deep anger among traditionalist Jews. Riots in the city in 168 BC provoked Antiochus brutally to repress Judaism. In 167 BC a rebellion broke under Mattathias of the Hasmonean family, a renegade priest who had defied an order to sacrifice to the Greek god Zeus. After Mattathias' death in 166 BC, his son Judas took over leadership of the revolt. Judas was a master of unconventional tactics and he won a series of victories over larger Seleucid armies that earned him the nickname Maccabeus, 'the hammer'. In 164 BC Judas captured Jerusalem and on 14 December he reconsecrated the Temple after removing the statues of the Greek gods placed by the Seleucids. The day is remembered annually by Jews in the festival of Hanukkah.

Antiochus died in 164 BC while campaigning in the east and was succeeded by his young son Antiochus V, whose regent Lysias concluded a peace with Judas in 163 BC. Antiochus was, however, overthrown and executed by his cousin Demetrius (r. 161–150 BC) in 161 BC. When Hellenized Jews complained they were being persecuted by traditionalists (who saw them as apostates), Demetrius used this as a pretext to reoccupy Jerusalem. Judas drove the superior Seleucid forces out again using guerrilla tactics but in 160 BC he was forced to battle at Elasa, where he was defeated and killed. Judas' brother Jonathan took over leadership of the rebellion and, reverting to guerrilla tactics, succeeded in further enlarging the area controlled by Hasmonean supporters. Jonathon proved adept at playing on the dynastic conflicts which plagued the Seleucids at this time and he was able to reoccupy Jerusalem in 153 BC and gain recognition as chief priest and leader of the Jewish people. For ten years Jonathon ruled in semi-independence but in 143 BC he was tricked into an ambush at Acre by the general Diodotus and executed. Diodotus seized the Seleucid throne in 142 BC but, after failing completely to subdue Jewish resistance, recognized Jonathon's brother Simon as the independent king of Judea.

149–146 BC

THE DESTRUCTION OF CARTHAGE ✦ Even with Hannibal dead, the Romans never felt easy about Carthage. Although shorn of its empire, Carthage quickly recovered from the war and paid off its war debts easily. The hard-line senator Cato made a point of ending every speech, no matter on what subject, with the phrase 'and Carthage must be destroyed'. He got his wish when Carthage broke its peace terms by retaliating against raids by the Numidians without asking Roman permission (which the Carthaginians knew perfectly well would not be given). Rome seized the chance to destroy the hated city once and for all in the Third Punic War (149–146 BC). The city fell only after a three-year siege in which the Roman forces were led by Scipio Aemilianus, the adoptive grandson of Scipio Africanus. An unknown number of its citizens were massacred and 50,000 survivors were sold into slavery. The city itself was systematically levelled and the site was cursed. Despite this, the site of Carthage was too good to be ignored and the city was refounded by Julius Caesar a century later.

In the same year that Carthage was destroyed the Romans also faced a Greek rebellion in the Peloponnesus. The Romans moved swiftly to suppress the rebellion, destroying the city of Corinth to make an example for the rest of Greece: its population was massacred or enslaved. Greece was annexed and became the province of Achaea. Only Sparta, whose austere military traditions the Romans admired, retained a nominal independence.

139 BC

THE RISE OF PARTHIA ✦ While the Romans and the Jews chipped away at the Seleucid kingdom from the west, the rising kingdom of Parthia carved deep inroads from the east. Parthia, now part of northeast Iran, became independent after its vassal king Arsaces I rebelled against his Seleucid overlords. The Seleucids tried several times to reconquer Parthia but by the early 2nd century BC its independence was secure. Taking advantage of the decline in Seleucid power after Magnesia, King Mithradates I (r. *c.* 170–138 BC) began aggressively expanding Parthian territory into Media (now northwestern Iran), and south and east into Afghanistan. In 148–147 BC he captured Hamadan on the western edge of the Iranian plateau. This became Mithradates' base for further campaigns, which brought Persia and Mesopotamia under his control by 141 BC. In 140 BC the Seleucid king Demetrius II launched a counteroffensive to regain control of Mesopotamia but in 139 BC he was defeated and captured by Mithradates, who treated him kindly. Mithradates died shortly after his victory but he had succeeded in bringing much of the old Persian empire under his control, turning Parthia into a power that was capable of resisting the growing might of Rome.

133 BC

ROME INHERITS PERGAMON ✦ Rome's main ally in Anatolia was Pergamon, a Greek kingdom that was created in 281 BC after the collapse of the kingdom of Thrace. The childless last king of Pergamon, Attalus III (r. 138–133 BC), was unpopular with his subjects, who accused him of neglecting the state in favour of pursuing his interests in botany and pharmacology. It was probably to quell internal opposition that

OPPOSITE **Bronze statue of a Parthian noble** *from Khuzestan, Iran. Parthia, now in northeast Iran, became an independent kingdom in 238 BC under Arsaces I (died c. 211 BC). The Parthians were a formerly nomadic Iranian people, renowned for their horsemanship and archery, with a culture that owed much to Persian and Greek civilization. Parthia prospered from its position astride the Silk Road, which linked China and the Mediterranean world.*

Attalus bequeathed his kingdom to the Roman republic: were he to be assassinated or overthrown the Romans would intervene. Attalus was still only in his early 30s but he died unexpectedly, of natural causes, in 133 BC. Roman rule was not, however, accepted by all Pergamenes. Aristonicus, who claimed to be a member of the royal family, together with the philosopher Blossius led a revolt by the lower classes. They aspired to create a utopian state called Heliopolis in which everybody would be free. The revolt was put down in 129 BC, Aristonicus was executed and Pergamon became the Roman province of Asia. Rome's empire had taken another step east.

133—122 BC

THE GRACCHAN REFORMS ✦ The rapid

growth of Rome's empire after the Second Punic War caused severe social and political strains. The spoils of empire went almost exclusively to the upper classes, particularly those who gained military commands and provincial governorships (the first by plunder and slaves, the second by embezzling taxes and other corrupt administrative practices). As a result, competition for political office became increasingly bitter. At the same time the burdens of constant campaigning fell heavily on the largest class of property owners, the smallholders, who supplied the greatest number of conscripts for Rome's armies. Despite military pay, the absence of men from their farms for long periods was ruinous, and many never came back. Families fell into debt and were dispossessed. Their lands were purchased by wealthy speculators who built up large estates, or *latifundia*. These were worked by cheap slave labour, which was in plentiful supply because of the mass enslavement of conquered populations. Once they had lost their lands, peasants drifted to Rome and joined the ranks of the *proletarii*, the lowest class of citizens who were not

THE MALIGNITY OF THE RICH

This is said to have been the first sedition in Rome, since the expulsion of the kings, in which the blood of any citizen was shed. ... Had Tiberius been dealt with moderately, it is probable that he could easily have been brought to a compromise, and, certainly, his influence might have been reduced without depriving him of his life, for he had no more than 3000 men about him. But it seems the conspiracy was formed against him to satisfy the resentment and malignity of the rich, rather than for the reasons they gave to the public.

PLUTARCH, *THE LIFE OF TIBERIUS GRACCHUS* (ADAPTED FROM 1848 TRANSLATION)

eligible for military service because they owned no property. The more far-sighted aristocrats feared this would undermine the basis of Roman power, its citizen armies. However, the majority had no interest in reforming a system which was making them spectacularly wealthy.

One member of the aristocracy who did see the need for reform was Tiberius Gracchus. Tiberius secured election as tribune of the plebs in 133 BC and proceeded to bypass the Senate by introducing land reform legislation through the popular assembly. Tiberius' proposal to confiscate illegally acquired state land and redistribute it among dispossessed smallholders aroused ferocious opposition among wealthy landowners. He also proposed that the royal treasure inherited from Attalus III of Pergamon be distributed among the new smallholders to help them stock their farms. This usurped the Senate's traditional control of finance. A mob of senators and their clients attacked the popular assembly and murdered Tiberius and around 300 of his supporters.

The cause of reform was taken up by Tiberius' brother Gaius, who was elected tribune in 123 and 122 BC. Gaius passed wide-ranging reforms through the popular assemblies, including state-subsidized corn for the urban poor, public works to provide employment and measures to tackle senatorial corruption. Gaius miscalculated, however, when he proposed extending full Roman citizenship to all of Rome's Italian subjects. The plebs did not want to share their privileges and he failed to win re-election to the tribunate. Once removed from office, Gaius became vulnerable to his senatorial enemies. When a political demonstration turned violent, the Senate invoked emergency laws and Tiberius and 3,000 of his supporters were rounded up and massacred.

The tribunates of the Gracchi proved to be a turning point in the history of the republic. The broad consensus

ABOVE **Souvenir of a migration.** *Detail of a silver ritual cauldron found in 1891 in a bog at Gundestrup in north Jutland, Denmark. This area was the original homeland of the Cimbri and Teutones tribes who went on a spectacular rampage through central and western Europe in the late 2nd century BC. It is thought they acquired the cauldron as loot in the Balkans and sent it to their homeland as an offering to their native gods. The richly decorated cauldron features scenes of Celtic gods, including horned Cernunnos the 'lord of the animals' (shown here), and was manufactured in southeast Europe by a Thracian craftsman working for a Celtic patron.*

that had supported the republican constitution was shattered and the Senate became divided into two factions: the reformist *populares* and the conservative *optimates*. The tribunate had emerged as a centre of opposition to senatorial government and murder was introduced to Roman politics.

105—102 BC

GERMANY AWAKES ✦ In 115 BC news that two migrating German tribes, the Cimbri and the Teutones, were heading in the direction of Italy awakened Roman memories of the Gauls' sack of Rome in 390 BC. Germany was beyond the limits of the world then known to the Romans and they were deeply shocked when the tribes annihilated the army they sent to stop them, at Noreia in the Austrian Alps, in 113 BC. The way to Italy lay wide open but the two tribes inexplicably turned northwest before reappearing on the western side of the Alps in 110 BC, threatening the recently conquered Roman province in southern Gaul. In 109 BC the Germans defeated another Roman army, sent to drive them off from the frontier. When they destroyed a third Roman army at Arausio (Orange) in 105 BC panic broke out in Rome. Once again the way to Italy lay open, but once again the Germans turned away, the Teutones heading to northern Gaul and the Cimbri heading to Spain.

The consul Marius used this breathing space to reorganize the Roman legions as a full-time professional army. When the Cimbri and Teutones again returned to Roman territory they were defeated and massacred: the Teutones at Aix-en-Provence in 102, the Cimbri, having finally invaded Italy, at Vercellae a year later. Marius' army reforms gave Rome one of the most effective instruments of imperial expansion known to history but they also led to the creation of client armies and fostered the rise of military dictators who would ultimately destroy the republic. The state was unwilling to grant land or pay pensions to discharged veterans so soldiers looked to their commanders to provide for them. Their dependence made it easy for power-hungry politicians to persuade their armies to back their political ambitions.

91—89 BC

THE SOCIAL WAR ✦ As Rome's empire grew, its Italian subjects became increasingly discontented. They shared the burdens of Rome's wars but received none of the spoils. The rejection of Gaius Gracchus' proposal to grant them Roman citizenship only fuelled their resentment. After a new attempt to enfranchise them was rejected in 91 BC, rebellions broke out all over Italy. The Social War (from *socii*, Latin for allies) was bitterly fought and in the end the Romans won only by giving in to the rebels' demands, granting Roman citizenship to all communities that stayed loyal and then to any that laid down their arms. The widening of the franchise completed the Romanization of Italy as the many local identities began to be replaced by a common Roman identity.

88–79 BC

THE ROAD TO DICTATORSHIP ✦ During the Social War Mithradates VI Eupator (r. 120–63 BC), the ambitious king of Pontus in northern Anatolia, seized the neighbouring kingdoms of Cappadocia and Bithynia. When the Romans ordered him to withdraw in 88 BC, Mithradates invaded and quickly occupied the Roman province of Asia. Because of abuses by Roman bankers, tax collectors and slavers, Mithradates was welcomed as a liberator and Roman citizens in Asia were massacred. Later in the year Mithradates sent a force across the Aegean in response to a call from Athens for him to liberate Greece.

The Senate appointed the consul Sulla to lead a campaign against Mithradates, to the disappointment of Marius, who wanted the command. Marius secured a vote in the popular assembly dismissing Sulla but Sulla had the support of the army and he marched on Rome, forcing Marius to flee into exile. While Sulla was campaigning successfully against Mithradates, Marius returned from exile, won over a legion to his cause, took Rome and massacred the leading *optimates*, only to die shortly afterwards. Sulla returned to Italy in 83 BC with his army and recaptured Rome. Thousands of Marius' supporters were hunted down and killed: Sulla gave their property to his followers. Land confiscated from Italian communities that had supported Marius was divided between 120,000 of Sulla's veteran soldiers. In 82 BC Sulla assumed the dictatorship and introduced measures intended to restore senatorial control, including abolishing the powers of the tribunate and the state-subsidized grain supply for the poor. Sulla resigned the dictatorship in 79 BC and died the following year. It was now clear that the surest way to political power was success in war. This brought prestige, the all-important support of an army, and wealth from plunder and slaves to reward followers: the relentless expansion of the empire in the years that followed was driven by internal Roman politics, not by an imperial master plan to conquer the known world.

> *Marius returned from exile, won over a legion to his cause, took Rome and massacred the leading* optimates, *only to die shortly afterwards.*

73–71 BC

SPARTACUS' SLAVE REBELLION ✦ Slavery in the ancient world took many forms. Many slaves, especially those with administrative, educational and craft skills, were often well treated and eventually given their freedom. Italy's huge population of rural slaves, on the other hand, lived in miserable conditions, and for those forced to become gladiators or sent to work in mines and quarries slavery was little better than a slow death sentence. Romans feared slave insurrections and runaway slaves faced severe beatings, even execution, if caught. The greatest slave rebellion faced by the republic was led by Spartacus, a Thracian gladiator who escaped with around 70 others from a gladiatorial school near Capua in 73 BC.

ABOVE **Mosaic of the 4th century** AD *showing a gladiator fighting a leopard, from Terranova, Italy. The earliest known Roman gladiatorial games took place in 264* BC *and by the end of the century had become a popular entertainment. Gladiator combats were more than a bloodthirsty spectacle: they were* *an opportunity to display Rome's martial virtues and courage and dignity in the face of death, something which all Romans aspired to. Although they were slaves, gladiators were often well cared-for because their training was a considerable investment for their owners. Few gladiators enjoyed long lives, however.*

The gladiators plundered the countryside around Capua, eventually recruiting over 120,000 escaped slaves to their cause, and set up their headquarters on Mount Vesuvius. Despite their lack of military training, the rebels held the Roman armies at bay for two years, winning battle after battle. The Senate appointed Marcus Crassus, a wealthy plebeian who had risen to prominence under Sulla, to put down the rebellion. Crassus contained Spartacus in Bruttium (the 'toe' of Italy). Spartacus struck a deal with pirates to transport his army to Sicily and start a slave insurrection there but he was betrayed: the pirates took the money and abandoned the slaves. Crassus was now reinforced by another rising star, Pompey (Gnaeus Pompeius), who brought an army from Spain. Spartacus made a hopeless last stand against the overwhelming odds in the mountains near Strongoli. Most of the rebels were slaughtered on the battlefield but 6,000 survivors were crucified along the Appian Way between Capua and Rome. Spartacus was said to have been killed in battle but his body was never identified. In the aftermath of the rebellion the Romans, it was said, out of pure fear, began to treat their slaves less harshly and the laws of slavery were slowly reformed.

THE DEATH OF SPARTACUS

Crassus pressed on to finish the struggle, ... Spartacus saw the necessity that was upon him, and drew up his whole army in order of battle. In the first place, when his horse was brought to him, he drew his sword, and saying that if he won the day he would have many fine horses of the enemy's, but if he lost it he would not need any, he slew his horse. Then pushing his way towards Crassus himself through many flying weapons and wounded men, he did not indeed reach him, but slew two centurions who fell upon him together. Finally, after his companions had taken to flight, he stood alone, surrounded by a multitude of foes, and was still defending himself when he was cut down.

PLUTARCH, *THE LIFE OF MARCUS CRASSUS* (1848)

70–61 BC

THE RISE OF POMPEY ✦ In 70 BC Pompey and Crassus were rewarded for their success against Spartacus with election to the consulship. Both were conservatives but they saw the need to court popular support and they restored the powers of the tribunes. In 67 BC Pompey consolidated his position at the heart of Roman politics when he secured a three-year command to suppress piracy in the eastern Mediterranean. Pompey completed his task in just three months. The grateful Senate gave him dictatorial powers in Asia to deal with Mithradates of Pontus, whose anti-Roman ambitions were destabilizing the region. Pompey crushed Mithradates' army in an ambush at the Battle of Lycus in 66 BC and occupied Pontus. Mithradates fled to the Crimea where he committed suicide in 64 BC. Before that, Pompey also defeated Mithradates' ally Tigranes of Armenia, leading his Roman army to the shores of the Caspian Sea. Another stunning success followed in 63 BC when Pompey conquered the Seleucid kingdom of Syria. In the same year Pompey captured Jerusalem after a short siege and

217

Spartacus made a hopeless last stand against the overwhelming odds in the mountains.

N

COLCHIS

IBERIA

ALBANIA

R. Cyrus

BLACK SEA

Sinope

Trapezus
(Trebizond)

Amisus

Artaxata

R. Araxes

BITHYNIA-PONTUS

ARMENIA

Nicomedia

Byzantium

Ancyra

CAPPADOCIA

Tigranocerta

GALATIA

R. Tigris

ASIA

Nyssa

COMMAGENE

Samosata

MESOPOTAMIA

PAMPHILIA

Aphrodisias

Cyrrhus

Zeugma

Tarsus

Pompeiopolis

Antioch

Aspendus

Side

CILICIA

Aleppo

R. Euphrates

Dura
Europos

Xanthus

SYRIA

Apamea

CYPRUS

Laodicea

Palmyra

Paphos

Citium

Berytus

Baalbek

Curium

Damascus

MEDITERRANEAN
SEA

Tyre

PHOENICIA

Bostra

Joppa

Gerasa

JUDEA

Jerusalem

Gaza

Masada

Pelusium

ARABIA

Alexandria

Petra

Memphis

R. Nile

EGYPT

RED SEA

0   100 km

0   100 miles

→ Pompey's first campaign

→ Pompey's later operations

3 Sequence of events

made Judea a Roman protectorate. Pompey had added more territory to the Roman empire than any previous individual and he had personally acquired so much loot that he paid his soldiers the equivalent of 12 and a half years' pay each. On his triumphant return to Rome in 62 BC, Pompey demanded recognition for his conquests in the east and land for his veterans. His demands were reasonable but the conservative *optimates* were afraid to enhance Pompey's status even more and they made sure that the Senate refused them.

Pompey had added more territory to the Roman empire than any previous individual and he had personally acquired so much loot that he paid his soldiers the equivalent of 12 and a half years' pay each.

60–53 BC

THE FIRST TRIUMVIRATE ✦ The Senate's refusal to meet Pompey's demands began the final descent of the Roman Republic into dictatorship and civil war. Pompey found an ally in Gaius Julius Caesar, an ambitious member of an old patrician family who had identified himself with the reformist *optimates*. After he was elected consul in 59 BC, Caesar persuaded Pompey to join with him and Crassus to push through a programme of reforming legislation. Their unofficial pact became known as the First Triumvirate ('rule of three'). Pompey's military prestige, Caesar's political ability and Crassus' immense wealth made them a formidable combination and they were able to work solely through the popular assemblies and sideline the Senate completely. Pompey's veterans were finally granted allotments of land, along with thousands of landless peasants. The triumvirate courted support in the provinces by reforming the all too easily exploited tax farming system. Caesar was granted a military command and the governorship of the province of Transalpine Gaul, giving him a golden opportunity to make a reputation as well as to enrich himself from the spoils of war. In 58 BC Caesar began a six-year campaign to conquer the Gauls (see pp. 221–4).

Crassus began to feel like the junior partner of the triumvirate and tried to emulate Caesar's military achievements. In 55 BC Crassus became governor of the wealthy province of Syria, which he planned to use as a base to conquer the Parthian empire. The Parthians were famous for their horse archers, while Crassus' force was mainly slow-moving legionary infantry. Crassus' ally, Artavazdes II of Armenia, advised him to invade though the Armenian mountains, where the

OPPOSITE **Pompey's campaigns in the east 67–62 BC.** *Pompey was initially sent east to deal with King Mithradates IV who had been a thorn in the Romans' side for many years. Pompey dealt quickly with Mithradates and moved on to campaign against his ally Tigranes of Armenia, forcing him to become a Roman vassal. In 63 BC, Pompey headed south to conquer the Seleucid kingdom of Syria and make Judea into a Roman client state. On his return to Rome, Pompey was given a triumph, a parade awarded to generals after successful campaigns, in which he was accompanied by his troops, his war booty, prisoners and an enormous pearl-studded portrait head of himself.*

Parthian cavalry would be unable to fight effectively. Crassus ignored his advice and invaded by a more direct route, crossing the Euphrates into the open deserts of northern Mesopotamia. Near Carrhae (Harran, southern Turkey) Crassus' legions encountered a force of 10,000 Parthian cavalry under General Surena. The Parthians repeatedly charged the legionaries, showering them with arrows, then retreating before coming within range of the Romans' javelins. The attacks continued until nightfall. The next day Crassus was murdered while attempting to parley with the Parthians and most of the surviving Romans were either captured or killed: it was one of the worst defeats ever suffered by Rome, with around 20,000 killed and 10,000 captured.

58—52 BC

CAESAR CONQUERS GAUL ✦ Gaul was the region of western Europe between the Pyrenees in the south and the Rhine and the Alps in the west. The Gauls, after whom it was named, were a Celtic people who were divided into dozens of tribes. The southern part of Gaul, along the Mediterranean coast, was conquered by the Romans in the 2nd century BC and became the province of Transalpine Gaul, also known as Provincia Romana, from which it is known today as Provence. By the time Caesar was appointed governor in 58 BC, Transalpine Gaul had become very Romanized. The Romans regarded the unconquered Gauls to the north as barbarians but they were actually well on the road to civilization. Tribal centres called *oppida* were developing into towns and cities, writing and coinage were coming into use, and the region had a prosperous agricultural economy based on cereals and stock rearing. Caesar could see that it was well worth conquering but the Romans liked to believe that they never fought wars without just cause.

Caesar's pretext for war was provided by the Helvetii, whose attempt to migrate from their homeland in modern Switzerland to Aquitaine threatened to destabilize Gaul. Caesar quickly intervened and drove them back by force. The Aedui, long-standing allies of Rome, then sought Caesar's help against an invasion by the German Suebi tribe. Caesar defeated them and drove them back across the Rhine. Caesar wintered in Gaul and the following year he campaigned against the Belgae of the northeast, defeating them in several pitched battles. In 56 BC Caesar extended his operations to western Gaul and by 55 BC he felt secure enough to mount expeditions against the Germans and Britons to

221

OPPOSITE **Palmyra,** *a caravan city on the edge of the Syrian desert, was one of the only regions to remain largely independent after Pompey's eastern campaigns. However, it later became an important bastion of the Roman defence against the Sasanian empire in the 3rd century. Its queen, Zenobia, tried to break free from Roman control but she was captured by the Roman emperor Aurelian in 272 and imprisoned.*

ABOVE **A coin with a portrait of a Parthian king** *of the 1st century BC. The Parthian empire was a decentralized state made up of semi-autonomous sub-kingdoms which paid tribute and supplied military support to a supreme 'king of kings'.*

discourage them from interfering in Gaul. By the beginning of 54 BC Caesar believed that he had broken Gallic resistance and decided to launch a second invasion of Britain. Again his confidence was premature: a rebellion by the Belgae brought him hurrying back. Caesar successfully crushed the Belgae in 53 BC but their resistance inspired a much more serious uprising in central Gaul under Vercingetorix, a chieftain of the Arverni. Believing this area to be friendly to Rome, Caesar had left his legions concentrated in the north against the Belgae, while he returned to Italy to promote his political career.

Vercingetorix invaded Transalpine Gaul late in 53 BC, hoping to tie Caesar down in the south while the isolated legions in the north were annihilated. Caesar reacted with decisive speed, first driving Vercingetorix out of the province, then making an unexpected crossing of the snow-covered Cévennes in January 52 BC in order to attack the Arverni before rushing north to join his legions. Caesar now tried to draw the Gauls into open battle by besieging their *oppida*, massacring or enslaving entire populations when they fell. Vercingetorix countered with a scorched earth policy intended to force the Romans to withdraw for lack of supplies. More tribes joined the uprising, supplies ran short and, after a defeat at Gergovia in May, Caesar began to withdraw to Roman territory. Vercingetorix now threw away his advantage with a badly planned attack on the retreating Romans, allowing Caesar to regain the initiative. In July Caesar besieged Vercingetorix in the *oppidum* of Alesia. Despite

ABOVE **The Battersea shield,** *a magnificent bronze shield decorated in the late Celtic La Tène art style, was dredged from the river Thames in London during bridge works in 1857. Dating to around the time of Caesar's invasions of Britain, the shield shows no signs of battle damage and was probably thrown into the river as a ritual offering.*

OPPOSITE **Julius Caesar** *as painted by the Dutch artist Peter Paul Rubens (1577–1640). Caesar's reputation grew after his death and he came to be regarded as one of the greatest men in world history. However, despite his undoubted military genius, Caesar had many limitations, including an ultimately fatal lack of political vision.*

heroic efforts to break the siege, both from within and by a relief army outside the Roman lines, Vercingetorix was forced to surrender in October 52 and Gallic resistance collapsed. By the end of 51 Gaul had been completely pacified.

49—45 BC

CIVIL WAR ✦ After Crassus' death in the east, the relationship between Caesar and Pompey broke down. While Caesar and Crassus had gone in search of military glory, Pompey had remained in Rome. Unfortunately, he found that this did not give him the controlling influence he expected because he faced continual political opposition not only from the *optimates* (which he had expected) but also from the tribunes. Gangs of rival supporters fought street battles and Rome became increasingly lawless. Fear of Caesar's growing influence with the plebeians, drove Pompey into

ABOVE **Caesar's camp.** *Caesar surrounded Vercingetorix's stronghold at Alesia with a double circuit of earth and timber ramparts, each of which totalled about 14 miles in length. The inner wall was to prevent Vercingetorix escaping from Alesia,* *while the outer was to prevent any supplies or reinforcements getting in. Caesar also built several camps around Alesia, one of which is reconstructed above. All the ramparts were protected by ditches and barriers of sharpened wooden stakes.*

alliance with the *optimates*, who secured his election by the Senate as sole consul in 52 BC. The Senate now voted to dismiss Caesar from his command, but tribunes allied to Caesar vetoed the order. In 51 BC Pompey decreed that Caesar could not stand for consul unless he demobilized his armies. This effectively blocked Caesar's political ambitions as demobilizing his army would leave him exposed to attack by his enemies. In spring 49 BC Caesar gave up trying to save his political career by negotiations and marched his army across the Rubicon, the small river that marked the border of his command in Gaul, and invaded Italy.

> *Caesar had no plans for constitutional reform. He was ruling as a king in all but name but, though he refused the royal title, he took to sitting on a gilded throne and wearing the purple robes of kingship in public.*

Pompey and the *optimates* were dismayed to find that they had little popular support and they abandoned Rome and fled to Macedon, hoping to recruit support in the east. With Italy secured, Caesar went to Spain, defeating Pompey's supporters there at the Battle of Ilerda (Lerida) in August before returning to Rome in October. Those senators who had not fled with Pompey appointed Caesar dictator. In January 48 BC Caesar crossed the Adriatic in pursuit of Pompey. Pompey's larger army defeated Caesar at Dyrrhachium (Durrës, Albania) but Pompey, overcautious, failed to take the initiative. Caesar regrouped and in August he completely destroyed Pompey's army at the Battle of Pharsalus in Thessaly. Pompey escaped to Egypt with Caesar in pursuit. Egypt had enjoyed stable rule and prosperity for over 200 years under the Greek-speaking Ptolemaic dynasty but it was militarily weak and had only maintained its independence because the Roman Senate did not trust any general enough to allow him to conquer it and get his hands on its enormous wealth. The weak government of the young king Ptolemy XIII was well aware of this and did not want to get involved in a Roman civil war. So, by the time Caesar arrived, Pompey had been murdered.

While in Egypt Caesar began an affair with Ptolemy's sister and queen, Cleopatra VII (brother–sister marriage was normal among the Ptolemies to preserve the purity of the royal bloodline). In December he helped Cleopatra overthrow Ptolemy and take the throne in her own right, though she named her younger brother Ptolemy XIV as a purely nominal co-ruler. Further campaigns were needed in Anatolia, Africa and Spain, where he defeated Pompey's sons at Munda in 45 BC, before Caesar had crushed all opposition and made himself the undisputed master of the empire.

CAESAR RALLIES HIS LEGIONS

'I have been your commander for nine years; under my leadership, your efforts on Rome's behalf have been crowned with good fortune; you have won countless battles and have pacified the whole of Gaul and Germany. Now I ask you to defend my reputation and standing against the assaults of my enemies.' The men of the Thirteenth legion clamoured that they were ready to avenge the wrongs done to their general and to the tribunes, and thus being assured of their support, he took them to Ariminum [Rimini], ordering the remaining legions to leave their winter quarters and follow him.

JULIUS CAESAR, *THE CIVIL WAR* (TRANS. JANE MITCHELL, 1967)

225

PTOLEMAIC EGYPT

The most successful of the kingdoms founded by the Diadochi was that founded by Ptolemy I (r. 305–283 BC) in Egypt in 305 BC. Ptolemy was a Greek-speaking Macedonian but he made his rule acceptable to the Egyptians by adopting the trappings of the pharaohs and becoming a patron of the traditional religious cults, a policy which was followed by all the kings who succeeded him, all of whom (15 in total) were also called Ptolemy. Alexandria became the capital of the Ptolemies, under whom it became the largest and richest Greek city in the world. Rivalling Athens as a cultural centre, Alexandria became the most important place in the ancient world for the study of the sciences. Its great library, the Museum, was the largest in the world. Dynastic conflicts weakened the kingdom from the time of Ptolemy IV Philopater (r. 221–205 BC) and from 168 BC it was effectively a Roman protectorate. The Ptolemies continued rule under Roman protection until 30 BC, when Egypt became a Roman province after the death of Cleopatra VII.

227

LEFT **The Nile mosaic** *from the temple of Fortuna Primigenia at Praeneste (Palestrina, Italy), made in the 2nd century BC, encapsulates the Roman view of Ptolemaic Egypt as an exotic and wealthy land.*

44 BC

BEWARE THE IDES OF MARCH ✦

Caesar was generous in victory and did not persecute his surviving opponents. In 46 BC he appointed himself dictator for ten years, extended to dictator for life in 44 BC, winning wide popular support for his dictatorship by cancelling debts and completely abolishing the hated tax-farming system in the provinces. Tens of thousands of landless citizens and discharged veterans were resettled in colonies in Italy and the provinces. The annual pay of legionaries was almost doubled. Roman citizenship was offered for the first time to Rome's subjects outside peninsular Italy. However, Caesar soon began to show his limitations as a politician. The republican constitution had been designed to govern a city state but decades of political conflict had shown that it was unsuited to the demands of ruling a world empire. Nevertheless, Caesar had no plans for constitutional reform. He was ruling as a king in all but name but, though he refused the royal title, he took to sitting on a gilded throne and wearing the purple robes of kingship in public. Caesar became the first living Roman to have his portrait shown on coins and by designating a personal *flamen* (a priest dedicated to the worship of a single god) began to pave the way for his own deification.

Caesar's actions caused growing dismay among the aristocracy – including some who had formerly been his supporters – who feared the introduction of a

ABOVE **Marble bust of Cleopatra VII,** *the last independent ruler of ancient Egypt. Like all rulers of her Ptolemaic dynasty, Cleopatra presented two faces to the world. Classical-style images such as this portrayed her as a Hellenistic ruler to her Greek-* *speaking subjects. To her Egyptian subjects, Cleopatra always presented herself as a traditional Egyptian queen, dressed in Egyptian costume, and portrayed in sculptures and temple reliefs in the traditional art styles of ancient Egypt.*

divine monarchy. In 44 BC, a group of 60 senators led by Marcus Junius Brutus and Gaius Cassius Longinus hatched a plot to assassinate Caesar. Though Caesar was said to have been forewarned about the plot by a soothsayer, and was well aware of the aristocracy's growing hostility, he took no precautions to ensure his personal safety. On 15 March, the Ides of March, Caesar was publicly stabbed to death in the Senate house. The conspirators proclaimed the restoration of republican liberty, fully expecting the news of Caesar's death to be greeted with celebrations. They had fatally misjudged the public mood: all republican liberty meant to most people was a return to the disorder, violence and corruption of the previous 90 years. One of Caesar's loyal commanders, the consul Mark Antony (Marcus Antonius), stirred up the Roman people against the conspirators, and Cassius and Brutus were forced to flee from Rome. A new civil war was inevitable.

ABOVE **Coin celebrating Julius Caesar's murder** *as tyrannicide. On one side is a portrait of Marcus Junius Brutus, one of the leaders of the senatorial conspiracy; on the other the legend 'Ides of March', two daggers and, between them, the cap of liberty given to freed slaves.*

OVERLEAF ***The Death of Julius Caesar*** *by the Italian artist Vincenzo Camuccini. Painted in 1793, at the height of the French Revolution, the theme of the killing of a ruler had strong resonances with contemporary viewers.*

RAGE AGAINST CAESAR'S MURDERERS

When upon the opening of Caesar's will, it was found that that he had left every Roman citizen a considerable legacy, and they beheld the body as it was carried through the Forum all mangled with wounds, the crowd could no longer be controlled. They stopped the procession and, tearing up benches, doors and tables, *heaped them into a pile and burned the corpse there. Then, snatching flaming brands from the pyre, some ran to the houses of the assassins, while others ranged the city to find the conspirators themselves and tear them in pieces.*

PLUTARCH, *THE LIFE OF JULIUS CAESAR*
(ADAPTED FROM 1848 TRANSLATION)

43–33 BC

THE SECOND TRIUMVIRATE ✦ In August 44 BC, Cassius and Brutus arrived in Greece. Caesar had been planning a campaign to avenge Crassus' defeat by the Parthians at the time of his death, and had been massing legions, supplies and money in the eastern provinces in readiness. Cassius and Brutus intended to use these resources to regain control of Rome, which was in the hands of Mark Antony and another of Caesar's supporters, the general Lepidus. During this period too, another player in the power struggle emerged: this was Octavian (Gaius Julius Caesar Octavianus), Caesar's ambitious 19-year-old nephew and adoptive heir. Despite his youth, Octavian was politically astute and he exploited his relationship with Caesar to raise a substantial army from among veterans his uncle had settled in Italy.

Mark Antony considered himself to be Caesar's successor and he refused to accept Octavian's claims to be his political heir. Octavian despised the republicans for murdering Caesar but he allied tactically with them, helping Decimus Brutus (one of Caesar's murderers but no relation of Marcus Junius Brutus) to defeat Antony at Mutina (Modena). When Decimus Brutus thanked Octavian for his support, Octavian answered coldly that he had come to oppose Antony, not support one of Caesar's murderers. When his army began to desert to Octavian, Decimus Brutus fled, hoping

OVERLEAF ***Antony and Cleopatra at the Battle of Actium*** *by the Austrian baroque painter Johann-Georg Platzer (1704–6). The importance of naval power in early modern Europe made the battle of Actium a popular subject for artists* *looking for spectacular historical themes to please aristocratic patrons. Details of costumes, weapons and ships shown here are largely imaginary: compare with the contemporary image of a Roman galley on p. 237.*

to join Marcus Brutus in Macedonia, but was murdered on the way by a Celtic chief loyal to Antony. He was the first of Caesar's assassins to die.

In August Octavian returned to Rome with his army and cowed the Senate into appointing him consul and recognizing him as Caesar's legal heir according to the terms of his will. He also forced the Senate to outlaw Caesar's murderers. Having broken decisively with the republicans, Octavian allied with Mark Antony and Lepidus in November, so forming the Second Triumvirate. Unlike the First Triumvirate, this was given legal recognition by the Senate, which conferred absolute powers on the triumvirs for five years 'to restore the constitution of the republic'. The triumvirs' first act was to institute a reign of terror to purge over 2,000 republican supporters in Rome and confiscate their property to fill the depleted treasury.

Cassius and Brutus were still in firm control of Rome's wealthy eastern provinces. Leaving Lepidus in Rome, Octavian and Antony invaded Greece in 42 BC and defeated Cassius and Brutus in two battles at Philippi in October. Cassius and Brutus committed suicide to avoid capture. Following Philippi, the triumvirs divided the empire in areas of responsibility. Lepidus, by now clearly the junior partner, got Spain and Africa; Octavian got Italy, Gaul and Dalmatia; Antony got Greece and Asia. Relations between Antony and Octavian were strained by conflicts between their families. In 40 BC Antony reached a new agreement with Octavian which increased his share of the empire at Lepidus' expense, whose share was now reduced to Africa alone. Antony agreed to supply Octavian with ships to help suppress a rebellion in Sicily led by Pompey's son Sextus. In return, Octavian agreed to supply legions for Antony's planned invasion of Parthia. To seal the agreement, Antony married

RIGHT **Bust of a young Octavian,** *the future emperor Augustus, made around 39 BC, showing him wearing an adolescent beard as a sign of mourning for his murdered uncle and adoptive father Julius Caesar. Although aged only around 14 at the time, he was already a master at manipulating his public image.*

GOING TO BED WITH CLEOPATRA

What's upset you? Because I go to bed with Cleopatra? But she's my wife and I've been doing so for nine years, not just recently. And, anyway, is Livia [Octavian's wife] your only pleasure? I expect that you will have managed, by the time you read this, to have hopped into bed with Tertulla, Terentilla, Rufillla, Salvia, Titisenia, or the whole lot of them. Does it really matter where, or with what women, you get your excitement?

ANTONY TO OCTAVIAN, FROM *THE TREASURY OF THE WORLD'S GREATEST LETTERS* (1948)

Octavian's sister Octavia in 41 BC, but by this time he had already met Cleopatra and become her lover.

In 38 BC the triumvirate was renewed for a further five years but there was little trust between them and it lasted barely two. After Octavian defeated Sextus in 36 BC, he stripped Lepidus of his powers and sent him into comfortable house arrest near Rome. In the same year Antony launched his invasion of Parthia but it was scarcely more successful than Crassus' had been and he withdrew after suffering heavy losses. Antony's desertion of Octavia for Cleopatra led to the final breakdown of the triumvirate. Octavian began a ferocious propaganda campaign against Antony and Cleopatra, portraying him as a decadent would-be oriental despot, and portraying her as a schemer who was using Antony to gain control over the Roman empire. Antony certainly gave Octavian plenty of ammunition, appointing his children by Cleopatra as kings and queens over nations that were under Roman rule. Worse, from Octavian's point of view, was Antony's declaration that he had forged his adoption papers and that Julius Caesar's legitimate heir was therefore Caesarion, his son by Cleopatra.

32–30 BC

OCTAVIAN AGAINST ANTONY ✦ When the triumvirate formally expired at the end of 33 BC it was not renewed. War was now inevitable. Antony divorced Octavia to marry Cleopatra and towards the end of 32 BC gathered a fleet and army at Actium on Greece's west coast in preparation for an invasion of Italy. Octavian accused Antony of treason and in 31 BC the Senate declared war on Cleopatra. On 3 September Octavian's fleet attacked Antony's fleet at Actium and destroyed it. During the night, Antony's army began to desert to Octavian, forcing him and Cleopatra to flee to Egypt. When Octavian invaded Egypt in July 30 BC, Antony's remaining troops deserted him too. On being misinformed that Cleopatra had committed suicide, Antony stabbed himself but survived long enough to be taken to her, dying in her arms. Cleopatra then surrendered to Octavian and Egypt was annexed to the Roman empire. Learning that Octavian planned to parade her in triumph through the streets of Rome, Cleopatra took her own life on 12 August 30 BC, supposedly by a snake bite. Octavian had Caesarion killed later in the year, thereby finally securing his claim to Caesar's legacy. Octavian's power was now unchallenged; the question was, what would he do with it?

ABOVE **Roman galley of the 1st century AD,** *from a relief at the temple of Fortuna Primigenia at Praeneste (Palestrina, Italy). This ship is probably very similar in general appearance to those that were used by both sides at Actium, though the crocodile figurehead may be meant to indicate that this particular ship came* *from Egypt. The tower at the bows provided an elevated firing platform for catapults and archers. After Actium there would not be another major naval battle in the Mediterranean for 500 years and the Roman fleet had little to do except patrol against pirates and transport troops.*

PAX
ROMANA
30 BC—AD 180

Ruling under the name Augustus, Octavian became Rome's first emperor. Despite bitter feuds and plotting within the royal families, Augustus' imperial constitution gave the Roman empire two centuries of almost unbroken internal peace known as the Pax Romana. The peoples of the empire enjoyed unparalleled security and prosperity in what was an enormous free trade area stretching from Britain in the north and Spain in the west, to the Euphrates in the east and Egypt in the south.

Rome was a tolerant empire; local identities and religions continued to flourish in parallel with a growing sense of common Roman identity. In the 2nd century the empire reached the practical limits of its expansion and by the end of the period it had been thrown onto the defensive behind heavily fortified borders.

29–2 BC

THE IMPERIAL SETTLEMENT ✦ Amid the general rejoicing over the end of the civil wars, many aristocrats were afraid that Octavian would turn out to be just another military dictator like Caesar. Octavian was a far more astute politician than Caesar had been, however, and he realized that Caesar's overt absolutism and public contempt for the institutions of the Republic had been his downfall. To allay these fears, Octavian immediately cut the size of the army, which had expanded enormously during the civil wars, from 60 legions to 28, retaining an equal number of auxiliary troops recruited from non-citizens. The surplus discharged veterans were resettled at Octavian's own expense. One of the main factors in the fall of the Republic was the emergence of client armies. To take the army out of politics, service in the legions became a lifetime career, with a minimum service of 25 years, regular pay and a guaranteed state pension on discharge.

Octavian's rule had no constitutional basis until 27 BC. At first he ruled as sole consul and submitted himself to the Senate every year for re-election until 23 BC.

PREVIOUS PAGES **Detail of a 2nd-century gilded bronze** *equestrian statue of the emperor Marcus Aurelius (r. 161–80), now in the Capitoline museum in Rome. Marcus Aurelius' great passion in life was philosophy, but it was during his reign that the empire's northern frontiers first came under serious pressure from the Germanic tribes, so he spent most his time in hard military campaigning.*

OPPOSITE **Marble statue of Augustus (r. 27 BC–AD 14),** *the first emperor of Rome, made around 20–17 BC. Roman emperors carefully cultivated their public image. Augustus presented himself in many guises: military commander (as here), chief priest, legislator, and family man – the father of his country. To the end of his reign, Augustus' public image was always portrayed as the young man he was when he came to power.*

In 27 BC he restored the magistracies – a slimmed-down Senate purged of his opponents – and the voting rights of the people, so technically restoring the Republic. It was a move calculated to force the Senate into creating a central constitutional role for him or risk a descent back into civil war. Having looked into the abyss, the Senate awarded Octavian proconsular powers in the provinces of Gaul, Spain, Syria and Egypt for ten years, in addition to the consulship. As most of the legions were stationed in these provinces, this effectively made him supreme commander of the army. The Senate also awarded him a new name, Augustus ('revered one'), by which he came to be known, and an official title *princeps* ('first citizen'), which disguised the monarchical nature of his rule. His successors preferred the title *imperator* ('commander-in-chief'), from which our word 'emperor' comes.

In 23 BC Augustus surrendered the consulship back into the control of the Senate in return for proconsular powers to intervene in all the empire's provinces, bringing all provincial governors under his direct control. He was also formally appointed supreme commander of the army, further strengthening his grip on the state. When the Roman people heard that Augustus had resigned the consulship, rioting broke out in the streets. To assure the people that he had not handed power back to the Senate, he accepted the authority of tribune for life. Further honours were awarded to Augustus in 12 BC when he became *pontifex maximus* ('chief priest') and in 2 BC, when he was acclaimed *pater patriae* ('father of the country'). Augustus came to be regarded as a semi-divine figure – especially in the east, where ruler-cults had been popular since the time of Alexander the Great – and after his death he was officially deified.

His rather untidy collection of offices allowed Augustus to exercise absolute power but the fact that these offices had been freely granted to him by the Senate and the people of Rome made his position constitutionally acceptable to the great majority of Roman citizens. Augustus was always careful to show respect to the Senate and its traditions and he consulted it about all important decisions. The consuls and other magistrates continued to be elected but from now on these were largely honorific positions. The institutions of republican government still stood but the Senate now retained only the appearance of authority. The legions were kept busy on the frontiers and Augustus made little show of his military authority, preferring a civilian government. All provincial governors and army commanders were appointed directly by Augustus while most administrators were recruited from the middle-ranking commercial equestrian class. Most of the corruption that blighted provincial administration under the republic was stamped out and the promotion of the imperial cult gave provincials a focus for positive loyalty to the empire.

OCTAVIAN SEDUCES THE ROMAN PEOPLE

Octavian discarded the name of triumvir, bore himself as consul, and said that a tribune's powers were enough for him to protect the common people. But when he had seduced the army by gifts, the common people by the provision of cheap food, and everyone by the blandishments of peace, then little by little he began to enlarge his powers, to encroach on the proper functions of the Senate, the magistrates and the laws. No one opposed him. Men of spirit had died on the battlefield or in the proscriptions. The remainder of the aristocracy were rewarded by wealth and position in proportion to their readiness to accept servitude. Having done well out of the revolution, they naturally preferred the existing security to the dangers and uncertainties of the old regime.

TACITUS, *ANNALS OF IMPERIAL ROME* (K. CHISHOLM AND J. FERGUSON, *ROME THE AUGUSTAN AGE*, 1981)

OPPOSITE **Peace and plenty.** *A scene symbolizing the peace and prosperity provided by Augustus' imperial regime, from the Ara Pacis ('Altar of Peace'). Finely sculpted from white marble, the altar was commissioned by the Senate to celebrate Augustus' return from a successful campaign in Spain in 13 BC and was consecrated in 9 BC. Other panels on the altar portray members of the Senate and the imperial family in procession to sacrifice to the gods.*

OVERLEAF **Detail of the Peutinger Map,** *an official road map of the Roman empire made in the 1st century AD. It is probably an updated copy of an original map made in the 1st century BC for Marcus Vipsanius Agrippa, a close friend of the emperor Augustus. Rome, naturally enough, is shown at the centre of the known world. This section of the map shows Mesopotamia.*

Map labels (top to bottom, left to right)

PVVAELI.

Sebaftopis.

anes. xii. Taffiros. iiii.   Stempeo. iiii.   Ex. ad fontem felicem. xxxv.   Cafniae.
                                                 Ad mercurium. xlv.   v. Apulum. vii.
RVERBES.   Pagas. xl. Caulita. xiii.
                                                                                Misium

R V E R B E S.   andaga.   Chadas.   Raugonia.
                    Barantea. xxvi.   xii. Armanas. xvii.   xxiii. Colchion. xxiii.   xxiii. Hari
aua. xii. aurifparate. xv.   Ad confluentes. xxx.   xxxviii.
OLCHI.   Charfidarate. xx. Vatanuffa.
                                                 Triganocarten. Zanserio. xx.   Cymiha. xxii.
                                                 xxx. xv. Thalbafaris. x.   Vyhanas. xxvii.
M ☉ S   xv. colchana. xlv.   Sitae. xii.   Iata
                                                              Hararra.   adpie. x.

Campi Veferti et in habitabiles.   Mahara. xvi. Colchis. xiii.   ☉   xxvii. adtygrem.   xii.
propter aque inopiam.   Coruhu. xiii.   arfina. xiii.   Coiffa.   P
                         Thirtonia. vii.   O

                    abaras. viii.   Reffaina.
                                                 xxxvi. Rene. xxvii.
Melentenis.   Sahal. xxxv.   Machu
    viii.   Corne. xiii.   Samofata.   Charris. xxxii.
    Mettita. xii. Glaudia. xlvi.   Barfalium. vii. Heba. xxx.   Charmobara. xii.   Batnis. xxx.   Edeffa. xl. Barbare. x.   Minnoc
                                                                        xxvi. Charra. xxvii.
Iordonnium.   Carbanum. iii.   ad ftapad[cem].   Smira. xxx.   fons Scabo
    ii.   Perre.   ii.   Tarfa. xxvii.   ad pont Singe.   Sathena. vii.   Haliag. xii. Chalama.
Heracome.   xxiii. drulis.   vicus. xxx.   xiii.
                                             xxiii.   Triar. xxxii.   Hoftra. xii.
    Sugga.   xii.   Zeugma.   xii.   vii. theibon.   ad fontes cob orem.
o Zociandem.   Cecihana. xvi. xxiii.   xii.   xxiii. Banata.   Hafte. xx. Amosta
    pas. xxiii.   xx. aladin.   Magrus. xx. Batita
    pas. xxiii.   Themeffat.
apammari   vii. Serren. Velamah. xii.   tharraha.   xv.
    dreq fines romanorum.   Veferta.   xviii. xxii.   Bofchrea. augubh. ad fonte Hadia
ha. xxviii.   Rolch   xvi.
                             Viotah.   igubis
                             l. x.   xvi.
fines exercituf fyriatice   Verta.   V E S E R T V M.
et conmertium Barbaroy.   pa   ludef.

Ardaschar (ru)

Pr. Djulva ?

Pr. Karadanny ?

Cyropolis (adnare Caspium) ?

Adlacum Urumia ?

Pr. Jenidscheh

Sindjar

Pr. Mianeh ?

Nisibin

El Hadhr (ru)   Ru. Kalaat -Scherlat.

Pr. Tekrit

pr. Hilla, Bâbil

El Madaien (Tak-i-Kesra)

AD 9

THE LOST LEGIONS ✦ The Roman empire expanded steadily throughout the earlier years of Augustus' reign. The last native resistance in Spain was crushed; in Europe, the Rhine and the Danube became the empire's northern frontier; and the client kingdoms of Galatia (in Anatolia) and Judea were annexed. In 12 BC Augustus began the conquest of Germany, the aim being to advance the frontier from the Rhine to the Elbe river. The strategic advantage to the empire would be a much shorter northern frontier to defend. The German tribes were at a simpler level of social and economic development than the Gauls had been in Caesar's time. Tribes had decentralized leadership, there were no towns or large villages, stock rearing was more important than settled farming, and the countryside was wilder and more forested than Gaul's. With their habitual contempt for barbarians, the Romans certainly underestimated the difficulties they would face in conquering the Germans.

Initially, the Roman conquest proceeded as planned under the command of Augustus' stepsons, Drusus and Tiberius. Wherever they stood and fought, the lightly armed Germans were routed by the legions and by AD 6 the Romans had apparently pacified the entire region between the Rhine and the Elbe. Beneath the surface, however, the Germans were deeply divided into pro- and anti-Roman factions and what one chief agreed was not binding on others. The Germans therefore needed careful handling. Unfortunately Varus, the general appointed governor of Germany in AD 7, had a well-deserved reputation for arrogance and brutality, and he ordered the Germans about 'as if they were actual slaves of the Romans'. He also demanded that the Germans meet the entire cost of building roads and towns themselves, an insupportable burden for an undeveloped economy like Germany's.

LEFT **The silver face mask** *of a ceremonial Roman cavalry helmet excavated at Kalkriese in Saxony, the site of the Romans' last stand at the battle of the Teutoburg Forest in AD 9. Such helmets looked magnificent and intimidating but gave little real protection for the wearer and were probably worn mainly on the parade ground.*

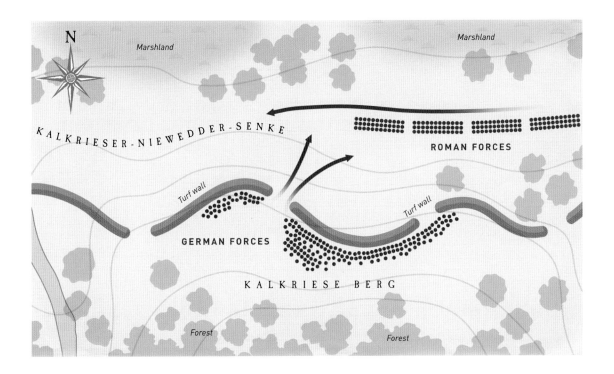

In September AD 9, resentment spilled over into open rebellion. The leader was Arminius, a chieftain of the Cherusci, who had, like many Germans, served as an auxiliary in the Roman army. Having been awarded Roman citizenship, Arminius was thought by Varus to be completely loyal and he used this misplaced trust to lead the Romans into a brilliantly planned ambush in the Teutoburg Forest, near the modern village of Kalkriese in Saxony. Trapped in a narrow corridor only 183 metres (200 yd) wide, with steep forested hills on one side and impassable marshland on the other, the Romans had no space to deploy in their regular battle formations. Three Roman legions, six cohorts of auxiliary troops and three cavalry regiments, around 15,000 men altogether, were massacred. Varus and many of his commanders committed suicide to avoid capture. As news of the battle spread, every German tribe joined the uprising and every trace of Roman occupation east of the Rhine was destroyed. Augustus was reputedly so shocked when he heard the news that

CHALLENGER OF ROME

[Arminius] *was unmistakably the liberator of Germany. Challenger of Rome – not in its infancy like kings and commanders before him, but at the height of its power – he had fought countless battles and never lost a war.*

TACITUS, ANNALS OF IMPERIAL ROME
(TRANS. MICHAEL GRANT, 1956)

ABOVE **Battle of the Teutoburg Forest, AD 9.** *The Germans were no match for Rome's disciplined and well-equipped legionaries in open battle. To neutralize the Romans' military superiority, the apparently loyal German chieftain Arminius led the Roman commander Varus, and his three legions and support troops, into an ambush in difficult forested countryside. Long before they reached the ambush site, the Roman forces had become straggled out over several miles on the narrow forest paths. They were constantly harassed by German warriors, who made sudden attacks before retreating to the cover of the forests. The Germans sprung their ambush when the Romans entered a narrow corridor between impassable marshes and forested hills where there was no space for the legionaries to deploy in their normal battle formations. The Germans launched their attacks from the protection of a zigzag turf rampart built along the margins of the forest. Trapped between the marshes and the rampart, and unable to fight effectively, the Romans were massacred to a man.*

LEFT **Maecenas Presenting the Liberal Arts to the Emperor Augustus** by *Giovanni Battista Tiepolo (1696–1770), now in the Hermitage, St Petersburg. A friend and advisor to the emperor Augustus, Gaius Maecenas was an important figure in Roman cultural life. Maecenas wrote poetry and philosophical dialogues, but the fragments that survive suggest that he was not a particularly talented writer. It is as the generous patron of many Roman poets, including Horace and Virgil, that he is chiefly remembered today. His spectacular gardens contained libraries and an auditorium, and were the first in Rome to have a heated outdoor swimming pool.*

EMPEROR WORSHIP

Ruler cults, focused on deified living kings, became popular in the Greek world from the time of Alexander the Great. These cults probably influenced Julius Caesar to prepare for his own deification in his lifetime. He was murdered before this could happen but he was posthumously deified by the Senate in 42 BC after the appearance of a comet was popularly interpreted as Caesar's soul in heaven. Augustus was the first emperor to be posthumously deified by the Senate; others who followed included Claudius, Vespasian, Trajan and Hadrian. The imperial cult was politically useful as a focus of loyalty to the emperors in the provinces and the army, and as a means for reigning emperors to publicly associate themselves with virtuous predecessors by promoting their deification. The imperial cult was also inseparably connected to the official Roman state gods, Jupiter, Juno and Minerva, whose worship it was treasonable to neglect. This was the main reason why early Christians, who refused to sacrifice to these cults, were persecuted.

BELOW **A relief, now in the Vatican,** *showing the apotheosis of the deified emperor Antoninus Pius (r. 138–61). A winged genius raises the emperor and his wife Faustina to heaven, escorted by two eagles. The fig leaf was added to this sculpture, and to many more surviving classical sculptures, during a papal campaign against nudity in art.*

he roamed his palace, banging his head against the walls and crying 'Quintilius Varus, give me back my legions!' The defeat convinced Augustus that the empire was nearing the practical limits of expansion and he advised his successors against making any new conquests.

AD 14

THE FIRST IMPERIAL SUCCESSION ✦ In 23 BC Augustus fell seriously ill. Though he recovered it brought the question of the succession to the forefront. Augustus' preferred successors had been his grandsons Gaius and Lucius but they both died young. In AD 4 Augustus formally adopted his stepson Tiberius, making him the heir apparent. However, Augustus' powers had been granted to him only for life so, in theory, they could not be inherited. Augustus knew better than to antagonize the Senate by trying to introduce a formal hereditary monarchy. Therefore, Tiberius, who was a fine soldier, was given plenty of opportunities to prove his suitability to rule so that the Senate could accept him as successor on merit. Fear of what might happen should Augustus die without an appointed successor was a powerful incentive for the Senate not to find too much fault with Tiberius. In 13 the Senate granted Tiberius the same powers that Augustus enjoyed, in effect making him co-emperor. When Augustus, now aged 76, fell ill with stomach pains and died at his family's villa at Nola near Naples on 14 August, Tiberius (r. AD 14–37) succeeded as emperor without opposition. Augustus' death was greeted with genuine and widespread grief, and he was accorded a lavish funeral ceremony in Rome before his body was publicly cremated. One senator claimed that he had actually seen Augustus' spirit soaring up to heaven through the flames. As had already been arranged, Augustus was formally deified and worshipped as one of the state gods alongside the high god Jupiter.

Augustus was reputedly so shocked when he heard the news of the Roman defeat by the Germans that he roamed his palace, banging his head against the walls and crying 'Quintilius Varus, give me back my legions!'

AD 27

TIBERIUS BECOMES A RECLUSE ✦ Tiberius' relations with the Senate were bad from the start. Tiberius thought senators were really fit only to be slaves and he lacked Augustus' ability to make them feel important and respected while at the same time excluding them from real power. In 22 Tiberius tried to disengage with day-to-day politics by sharing his powers with his son Drusus but Drusus died the following year – murdered, it is thought, by Sejanus, the commander of the emperor's elite Praetorian Guard, who was having an affair with Drusus' wife Livilla. No suspicions were aroused at the time, however, because Drusus was a notoriously heavy drinker. Sejanus asked Tiberius to allow him to marry Livilla, hoping thereby to be adopted into the ruling family, but Tiberius refused. Encouraged by Sejanus, Tiberius began to spend long periods away from Rome and in 27 BC he went to live permanently at his villa on the island of Capri; salacious rumours soon circulated about the depraved sex life he was supposed to be enjoying there.

Tiberius' absence created a power vacuum in Rome which was filled by Sejanus and the Praetorians. Sejanus controlled the flow of information to Capri, feeding Tiberius' growing paranoia about disloyalty in the Senate and exploiting it to purge his political opponents, and thus becoming the most powerful man in the empire. Statues were erected in his honour and his birthday was publicly celebrated. In 31 Sejanus was finally betrothed to Livilla and he shared the consulship with Tiberius but by the end of the year he was dead. Informers had alerted Tiberius to Sejanus' self-aggrandizement and he ordered his arrest and summary execution.

Any sense of relief in the Senate was short-lived as Tiberius now ruthlessly persecuted anyone he suspected of complicity with Sejanus. Tiberius was particularly hated for his use of the *lex maiestatis*, a treason law against anything that diminished the majesty of the Roman people, to punish disrespect to the emperor and restrict free speech. Since an accuser who obtained a successful prosecution under the law was entitled to a share of the defendant's property (the rest going to the state), this encouraged trumped-up charges. Tiberius used the law to destroy his enemies, even members of his own family, while senators used it to pursue their own feuds. As the death penalty was frequently applied, an atmosphere of general terror pervaded the aristocracy. None of this impacted at all on people outside the small political class, however, and the administrative structures created by Augustus ensured the smooth running of the empire even without the active engagement of the emperor.

AD 8

POET BANISHED ✦ Augustus may have transformed the politics of Rome but he was at heart a social conservative. He introduced sumptuary laws in an (unsuccessful) attempt to curb what he considered the decadent and immoral conspicuous consumption of the rich, supported the traditional state religious cults, and in 18 BC introduced laws to encourage monogamous marriage and family life.

OPPOSITE **This 3rd-century mosaic** *from North Africa shows the poet Virgil composing his epic poem the Aeneid, flanked by Melpomene, the Muse of tragedy, on the right, and Clio, the Muse of history, on the left. The Muses were nine Greek goddesses who inspired works of art, literature and science. Apart from Clio and Melpomene, the other Muses were Calliope (epic poetry), Erato (love poetry), Euterpe (flutes and lyric poetry), Polyhymnia (sacred poetry), Terpsichore (dance), Thalia (comedy and pastoral poetry) and Urania (astronomy).*

In this atmosphere of official puritanism it was probably unwise of the prominent poet Ovid (Publius Ovidius Naso) to publish the *Ars Amatoria* (*The Art of Love*), an erotic poem celebrating seduction and adultery, which Augustus considered to be a serious crime. In AD 8 Augustus banished Ovid to the gloomy port of Tomis (Constanta, Romania) on the Black Sea. Ovid wrote that he had been banished for 'a poem and an error': the error is thought to have been his implication in a scandal involving Augustus' granddaughter Julia. No amount of pleading could persuade Augustus to change his mind and Ovid died in exile in AD 17.

Ovid's fate contrasts with that of writers who promoted the ideals of the regime, such as the poet Virgil, whose epic *Aeneid* recounts the adventures of Aeneas, the legendary ancestor of the Romans, and the historian Livy, who wrote a massive history of Rome from its foundation. Such writers were actively encouraged by Augustus. Augustus also used art and architecture to glorify his rule. Countless official statues of the emperor were sent out to the provinces. Rome was embellished with public baths, theatres, triumphal arches, aqueducts and temples so that Augustus was able to boast that 'I left Rome a city of marble, though I found it a city of bricks.' A fire brigade and a police force improved public safety in the city and the people were kept happy with 'bread and circuses' – a corn dole and free entertainments like gladiator shows, plays and chariot races. Support for Augustus among the Roman people was solid.

AD 37–40

MAD AND BAD ✦ Tiberius' death, aged 77, in AD 37 was greeted with a sense of relief but worse was to come with his successor Gaius, who is much better known by his nickname of Caligula. Born in AD 12, Caligula was the son of Tiberius' nephew Germanicus. As a child he accompanied his father on military campaigns and was given his nickname, which means 'little soldier's boot' for the child-sized army boots he liked to wear. After Germanicus died in Syria in 19 – he was poisoned, many thought, on Tiberius' orders to remove a dynastic rival – his mother Agrippina became involved in a bitter feud with Tiberius which ended only when she died in prison in 33. From 31 Caligula lived under supervision at Tiberius' villa on Capri and was designated his

Caligula's behaviour became increasingly erratic: he proposed appointing his horse Incitatus as consul; he demanded that he be worshipped as a living god; he was accused of incest with his sisters and every other imaginable sexual perversion.

BELOW **The Aqua Claudia (Claudian aqueduct) near Rome.** *The aqueduct was built during the reign of the emperor Claudius to carry water to the city from springs 45 miles away. For most of its course the aqueduct ran underground. Rome's first aqueduct, the Aqua Appia, was built in 312 BC. By the 2nd century AD Rome was supplied with 300 million gallons of water a day by ten aqueducts with a total length of over 280 miles.*

heir in 35. To begin with, Caligula showed no inclination to tyranny. He announced an end to Tiberius' politically motivated treason trials, allowed those he had exiled to return, reformed the tax system, gave back to the popular assembly the right to elect magistrates and put on magnificent free entertainments. He was wildly popular.

In 39 Caligula's relations with the Senate suddenly deteriorated. His lavish spending had emptied the treasury. He began new treason trials with the sole purpose of seizing the defendants' estates: several senators were executed. New taxes were introduced and citizens were pressured into 'lending' money to the state. Wills were reinterpreted to justify seizing estates. The financial crisis caused an interruption to Rome's grain supply, leading to a brief famine in the city. Caligula's popularity faded quickly and several conspiracies against him were discovered. His behaviour became increasingly erratic: in spring 40 he gathered an army on the Channel coast, everyone thought in preparation for an invasion of Britain, and ordered his soldiers onto the beaches to collect seashells as tribute from the ocean; he proposed appointing his horse Incitatus as consul; he demanded that he be worshipped as a living god; he was accused of incest with his sisters and every other imaginable sexual perversion. Contemporary

CALIGULA CONQUERS THE SEA

[Caligula] *drew up his army in battle array facing the Channel and moved the siege-engines into position as though he intended to bring the campaign to a close. No one had the least notion what was in his mind when, suddenly, he gave the order: 'Gather sea-shells!' He referred to the shells as 'plunder from the sea, due to the Capitol and to the palace' and made the troops fill their helmets and tunic laps with them.*

SUETONIUS, *THE TWELVE CAESARS* (TRANS. GRAVES)

LEFT **Gilt bronze bust of the emperor Caligula (r. 37–41).** *Caligula is remembered as the archetypical 'mad and bad' Roman emperor. His reign began amid popular acclaim but his increasingly bizarre behaviour led to his murder after a reign of only four years.*

writers believed that Caligula had gone insane but his tyranny may really have been an ill-judged attempt to create an absolute divine monarchy. Caligula's misrule revealed a serious weakness in the imperial system: there was no constitutional way to remove a mad or bad emperor.

AD 41

CALIGULA ASSASSINATED ✦ On 24 January 41 Caligula was stabbed to death in his palace by officers of the Praetorian Guard led by Cassius Chaerea. Caligula had frequently mocked Chaerea for his effeminate voice and had unjustly questioned his loyalty and that of other officers. Knowing the inevitable consequences of being charged with treason, Chaerea acted first. Once Caligula was dead, the conspirators searched out his wife and young daughter and killed them too: they did not find Caligula's uncle, Claudius, who hid behind a curtain, where he was found later by a loyal Praetorian guardsman. When the news broke, the Senate met in emergency session to debate restoring the republic. But while the senators debated, the Praetorian Guard decided. Chaerea could not persuade the Praetorians to support the restoration of the republic – they could see that it was not in their interests – and they proclaimed Claudius as emperor. Claudius' offer of a gift equivalent to nearly three months' pay for each guardsman no doubt helped them make their minds up but it was an unfortunate precedent to set for the future. The Senate called on Claudius to surrender but it lacked both popular and military support. The day after Caligula's murder, the Senate recognized Claudius as emperor but it was clear that this was merely a formality. What really counted from now on was that a candidate for the throne had the support of the army: the Senate was a mere rubber-stamp assembly.

RIGHT **Idealized marble statue of the emperor Claudius (r. 41–54),** *from Leptis Magna in Libya. Claudius was in reality slightly disabled and physically unimpressive. Although he avoided Caligula's excesses and was a competent administrator, Claudius was never a popular emperor. As a result of being proclaimed emperor by the Praetorian Guard, his relations with the Senate, who regarded proclaiming a new emperor as their prerogative, never really recovered. Nor did his practice of promoting freedmen of proven ability to high administrative office endear him to senators, who expected these jobs to go to members of their own families.*

AD 43

ROMAN CONQUEST OF BRITAIN BEGUN ✦ Claudius' claim to the throne was a good one – he was the last surviving adult male member of the royal family – but he was in many ways an unlikely emperor. Already 50 years old, Claudius was disabled as a result of infant paralysis: he slobbered, limped, his head shook and he was slightly deaf. His disabilities, which he claimed later to have exaggerated, probably saved his life. As no one thought him a credible candidate for the throne, he was untouched by the murderous feuding within the royal family. During his years in the background, Claudius kept himself busy writing numerous books on Roman history, none of which have survived. His methodical mind made him an able administrator in office yet from the beginning of his reign he was seen as a weak emperor. The Senate always remained hostile to Claudius and several senators were executed for plotting against him.

Claudius slobbered, limped, his head shook and he was slightly deaf. His disabilities probably saved his life.

It was to strengthen his standing with the army, the ultimate guarantor of his position, that Claudius began the conquest of Britain in early spring 43. Since Caesar's invasions nearly a century before, the Britons had been exposed to strong Roman influences, which some welcomed and others opposed. The pretext for this Roman invasion was the fact that the pro-Roman king, Verica of the Atrebates tribe, had been driven into exile by Caratacus and Togodumnus, the anti-Roman kings of the Catuvellauni and the Trinovantes. Claudius embarked four legions for the invasion, under the command of Aulus Plautius. Despite Caesar's invasions, most Romans still regarded Britain as being beyond the edge of the known world and the legionaries almost mutinied on being told their destination. The main Roman force landed in Kent, at Richborough (then a fine natural harbour, now a few miles inland), where the Romans later erected an enormous commemorative arch. The Britons did not contest the Roman landings but waited until they advanced inland. They then made a stand at the Medway river, but were defeated in a hard two-day battle and pursued by the Romans to the Thames. With a bridgehead secured, Claudius joined the army and led it on across the Thames to capture the Trinovantes' capital at Camulodunum (Colchester, Essex), which he entered triumphantly on the back of an elephant. Togodumnus died in the fighting and Caratacus fled. He continued to organize resistance against the Romans but was eventually captured in 51 and sent to a comfortable imprisonment in Rome.

Claudius rewarded friendly British rulers with client kingdoms; Verica had died in the meantime so his territory was given to a relative. Camulodunum, meanwhile, became the first capital of Roman Britain. Claudius had the symbolic victory he needed and he left almost immediately, probably around the end of the June 43, to hurry back to Rome to celebrate a triumph. The real business of conquering Britain and organizing it as a Roman province was left to his generals.

54

A CASE OF FOOD POISONING ✦ Claudius' addition of Britain to the Roman empire did not win him the popularity he hoped for and he was not much mourned when he died suddenly in October 54. Claudius' death was the result of a conspiracy by his fourth wife, his niece Agrippina (Caligula's sister). Claudius married Agrippina in 48 after he had ordered the execution of his promiscuous third wife Messalina for her part in a senatorial conspiracy against him. Agrippina had already been married twice and by the first marriage she had an eleven-year-old son, Lucius Domitius Ahenobarbus, better known by his adopted name, Nero. Claudius already had a seven-year-old son, Britannicus, by Messalina, but Agrippina immediately began scheming to secure the succession for Nero, winning over many of the senior palace officials to her cause.

In 50 Claudius formally adopted Nero, ostensibly to act as guardian for Britannicus, and when he came of age a year later he was granted proconsular powers (the powers appropriate for a provincial governor). In 53 Nero married Claudius' daughter Octavia. Nero's claim to the throne was now secure, but Agrippina was in a hurry: she wanted Nero to inherit the throne while he was still young enough for her to dominate him. Though not proven beyond all doubt, it is generally believed that Agrippina murdered Claudius by arranging for him to be served with a poisoned dish of his favourite wild mushrooms. His food taster and most of the palace officials were in on the plot. However, Nero proved to be a stronger character than Agrippina had imagined and he immediately rejected her interference in state affairs. Thwarted, Agrippina transferred her support to the claims of Britannicus, who was now nearly 14, the official age of adulthood in the Roman world.

After Britannicus was poisoned on Nero's orders in February 51, Agrippina was banished from court. She did not learn her lesson. Because of her continued meddling, in 59 Nero decided to kill Agrippina. He first attempted to drown her in a contrived shipwreck, using a specially designed collapsing boat, but she swam ashore. Nero then ordered sailors from the Roman fleet to batter her to death. Nero's brutal murder of his mother shocked Roman opinion and set the tone for the rest of his reign.

> *Because of her continued meddling, in 59 Nero decided to kill his mother Agrippina. He first attempted to drown her in a contrived shipwreck, but she swam ashore. Nero then ordered sailors from the Roman fleet to batter her to death.*

259

60

BOUDICCA'S REVOLT ✦ The Roman conquest of Britain progressed steadily until by 60 the southeastern third of the island was apparently firmly under their control. However, the high-handed Roman decision to annexe the client kingdom of the Iceni (in East Anglia) caused its queen Boudicca to rebel.

It was said that Roman soldiers had even flogged the queen and raped her daughters. The Britons fell upon Camulodunum, which they saw as the symbol of their subjection. The city was completely unfortified and had only a small garrison – most of the Roman forces were away on campaign in Wales with the governor Paulinus – and its population was massacred. The city was levelled to the ground block by block. Rebel forces also sacked Verulamium (St Albans), a pro-Roman British settlement, and the small port of Londinium (London).

While the rebels were busy plundering and burning, Paulinus hurried back from Wales with a force of about 10,000 legionaries and auxiliaries. At an unknown battlefield somewhere in the English Midlands, Boudicca confronted Paulinus with a huge army, claimed to have been over 200,000 strong.

The rebels were so confident of victory that the warriors even brought their wives and children along in wagons to watch the battle. Boudicca raced around this vast but undisciplined throng in a chariot, encouraging her warriors with stirring speeches. Her battle plan seems to have been simply to overwhelm the Romans by sheer weight of numbers. However, Paulinus had taken up a good defensive position in a natural defile which could only be attacked easily from the front, making it impossible for the Britons to use their superior numbers to outflank and envelop the Roman army.

The Romans easily broke up the initial British attack with their javelins – few of the Britons had any body armour – before going over to the offensive. The Roman infantry adopted a wedge formation and, flanked by the cavalry, charged the Britons and drove them back. The wagons that the Britons had left in a semi-circle to their rear as a grandstand for the spectators now became a trap, obstructing their flight. The Romans broke ranks and fell upon the panic-stricken Britons, indiscriminately slaughtering men, women, children and beasts of burden. One report estimated that the Britons suffered 80,000 casualties to the Romans' 400. The Roman victory broke the back of the rebellion. Boudicca escaped

BREAD AND CIRCUSES

Roman emperors made great efforts to keep the people of Rome fed and entertained.

They gave out doles of bread or grain, held public feasts at religious festivals, put on spectacular gladiator shows and wild beast hunts in the arena, provided plays, horse racing and chariot racing, and subsidized public baths. Traditionally, public entertainments in Rome were free, paid for either by the emperor himself or by ambitious senators trying to win popular support for consular elections. Seating at entertainments was not a free-for-all, however. The wealthiest classes had the best seats and slaves sat right at the back.

The most popular entertainment was not gladiator shows but chariot racing. The different racing teams attracted fanatical supporters who frequently fought street battles against one another. Spending lavishly on entertainments was the quickest way for an emperor to court popularity with the masses: failing to maintain the bread supply was the quickest way to fall from favour.

RIGHT **Riot.** *Sports-related violence was common in the Roman empire. This fresco from Pompeii depicts a riot that broke out at gladiatorial games in the city's amphitheatre in AD 59. Supporters of rival teams of gladiators from Pompeii and nearby Nucera began trading insults. This escalated to stone throwing and fighting between the Nucerians and Pompeiians, which spilled out onto the streets. Many people were killed and injured. The emperor Nero temporarily banned gladiator fights in Pompeii as a punishment.*

the battlefield but committed suicide shortly afterwards. In the aftermath of the rebellion, the Romans adopted a more sensitive approach towards the Britons aimed at encouraging the native aristocracy to develop a positive loyalty to the empire. The Roman administration was moved to Londinium, which quickly became Britain's largest city.

64

THE GREAT FIRE OF ROME ✦ On the night of 19 July a fire broke out at the Roman Circus (a chariot-racing course). Fanned by a strong wind, the fire spread to nearby commercial premises full of combustible materials and was quickly burning completely out of control. It was six days before the fire burned itself out. By that time, three of Rome's 14 districts had been completely destroyed and another seven seriously damaged. The imperial palace on the Palatine Hill was also destroyed. Nero was at Antium (Anzio), south of Rome, when the fire broke out. On hearing the news he hurried back to organize relief efforts: opening public buildings and building temporary accommodation for the homeless, and providing food aid to prevent starvation, all at his own expense. Nero's generosity earned him no thanks because a rumour had spread that while the city burned, he had gone on stage to play the lyre and sing about the sack of Troy (Nero believed that he was a prodigiously talented actor). Whether true or not, Nero's well-earned reputation for cruel and bizarre behaviour meant that the rumour was widely believed. In reality, Nero also paid for much of the rebuilding of Rome. Strict standards were enforced on builders to reduce the amount of timber used in houses, which all had to have fireproof stone partition walls. Private landlords had to keep fire-fighting equipment in their houses and big improvements were made to the public water supply system. Again, Nero got no thanks. He appropriated a large part of the ruined city to build himself a magnificent new palace, the 'Golden House', and private gardens. This gave rise to a new rumour, that Nero had started the fire deliberately to clear the city to make room for the palace. There is no evidence

WOMAN WARRIOR

Boudicca drove round all the tribes in a chariot with her daughters in front of her. 'We British are used to women commanders in war,' she cried. 'I am descended from mighty men! But now I am not fighting for my kingdom and wealth. I am fighting as an ordinary person for my lost freedom, my bruised body, and my outraged daughters.'

TACITUS, *ANNALS OF IMPERIAL ROME* (TRANS. MICHAEL GRANT 1956)

OPPOSITE ***Boadicea,*** **[Boudicca]** ***Haranguing the Britons*** *by the English historical painter John Opie (1761–1807), depicts the beginning of the British queen Boudicca's anti-Roman rebellion in AD 60 as she demands that her subjects avenge her daughters who had been raped by the Romans. Boudicca's rebellion was largely forgotten about during the Middle Ages. When she was rediscovered by antiquarians in the 16th century, the warrior queen quickly became a symbol of Elizabeth I's resistance to the Spanish Armada. Ironically, in the 19th century the anti-imperialist rebel Boudicca came to be identified with Queen Victoria, the head of the greatest empire the world had ever seen.*

ABOVE **Human torches.** The Torches of Nero by the Polish painter Henryk Siemiradzki (1843–1902) was inspired by Nero's scapegoating of the Christians for the disastrous Great Fire of Rome in AD 64. Nero was widely suspected of starting the fire deliberately to clear space for a new palace. To divert attention from the rumours, Nero blamed Christians, whose refusal to sacrifice to the state gods made their loyalty to the state suspect in the eyes of most Romans. Hundreds of Christians were subjected to cruel deaths, such as being burned alive as human torches. Regarded by their fellows as martyrs, the bravery that these Christians showed in the face of death actually spread sympathy for their beliefs.

NERO'S SCAPEGOATS

Nero fastened the blame for the fire and inflicted the most exquisite tortures on a class hated for their abominations, called Christians by the populace. Christ, from whom the name had its origin, suffered the extreme penalty during the reign of Tiberius at the hands of one of our procurators, Pontius Pilate, and a most mischievous superstition, thus checked for the moment, again broke out not only in Judea, the first source of the evil, but, even in Rome, where all things hideous and shameful from every part of the world find their centre and become popular. In accordance, an arrest was first made of all who pleaded guilty; then, upon their information, an immense multitude was convicted, not as much of the crime of firing the city as of hatred against mankind. Mockery of every sort was added to their deaths. Covered with the skins of beasts, they were torn by dogs and perished, or were nailed to crosses, or were doomed to the flames and burnt, to serve as a nightly illumination, when daylight had expired.

TACITUS, *ANNALS OF IMPERIAL ROME* (1876 TRANSLATION)

that the rumour contained any truth but Nero was sufficiently worried by it to search for a scapegoat to blame for the fire. He found it in a new religious sect, the Christians, whose refusal to sacrifice to the state gods made them (like the Jews) suspect to the Roman people. Nero's vicious persecution of the Christians backfired, creating popular sympathy for the victims and adding to his reputation for wanton cruelty.

69

THE YEAR OF THE FOUR EMPERORS ✦ Following the Great Fire of Rome Nero faced a serious Senatorial plot against his life. The conspiracy was betrayed, and the ringleaders were executed, but it frightened Nero and his behaviour became more arbitrary and megalomaniac. He identified himself with Hercules and the sun god Apollo and he contemplated renaming Rome Neropolis. Deciding that the people of Rome were unworthy of him, in 66 Nero embarked on a year-long tour of Greece during which he took part in all the major pan-Hellenic drama and athletic festivals. He was so successful that he won 1,808 first prizes, including that for the Olympic chariot race, which he was awarded

OPPOSITE **Backstage at the Roman theatre.** *This 1st-century mosaic from a house in Pompeii shows actors getting dressed for a comic satyr play. Satyr plays were full of ribald humour, slapstick gags, drunkenness and sex: actors frequently wore enormous false phalluses. Satyr plays originated in Athens c. 500 BC, where they were performed to provide a bit of light relief after an audience had sat through a tragic play. Because many in the audience had to sit a long way from the stage, actors (always men) in Greek and Roman theatres always wore masks with exaggerated expressions to make it easy to identify what sort of characters they were portraying.*

despite falling out of his chariot. Meanwhile rebellions broke out in northern Gaul, under a Romanized German chieftain called Julius Civilis, and in Judea, where the extreme Jewish Zealot sect wiped out the small Roman garrison and seized Jerusalem. These rebellions proved fatal to Nero because they lost him the support of the army.

In March 68 Vindex, the disaffected governor of Lugdunensis in central Gaul, rebelled against Nero and persuaded Galba, the governor of Tarraconensis in Spain, to join him. The governors of the other Spanish provinces and of North Africa joined the rebellion. Vindex committed suicide after he was defeated in battle by Verginius, the loyal commander of the Rhine legions. Following their victory, the legions showed their own discontent with Nero by trying to proclaim Verginius emperor. Nero seemed paralysed by the rebellion and at a loss as to how to respond. Seeing Nero's lack of resolve, the Praetorians joined the rebellion in June and recognized Galba as emperor. Nero fled from Rome and ordered a loyal servant to kill him when he heard the news that the Senate had declared him a public enemy. His last words were 'What an artist dies in me!'

Nero's death brought to an end the first dynasty of imperial Rome but it did not bring political stability. Nero had spent freely and the state finances were ruined. Galba made remedying this his priority and he courted unpopularity by raising taxes. However, it was his high-minded refusal to reward the Praetorians for their support – Galba saw it as bribery – that was his undoing: in January 69 they murdered him and proclaimed Otho, another general, emperor in his place. By this time, the legions on the Rhine had proclaimed their own general, Vitellius, emperor. Following Galba's murder, Vitellius invaded Italy and defeated Otho's legions at Cremona in April. Although Otho's cause appeared far from lost, he committed suicide – it was said he did so because he abhorred the thought of plunging the empire into a protracted civil war for the sake of his ambition.

Vitellius ruled unchallenged for only a few months. In July he learned that the legions fighting the Zealot rebels in Judea had proclaimed their commander Vespasian as emperor. When the Danube legions also declared for Vespasian in August, Vitellius attempted to negotiate his abdication from the throne but the Praetorians refused to allow it. Leaving his elder son Titus to prosecute the war against the Zealots, Vespasian occupied Egypt, the source of most of Rome's corn supplies. Vespasian sent his trusted ally Licinius Mucianus, the governor

OPPOSITE **The Colosseum in Rome** *was the largest of all Roman amphitheatres, with a capacity for 50,000 spectators. The amphitheatre was begun under the emperor Vespasian in 72 and completed eight years later under his son and successor, Titus. It was paid for with booty taken from Judea during Vespasian's war against the Zealots. During its inaugural games in AD 80, over*

8,000 wild animals were killed in the arena in mock hunts and at one point it was flooded for the recreation of a sea battle. The amphitheatre's popular name is thought to be derived from a colossal statue of Nero which once stood nearby: its official name, the Flavian amphitheatre, was derived from its founder Vespasian's family name, Flavius.

of Syria, to Italy but by the time he reached Rome Vitellius was already dead. Marcus Antonius Primus, the commander of the legions on the Danube, led his forces into Italy and defeated the Vitellians at a second battle at Cremona in October. When Primus' forces fought their way into Rome in December, Vitellius was found hiding alone in the palace caretaker's lodge and was executed. That night, the Senate recognized Vespasian as emperor. When Mucianus arrived in Rome a few days later he took over effective control of the city until Vespasian arrived in person to take up the reins of government in September 70. For the first time, an emperor had been made somewhere other than at Rome.

LEFT **The Destruction of the Temple of Jerusalem,** by the Italian Romantic painter Francesco Hayez (1791–1882), was inspired by the destruction of the second Temple of Jerusalem by the Romans in AD 70 during the suppression of the Zealot revolt. The first Temple, built by Solomon in the 10th century BC, was destroyed by the Babylonians in 586 BC. Construction of the second Temple began in 535 BC, after the Persian king allowed the Jews to return home after the Babylonian exile. This Temple was reconstructed on a lavish scale by Herod the Great around 19 BC. The temple precinct's massive walls and towers made it a natural fortress. Following its destruction, the Temple's ruins were quarried to build a palace for the Roman governor of Judea and a temple of Zeus.

70

THE DESTRUCTION OF THE TEMPLE ✦

When Vespasian left Judea to pursue his claim to the imperial throne, he left his elder son Titus in command of operations against the Zealots. In March 70 Titus laid siege to Jerusalem with four legions. He made the supply situation for the defenders worse by allowing pilgrims to enter the city to celebrate Passover and then refused to let them leave. Jerusalem was strongly fortified, with several lines of defences, while the Temple precinct itself was a natural stronghold, protected by double walls and the Antonia fortress. The Temple itself had been rebuilt on a massive scale by King Herod in *c.* 19 BC. Despite fierce resistance, by May Titus had breached the two outermost lines of defences, bringing half the city under his control. The Temple precinct and the Upper and Lower City quarters, which remained in Zealot hands, Titus encircled with a siege wall and siege towers, to prevent Zealot raiders sallying out to destroy his siege engines or forage for food. The Antonia fortress overlooked the Temple and it was this that Titus now focused on taking. The walls resisted all attacks by catapults and battering rams and the Zealots fought off several Roman attempts to take the fortress by storm. The Antonia finally fell in early July, to a stealthy attack at the dead of night when the Zealot sentries had fallen asleep at their posts.

At the beginning of August the Romans brought up battering rams to try to breach the walls of the Temple precinct but a week of battering made no impression on the massive masonry. On 8 August, Titus ordered the gates to be set on fire. When the fire spread to timbers in the walls, the defenders were forced to retreat and the Romans stormed in. Resistance continued in the Temple itself. Titus wanted to preserve the Temple if possible, probably to turn it into a pagan sanctuary to humiliate the Jews, but it caught fire after a soldier hurled a burning brand through a window into a side room. The Romans plundered the Temple of its rich ornaments before the flames forced them out. The Zealots counterattacked desperately, trying to retake the Temple and extinguish the flames. Thousands of civilians who had taken refuge in the Temple precinct got caught up in the fighting and were massacred by the Romans. The Lower City fell a few days later but the Upper City held out for another month. The Romans faced little resistance when they launched their final assault on 7 September as the defenders were so demoralized and weakened by starvation. The Romans spent the night in plundering and indiscriminate slaughter; those inhabitants who managed to hide until morning, by which time the soldiers had tired of killing, were enslaved.

72–73

THE SIEGE OF MASADA ✦ After the fall of Jerusalem, the Romans began mopping up the last centres of Zealot resistance in Judea. The last important stronghold to fall was the mountain-top fortress of Masada in the Judean desert overlooking the Dead Sea. When the Jewish revolt broke out in 66 an extreme Zealot group called the *Sicarii* ('dagger men') surprised the Roman garrison and seized the fortress. In late summer 72 the new governor of Judea, Flavius Silva, laid siege to Masada. It was a formidable undertaking. Built by King Herod *c.* 37–31 BC, Masada had deep cisterns to store rainwater and the defenders had sufficient food supplies to sit out a siege for years if necessary. All the besiegers' food and drinking

LEFT **Vespasian and Titus celebrate a triumph** *on their return to Rome in AD 71, depicted here by the 16th-century Italian artist Giulio Romano. Triumphs were originally awarded by the Senate to reward victorious generals, but after the introduction of imperial rule they became the sole prerogative of the emperor.*

DEATH WITH HONOUR

It is evident that daybreak will end our resistance, but we are free to choose an honourable death with our loved ones. This our enemies cannot prevent, however earnestly they may pray to take us alive; nor can we defeat them in battle.

ELEAZAR BEN Y'AIR ACCORDING TO JOSEPHUS, *THE JEWISH WAR* (TRANS. G.A. WILLIAMSON, 1959)

water had to be brought in from many miles away by Jewish forced labourers. Silva decided that the fortress would have to be taken by storm. First, the Romans built siege camps and a wall to surround Masada. Masada is a cliff-girt plateau and the summit was accessible only by narrow and easily defended paths. The weakness in these natural defences was a 122-metre (400-ft) high spur on the western flank of the mountain. The Romans spent months building a ramp on top of this spur. In April they pushed a siege tower and battering ram to the top of the ramp and prepared to breach the fortress walls. The defenders built a counterwork but the Romans destroyed it with fire on 14 April. The Romans spent the night preparing for their final assault but when they stormed the walls the next day they met no resistance. Realizing that the fortress's fall was now inevitable, Eleazar ben Y'air, the leader of the Sicarii, persuaded the defenders to draw lots to kill one another (so avoiding the sin of suicide) rather than face enslavement by the Romans. The Romans counted 960 bodies and found alive only two women and five children who had hidden in a cistern.

79

ERUPTION OF VESUVIUS ✦ In February 62 a powerful earthquake caused widespread damage to the Roman holiday resorts around the Bay of Naples. Pompeii, lying at the foot of Mount Vesuvius, was particularly badly damaged. Another powerful earthquake followed two years later. Vesuvius was recognized as having a volcanic origin but the rumblings in the earth were not seen as portents of an impending disaster. In fact, earth tremors became so common in the years that followed that the locals were quite blasé about them and they were entirely unprepared when Vesuvius exploded into life in 79. The exact date of the eruption is not known for certain but it was probably 24 October.

According to the only eyewitness account, by Pliny the Younger who watched from the Roman naval base at Misenum on the far side of the Bay of Naples, the eruption began around midday when an explosion threw a column of ash high into the sky: as it spread it began to fall on the surrounding countryside. Those who decided to flee now were the lucky ones. Early the next day pyroclastic flows – fast-moving clouds of incandescent ash and poisonous gas – began rolling down the

LEFT **The fortress of Masada** *on a mountain top overlooking the Dead Sea was the last major stronghold of the Jewish Zealot rebels. The fortress was surrounded on all sides by cliffs and the Romans were only able to storm it by building a huge ramp, the remains of which can be seen on the right-hand edge of the picture.*

ABOVE **Shortly after Titus' death in AD 81,** *his brother Domitian erected a permanent memorial to his defeat of the Zealot rebellion in the form of a triumphal arch near the Forum. Sculpted panels on the arch depicted scenes from the triumph held in 71, including Roman soldiers parading the menorah and other loot from the Temple. Traditionally Roman Jews refused to walk under the arch.*

mountainside, flattening buildings and incinerating or suffocating anyone caught in their path. The eruption continued for about 20 hours by which time the towns of Pompeii, Herculaneum, Oplontis and Stabiae were completely buried under ash, lava or pyroclastic deposits. At least 16,000 people are believed to have died. One of the casualties was Pliny the Younger's father, Pliny the Elder. Pliny the Elder was commander of the fleet at Misenum but his passion was natural history. Pliny took ship across the bay to the resort of Stabiae to study the eruption at closer quarters and rescue people trapped there: he was overcome by poisonous gases but his companions managed to escape back to sea. The gentle ash fall which buried Pompeii preserved almost everything it covered: wall paintings, furniture, garden ornaments, foodstuffs, tools – even graffiti. As a result Pompeii is a perfect time capsule of everyday Roman life in the 1st century AD. As the bodies of people, and animals, who failed to escape the eruption, decayed, they left cavities in the ash. These were filled by excavators, revealing something of their final agonies.

INTO THE INFERNO

[Pliny] hurried to the place everyone else was hastily leaving, steering his course straight for the danger zone. He was entirely fearless, describing each new movement and phase of the portent to be noted down as he observed them. Ashes were already falling, hotter and thicker as the ships drew near, followed by bits of pumice and blackened stones, charred and cracked by the flames; then suddenly they were in shallow water, and the shore was blocked by debris from the mountain. For a moment my uncle wondered whether to turn back, but when the helmsman advised this, he refused.

PLINY THE YOUNGER (TRANS. BETTY RADICE, 1963)

83

CONQUEST DENIED ✦ The task of completing the Roman conquest of Britain was given to Gnaeus Julius Agricola, who became governor in 77. By the end of 82 only the Caledonian tribes of the Scottish Highlands still resisted Roman rule. In 83 Agricola advanced north from his base on the Tay river

LEFT **The Last Day of Pompeii** by the Russian painter Karl Pavlovich Bryullov (1799–1852) depicts the destruction of the Roman city during the explosive eruption of the volcano Vesuvius. The story of Pompeii has inspired countless works of art, literature, and more recently film, since the first archaeological excavations began to uncover the city in 1764. Bryullov personally visited the site in 1828 to make sketches for the dramatic painting, which caused a sensation in Italy when it was first exhibited in 1833.

along the eastern edge of the Highlands. Over a dozen of his marching camps have been identified: the most northerly is at Cawdor, a few miles from Inverness. Somewhere on his march north, Agricola met and defeated a confederate army of the Caledonian tribes at the Battle of Mons Graupius, the site of which has never been identified. At around 30,000 strong, the Caledonians' army was probably only slightly larger than the Roman army and the outcome of the battle was never in doubt. The Caledonians fought desperately, and even after they had been driven from the battlefield they constantly regrouped to try to ambush the pursuing Roman forces. Only nightfall ended the fighting, by which time some 10,000 of the Caledonians had been killed. Roman losses were only 360.

Roman historians presented Mons Graupius as a decisive Roman victory: in reality it was anything but. Two-thirds of the Caledonian army escaped and during the night it simply melted away into the landscape. The next day, Roman patrols found only burned and deserted farms. From now on the Caledonians resorted to guerrilla warfare. Agricola wintered in the Highlands but in 84 the emperor Domitian recalled him to Rome and he never returned to Britain. Faced with a serious threat from the Dacians on the Danube frontier, Domitian began to withdraw troops from Britain and the aim of total conquest was quietly abandoned. In the years that followed the Romans gradually withdrew from Agricola's northern conquests but it was many decades before the frontier of Roman Britain was finally settled.

96–98

SUCCESSION BY ADOPTION ✦ Under Vespasian's capable rule, peace and stability returned to the Roman empire and after his death the throne passed unchallenged to his sons Titus (r. 79–81) and Domitian (r. 81–96). However, Domitian turned out to be another autocratic tyrant who saw conspiracies everywhere. In September 96 Domitian fell victim to a real conspiracy when he was stabbed to death by his servants. Later the same day, the Senate proclaimed Marcus Cocceius Nerva as emperor. The Senate revenged itself on Domitian by

THE TRUE NATURE OF ROMAN IMPERIALISM

Here at the world's end, on its last inch of liberty, we [Caledonians] have lived unmolested to this day, defended by our remoteness and obscurity. Now the uttermost parts of Britain lie exposed. There are no more tribes to come; nothing but sea and cliffs and these more deadly Romans, whose arrogance you cannot escape by obedience and self-restraint. ... To plunder, butcher, steal, these things they misname empire: they make a desolation and they call it peace.

CALGACUS AT THE BATTLE OF MONS GRAUPIUS, ACCORDING TO TACITUS, AGRICOLA (TRANS. M. HUTTON, 1914)

279

OPPOSITE **A fine Roman mosaic** *from Pompeii with a seafood theme, well-preserved after the eruption. Romans ate enormous quantities of seafood and flavoured almost everything they cooked with garum, a rich sauce made by fermenting fish. As a result seafood was a popular subject for the mosaics that decorated the dining room floors of well-to-do Roman houses. The patterns of mosaic pavements were created using tesserae, pieces of coloured stone or tile that had been cut into small squares. The art developed in the 3rd century BC and reached its peak in the medieval Byzantine empire.*

passing an act of *damnatio memoriae* (condemnation of memory) by which his name was to be erased from public inscriptions and images of him were to be destroyed.

Old and childless, Nerva was an experienced administrator but his lack of military experience made it impossible for him to establish his authority over the army. Domitian had been popular in the army and in October 97 the Praetorian Guard held Nerva hostage until he agreed to order the execution of Domitian's murderers. After this humiliation, Nerva realized that his position was untenable without the support of a colleague who could command the loyalty of the army. After some deliberation, Nerva adopted 45-year-old Marcus Ulpius Trajanus (Trajan), a respected and able administrator and soldier, as his son and heir. On New Year's Day 98 Nerva suffered a stroke: when he died four weeks later Trajan succeeded to the throne without opposition. Born in Spain, Trajan (r. 98–117) was the first provincial to become Roman emperor. Nerva's decision to adopt an adult heir with proven abilities was nothing but a short-term expedient to keep him in power, but the practice was continued by the next five emperors, providing Rome with almost a century of unparalleled political stability.

THE DACIAN WARS ✦ Trajan proved to be a strong ruler but he was no tyrant. He won immediate popularity with the people with generous cash handouts and spectacular entertainments. He pursued policies to support agriculture, stimulate trade and provide employment with building projects. Ostia, the port of Rome, was given a new all-weather harbour – before this, Rome's corn supply, which was imported by sea mainly from North Africa and Egypt, was easily disrupted if bad weather prevented ships from docking. Rome itself was given a fine new market. People wrongly imprisoned by Domitian were freed and confiscated property was returned to their original owners. A grateful Senate awarded Trajan the title *optimus princeps*, the best emperor.

Abroad, Trajan pursued an aggressive policy of expansion by conquest. Trajan's first major war was the conquest of

WISE AFTER THE EVENT

[Domitian] *used to say that the lot of emperors was most unfortunate, since when they discovered a conspiracy, no one believed them unless they had been murdered.*

SUETONIUS, *LIFE OF DOMITIAN* (1914 TRANSLATION)

BELOW **Hadrian's Wall** *cuts across the breadth of northern England, extending 70 miles from the Irish Sea in the west to the North Sea in the east. Hadrian built the wall in 122–3 to protect the Roman province of Britannia from the unconquered British tribes to the north. For much of its length the wall follows the crest of a steep escarpment, giving good views to the north.*

Dacia, a region of eastern Europe approximating to modern Romania. Raids across the Danube frontier by the Dacian king Decebalus provoked a punitive expedition by the emperor Domitian in 87. Decebalus, a master of ambushes, defeated Domitian's expedition as well as a second Roman invasion the following year. Domitian was forced to accept an unfavourable peace deal, which gave Decebalus large financial subsidies, craftsmen and supplies of weapons in return for his nominal submission.

Decebalus escaped but committed suicide to avoid capture when cornered by Roman cavalry.

Decebalus had no intention of keeping the peace. When he allied with hostile German tribes in 101, Trajan decided to invade Dacia in force. The first permanent bridge across the Danube was built, near the Iron Gates, to make supplying the invading legions faster and easier. After Trajan won a decisive victory at Tapae in 102 Decebalus submitted and for a few years the border was quiet. However, Decebalus began crossing the Danube to raid Roman settlements so Trajan invaded Dacia again, in 105. This time his aim was outright conquest, which would give Rome control of Dacia's gold mines. Trajan captured the Dacians' strongholds one by one until he reached Sarmizegetusa, Decebalus' strongly fortified mountain-top capital, in summer 106. The city fell after a traitor helped the Romans find and destroy its underground water supply pipes. Decebalus escaped but committed suicide to avoid capture when cornered by Roman cavalry. By the year's end the last Dacian resistance was crushed. Decebalus' treasure, consisting of 182 tons of gold and 365 tons of silver, was found hidden in a river, repaying the costs of conquest several times over.

113–17

THE PARTHIAN WAR ✦ After Mark Antony's disastrous expedition in 33 BC, peaceful relations between Rome and Parthia were broken only by two inconclusive wars over spheres of influence in Armenia, in 36 and 58–63. War broke out again in 113 when the Parthian king Osroes tried to turn Armenia into a Parthian puppet state by installing his brother Parthamasiris as king. In 114 Trajan invaded and occupied Armenia and in 115 he used it as his base to begin the conquest of Mesopotamia, one of the richest provinces of the Parthian empire and home to their capital, Ctesiphon. In 116 Trajan captured Ctesiphon and led a fleet down the Euphrates to the Persian Gulf. Osroes was deposed and a puppet ruler, Parthamaspates, was imposed on Parthia.

Trajan's success was transitory. While he was still at the Persian Gulf, dreaming of recreating the empire of Alexander the Great, rebellions broke out throughout Mesopotamia: at the same time a serious Jewish rebellion broke out in Palestine. Trajan was forced to retreat and though he managed to restore Roman control in Mesopotamia, the situation remained very precarious. Now in his mid-60s, Trajan's health began to fail him and early in 117 he decided to return to Italy. Trajan got no further than Selinus in Cilicia (now southern Turkey) where he died suddenly on 8 August, shortly after formally adopting Hadrian (r. 117–38), another Spaniard, as his son and heir. Hadrian's first act as emperor was to give up all of Trajan's Parthian conquests apart from the strategically important city of Edessa (now Şanliurfa, Turkey), believing them to be undefendable. Deprived of Roman support, Parthamaspates was quickly overthrown and Osroes returned to power.

122–3

THE LIMITS OF EMPIRE ✦ With Trajan's death, the great days of Roman expansion came to an end. Hadrian's reign was mostly peaceful, the only serious war being the suppression of a Jewish revolt under the messianic leader Simon bar Kochba in 133–5. Hadrian put enormous resources into strengthening the defences of the empire's northern borders: his most famous frontier system was the 70-mile (113-km) long wall, which still bears his name, which he ordered to be built 'to separate the Romans from the barbarians'. This finally defined the northern border of the Roman province of Britannia and for most of the next 300 years marked the outer limits of Roman power. Hadrian's policies gave the empire a long period of peace, which continued through the reign of his chosen successor Antoninus Pius (r. 138–61) and beyond. To later generations this seemed like a golden age for humanity.

ABOVE **A souvenir of Hadrian's Wall.** *A minor industry developed in Britain making souvenirs of Hadrian's wall for Roman soldiers to take home with them at the end of their postings there. The Rudge Cup, actually a bronze bowl, which was found at a ruined Roman villa in southern England in 1725, is decorated with a stylized depiction of the 70-mile-long wall which protected the Roman province of Britain from the unconquered tribes to the north. In a strip around the rim are the names of five forts at the western end of the wall, including Camboglans (modern Castlesteads) and Banna (modern Birdoswald).*

All of Rome's blood-soaked conquests seemed to be justified by the peace and prosperity which it had brought to the known world. However, the end of imperial expansion had serious long-term consequences. In pre-industrial societies agriculture was the primary source of wealth. Technological innovations which could increase the productivity of agriculture were slow to come, so the easiest way for a society to increase its resources was to conquer new territory. Now that it had reached the limits of practical expansion, the Roman empire was going to have to learn to live on a budget that was essentially fixed. This was going to work only so long as its commitments did not increase.

161–79

END OF THE PAX ROMANA ✦ Antoninus Pius was succeeded on his death by his adopted sons Marcus Aurelius (r. 161–80) and Lucius Verus (r. 161–9). It was the first time that two emperors had jointly ruled the Roman empire. Marcus held more *auctoritas* ('authority') than Lucius and was the senior emperor. From the very beginning, theirs was a reign troubled by foreign wars. The Parthian king Vologases IV saw Antoninus' death as an opportunity to invade Armenia and install a member of his own family on the throne. Parthian rule in Armenia was unacceptable to the Romans and war immediately broke out. Wars threatened too in Britain and Germany. Marcus sent Lucius to take command of the war against Parthia. Five years of tough campaigning brought decisive victory in 166 but Lucius' returning army brought more than war booty with them. In the later stages of the campaign an epidemic, believed to be smallpox, broke out in the Roman army. As the soldiers returned to their home bases after the war, they spread the epidemic to all parts of the empire. In some areas up to a third of the population died: its most illustrious victim was Lucius Verus. The loss of population had a severe effect on agricultural production for years afterwards and the army found it difficult to find enough recruits when a major war broke out with the German Marcomanni tribe on the Danube frontier in 167.

THE BEST OF TIMES

If a man were called to fix the period in the history of the world during which the condition of the human race was most happy and prosperous, he would without hesitation name that which elapsed from the death of Domitian [AD 96] *to the accession of Commodus* [180].

EDWARD GIBBON, *THE DECLINE AND FALL OF THE ROMAN EMPIRE* (1776–88)

OPPOSITE **Mass execution.** *A brutal expression of imperial authority, this scene from the column of Marcus Aurelius depicts the execution of German nobles captured in AD 172 or 173 during the emperor's Marcomannic Wars. Once they had been deprived of their leaders, the defeated Germans were resettled on lands abandoned because of the high mortality during a plague epidemic which broke out in AD 166. The 130-foot-tall column, which was inspired by Trajan's Column, was begun shortly before Marcus Aurelius' death in AD 180 and was completed by 193.*

Since defeating the Romans in Augustus' time, the Germans had been getting steadily stronger and better organized. Many of the smaller tribes had joined together in confederations, the better to defend themselves or wage war against their neighbours. Roman border provinces had prospered by supplying food, weapons, pottery and entertainment to their large military garrisons. The Germans too prospered by trading with the Roman army, or by serving as mercenaries in auxiliary regiments. However, the weakening of the border defences during the Parthian War offered the Germans an opportunity to take Roman wealth by raiding. These raids were successfully contained until, in 167, the Marcomanni, in confederation with the Quadi, Langobardi, Vandals and other tribes, invaded and crossed the Alps, advancing as far as Aquileia in northern Italy before they were stopped.

Marcus Aurelius made Carnuntum, on the Danube in present-day Austria, his main base for campaigning against the Germans. By 176

Five years of tough campaigning brought decisive victory in 166 but Lucius' returning army brought more than war booty with them. As the soldiers returned, they spread an epidemic, believed to be smallpox, to all parts of the empire.

ABOVE **The Triumph of Marcus Aurelius** by Giovanni Domenico Tiepolo (1727–1804) depicts a triumph celebrated by the emperor after his victory over Parthia in AD 166. This image of Marcus Aurelius as a martial ruler is out of fashion today. The popularity of his wistful and compassionate reflections on Stoic philosophy, Meditations, in the 19th century helped create a new image of Marcus Aurelius as a careworn philosopher-emperor. This image has been reinforced in modern times by his sympathetic portrayal in films such as The Fall of the Roman Empire (1964) and Gladiator (2000).

the Marcomanni had been defeated and large numbers were forced to resettle in the empire, on lands left untilled because of the population decline caused by the plague. While Marcus was busy fighting the Marcomanni, other tribes along almost the whole length of the northern frontier started raiding the empire. It took Marcus most of the remainder of his reign to finally secure the frontier. Despite his success, German power was far from broken and their numbers were growing constantly. From now on, German pressure on the empire's frontiers was to be continuous.

180

DEATH OF A PHILOSOPHER EMPEROR ✦ Marcus Aurelius had no military experience when he became emperor and he probably surprised himself when it turned out that he was a good soldier. Marcus never came to enjoy war, however, and he longed to have the leisure to return to his main interest, the study of philosophy. A Stoic, Marcus took comfort from philosophy through the difficult years of campaigning and kept with him a notebook, known as the *Meditations*, in which he recorded his own reflections on the mysteries of life and death. Marcus was also devoted to his family, so much so that this deeply sensitive and moral man was apparently blind to the all too obvious failings of his son Commodus. Rather than follow the practice of his predecessors and adopt as heir a man of proven ability, Marcus named Commodus as his successor in 176 and he succeeded without opposition when Marcus died while preparing for a new expedition on the Danube frontier in 180. Commodus proved to be one of the worst tyrants in Roman history and Marcus has ever since been much criticized for allowing him to succeed. However, there was strong support in the army for the hereditary principle and in such troubled times Marcus probably believed that this was the best way to ensure political stability.

RIGHT **Marble bust of the empress** *Faustina the Younger, the wife for 30 years of the emperor Marcus Aurelius. Faustina accompanied her husband on his military campaigns and for that was revered by the army. Marcus was unmoved by accusations against her of adultery, murder and other crimes, and remained devoted to Faustina until her death, aged around 45–50, in camp in Anatolia in AD 175.*

DECLINE AND FALL

AD 180–476

In the 3rd century the Roman empire came close to collapse under the impact of German and Persian invasions, economic crisis, and political instability and civil war. The empire that survived by the end of the century had been transformed into a military state which sought to control almost every aspect of its citizens' lives.

The better to manage the threats to the frontiers, it became normal to divide the empire into eastern and western halves, each under its own emperor. This division became permanent after 395. A cultural and spiritual transformation followed close behind the political transformation after the legalization of Christianity by Constantine the Great in 313. In the 5th century, the empire's northern frontier finally cracked and a succession of migrating Germanic tribes moved in, carving out their own kingdoms. In 410 Rome itself was sacked by the Visigoths. The western empire was reduced to little more than Italy, and when the last emperor was deposed in 476 it too came under Germanic rule.

193

THE YEAR OF THE FIVE EMPERORS ✦ Commodus' reign brought a welcome respite after the near constant warfare of Marcus Aurelius' reign: the British, Rhine, Danube and North African frontiers all suffered from barbarian plundering raids but there were no major wars. The peaceful conditions allowed Commodus to leave the day-to-day business of government in the hands of favourites and indulge himself in a thoroughly debauched lifestyle: his main interests were horse racing and chariot racing, and gladiatorial combats, in which he often took part. The many spectacular shows he staged made Commodus popular with the Roman people but the senatorial class hated him for excluding them from government. Almost from the beginning of his reign, Commodus faced conspiracies to overthrow him. Fearing for his life, Commodus spent most of his time living on family estates outside Rome.

In spring 190 Rome suffered from a serious food shortage, for which Commodus' chief minister Cleander got the blame. Faced with rioting in the streets, Commodus executed Cleander and took up the reins of government in person. He soon began

PREVIOUS PAGES **Colossal bronze head** *of the emperor Constantine the Great in the Capitoline museum, Rome. Constantine's legalization of Christianity in 313 paved the way for a transformation of Roman art, architecture and literary culture that began the transition from the ancient world to the Middle Ages.*

OPPOSITE **The emperor Commodus** *dressed as Hercules in a lion skin and carrying a club. Commodus was the first emperor to be 'born in the purple', that is, while his father was a reigning emperor. The murder of the notoriously megalomaniac emperor in 193 without an obvious successor caused a brief civil war between five rival claimants.*

to show megalomaniac tendencies, identifying himself with the demi-god Hercules and renaming Rome Colonia Commodiana after himself. He disgusted the Roman people by his antics in the arena, which included killing cripples and disabled veteran soldiers. At the end of December 192, conspirators, including his mistress Marcia, sent Commodus' wrestling trainer to strangle him while he bathed.

On New Year's Day 193 Pertinax was proclaimed emperor by the Praetorian Guard. He was an experienced soldier and administrator with a reputation as a disciplinarian. The Praetorians expected Pertinax to reward them generously for their support and when he instead tried to impose stricter military discipline on them, the Praetorians murdered him after a reign of only three months. Pertinax's successor Didius Julianus was a wealthy senator who won the throne by outbidding his rivals in an auction held by the Praetorians. The manner of Julianus' succession was greeted with outrage by the people of Rome, who threw stones at him and jeered whenever he appeared in public.

Reports of the public anger in Rome encouraged three generals to proclaim themselves emperor: Septimius Severus on the Danube frontier, Pescennius Niger in Syria and Clodius Albinus in Britain. Severus had the shortest distance to march; he took Rome at the beginning of June and executed Julianus. Severus immediately headed east and defeated Niger in March 194 on the same battlefield at Issus where Alexander the Great had defeated the Persians in 333 BC. Niger was captured and executed shortly afterwards. Albinus survived until February 197 when he committed suicide after being defeated by Severus near Lugdunum (Lyon) in Gaul.

211

FRATRICIDE ✦ Severus' competent rule and successful military campaigns in Britain and Parthia seemed to promise a return to stable dynastic rule and secure borders. He appointed his two sons, Caracalla and Geta, as his joint successors and when he died in February 211 at the legionary fortress of Eboracum (York) in Britain he advised his sons, on his deathbed, to 'stick together, pay the soldiers, and forget the rest'. It was good advice but they did not take it. Both aspired to hold power alone and relations between them were hostile. At a reconciliation meeting arranged by their mother in December that year, Caracalla had Geta murdered by Praetorian guardsmen and then ordered the Senate to pronounce a *damnatio memoriae* against him, erasing his image from all coins, portraits and statues.

> ## CITIZENSHIP FOR ALL
>
> *Caracalla made all the people in his empire Roman citizens; nominally he was honouring them, but his real purpose was to increase his revenues.*
>
> CASSIUS DIO (1927 TRANSLATION)

212

CITIZENSHIP FOR ALL ✦ Throughout the history of Roman expansion, citizenship had been gradually extended to conquered peoples as a reward for loyalty, and military or political service, and to encourage them to assimilate Roman ways. By the 2nd century AD most provincials were beginning to feel as Roman as the people of Rome itself, while provincial birth was no longer an obstacle to holding the highest offices of state, including the emperorship itself. Caracalla brought this process of Romanization to its final conclusion in 212 when he issued an edict granting full Roman citizenship to all free men in the empire. All free women in the empire were given the same rights as Roman women. As cynical contemporaries were quick to point out, provincials, as well as having fewer rights than full citizens, were also exempt from many taxes. While Caracalla was elevating the legal status of the provincials, he was at the same time expanding the empire's tax base. This act apart, Caracalla's reign was one of undistinguished tyranny: he was murdered in 217 while preparing a campaign against Parthia and the empire was plunged once more into political chaos as emperors began to come and go in rapid succession.

OPPOSITE **Unhappy families.** *A family portrait of the emperor Septimius Severus, his wife Julia Domna, and their sons Caracalla and Geta. Geta's portrait has been deliberately defaced. After their father's death, Caracalla murdered Geta and ordered the Senate to pronounce a* damnatio memoriae *to erase any trace of his existence.*

OVERLEAF **Thomas Couture's painting** The Romans in the Decadence of the Empire *(1847) brilliantly expresses the belief, common in the 19th century, that the decline of the Roman empire was the result of moral collapse. In fact, Roman writers of all periods seem to have harboured the gloomy belief that their morals were going from bad to worse: there is no evidence that Romans of the late empire were any more or less decadent than those of any other period.*

218–84

AN EMPIRE IN CRISIS ✦ The 65 years following the murder of Caracalla were among the most disastrous in Roman history. German pressure on the northern frontiers was unrelenting and to this was added a new and formidable threat in east when the Persians overthrew their Parthian overlords in 224–6. The new and energetic Sasanian dynasty was ambitious to recreate the Achaemenid empire of Cyrus the Great and Darius and it inflicted a series of humiliating defeats on the Romans, culminating in 260, when the emperor Valerian was captured at Edessa.

In these conditions of almost continual war, the legions came to dominate the political life of the empire, with destabilizing results. The emperor had to be first and foremost a good soldier who could command the support of the army. But the legions had learned that they had the power to make and unmake emperors and an emperor who was a poor soldier would not rule for long. Rival candidates for the throne, proclaimed by different legions, fought each other for control of the empire, while the frontiers were left denuded of troops and exposed to German or Persian attack. Even when one claimant emerged supreme for a time, he had to be ever watchful of his more successful and popular generals in case they should take the opportunity presented by a military crisis to attempt to seize power. This created an atmosphere of mutual distrust, so a general who felt the eye of imperial suspicion upon him often felt forced to rebel as the only means of self-defence against a treason charge and inevitable execution. Of the 29 emperors who were recognized by the Senate in this period, all but one died by violence (the not so lucky exception died of plague), while the ambitions of dozens of pretenders ended in their execution

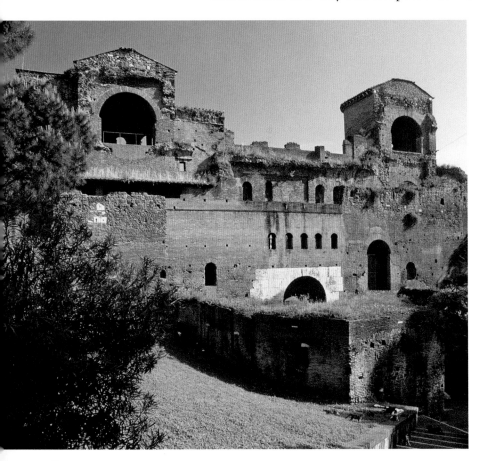

ABOVE **The Porta Asinaria,** *a gateway in Rome's Aurelian Walls, constructed between 271 and 275. By the 3rd century Rome had long outgrown its defensive walls built during the Republican period but in the years of the Pax Romana, with no credible threat to Rome's security, there seemed no point in replacing* them. *Frequent barbarian invasions in the 3rd century reawakened Roman fear of a repeat of the Gallic sack of 390 BC. The emperor Aurelian (r. 270–75), therefore, commissioned this new 12-mile-long circuit of walls, now named after him, to enclose almost all of Rome's urban area.*

ABOVE **The Sasanian court** *depicted in a 15th-century illuminated copy of the Shanameh, an epic history of the Persian kings by the poet Firdawsi (c. 940–1020). The Sasanians were far more aggressive than the Parthian dynasty they overthrew in 224–6. The Sasanians consciously tried to recreate the Persian empire of Cyrus the Great and Darius I and several* *times overran large parts of the eastern Roman empire. The eastern Roman (Byzantine) emperor Heraclius finally inflicted a crushing defeat on them in 628, ending a 26-year-long war that brought both empires to their knees. The Sasanians were so weakened by their defeat that they were easily conquered by the newly Islamized Arabs in 637.*

or assassination. The emperor Gallienus alone defeated 18 usurpers in his nine-year reign (259–68) only to be murdered at the end by his officers. At the same time, constant attempts by the emperors to buy the loyalty of the soldiers created a financial crisis. To raise extra revenue the emperors progressively debased the coinage but this led in turn to disastrous inflation. Depopulation caused by repeated plagues added to the empire's economic woes.

These triple stresses of civil war, invasion and economic crisis brought the empire close to collapse during the 260s. After Valerian's death, Odenathus, the client ruler of Palmyra in Syria, seized control of the empire's eastern provinces. The general Postumus seized Gaul, Spain and Britain and declared them an independent empire. The Goths overran Dacia and plundered the Balkans. Saxon pirates raided Britain. It was the unlucky emperor Gallienus who began to turn the empire around by radically reforming the army. During the imperial peace of the 1st and 2nd centuries, the armies had become largely static garrisons stationed on the fortified frontiers. This left the empire without defence in depth. Once invaders broke through the frontier defences, they were free to roam at will on the empire's extensive road system. Gallienus' solution was to create highly mobile field armies, with strong cavalry elements that could operate independently of the legions, most of which were broken up into smaller, more flexible, units. He also ended the system which reserved the highest commands for members of the aristocracy, promoting instead soldiers of proven talent such as Traianus Mucianus, a Thracian who had joined up as an ordinary infantryman and rose to the rank of general. These reforms allowed Gallienus' successors to restore the territorial integrity of the empire (though Dacia was abandoned to the Goths) but its internal stability showed no signs of improving. When the emperor Carus was murdered after a reign of only a year, another succession struggle broke out.

> *Of the 29 emperors who were recognized by the Senate in this period, all but one died by violence (the not so lucky exception died of plague).*

284–305

A NEW BEGINNING ✦ Carus' eventual successor, Diocletian (r. 284–305), may have seemed to be just another power-hungry general but his reign was the most important in Roman history since Augustus'. Not the least of his achievements was that he became the first emperor to die in old age of natural causes for nearly a century.

Diocletian faced three major tasks: restoring stability and prestige to the imperial office; securing the empire's frontiers; and reviving the economy. He was not entirely successful in any of them but his reforms did succeed in giving the empire a new lease of life. Diocletian tackled the first problem by introducing a system known as the tetrarchy (rule of four). Diocletian recognized that the empire was too large, and its problems too numerous, to be adequately governed by one emperor so he appointed another general, Maximian, as equal co-ruler with the title Augustus, along with two junior colleagues, Constantius and Galerius, with the title Caesar. Diocletian's idea was that when he and Maximian died or retired, Constantius and Galerius would replace them as Augusti and appoint two new Caesars, so ensuring smooth successions. The empire was divided into four areas of military responsibility. Diocletian ruled the east from Nicomedia (İzmit, Turkey) and his Caesar Galerius ruled the Balkans from Sirmium (Belgrade); Maximian ruled Italy, Spain and Africa from Mediolanum (Milan) and his Caesar Constantius ruled Gaul and Britain from Augusta Trevorum (Trier, Germany). Dividing power in this way meant that threats to the frontiers could be responded to more quickly and it also prevented the frontier armies proclaiming their own candidates for the throne: over the course of the next century it became the normal practice. Rome, too remote from the frontiers to be a useful base, was abandoned by the emperors. Diocletian, who was born in the Balkans, had been emperor for 20 years before he ever visited the city.

Augustus veiled the monarchical nature of imperial rule with the pretence that he was *princeps*, merely the first citizen. Diocletian abandoned this title (he preferred *dominus*, 'lord') and turned the empire into an undisguised absolute monarchy. The emperor's authority came not from the Senate as representative of the Roman people but directly from the high god Jupiter. There was no need for an emperor to seek the Senate's approval or consult it about anything: it became little more than Rome's city council. Anyone who refused to sacrifice to the state gods was deemed an enemy of the state and Christians were brutally persecuted. To restore respect to the imperial office, Diocletian introduced elaborate court ritual. Emperors appeared in public wearing jewelled diadems and slippers and robed in purple and gold silk. Anyone seeking an audience with the emperor was expected to prostrate themselves before him and kiss the hem of his robe.

Diocletian increased the size of the army from 300,000 to over 400,000 and raised taxes to pay for it. The tetrarchs were all good soldiers and vigorous campaigning secured peace on all the empire's borders. Price controls were introduced to control inflation but they were only partly

RIGHT **Coin bearing a portrait of the emperor Diocletian** *whose root-and-branch reform of the Roman empire's government and military institutions restored stability and security after years of invasions, civil wars, and economic problems. Diocletian began the practice of dividing the empire into eastern and western halves, each with their own emperor.*

299

effective as they simply drove many goods off the market. The empire's population had declined as a result of the wars and plagues of the 3rd century so, to insure against labour shortages, Diocletian made many key occupations, including bakers, shippers, farmers and soldiers, into hereditary obligations. A huge bureaucracy was created to manage the economy and the tax system.

In 305 Diocletian abdicated and retired to a heavily fortified palace at Split in Croatia. Maximian reluctantly followed suit. As Diocletian had planned, Galerius became the new Augustus in the east and Constantius the Augustus in the west. Two relative unknowns, Maximinus and Severus, were appointed as the new Caesars. It was a poor choice because it was well known that Maximian's son Maxentius, and Constantius' son Constantine, both had political ambitions.

306–12

THE RISE OF CONSTANTINE ✦ Diocletian's system of succession very quickly broke down. There was a strong preference in the army for hereditary succession and when Constantius died at Eboracum in July 306 his troops immediately proclaimed Constantine (r. 306–37) as the new Augustus. Galerius meanwhile had promoted the Caesar Severus as the new Augustus in the west. To avoid war, Galerius admitted Constantine to the tetrarchy as the new Caesar to fill the vacancy left by Severus' promotion. In 307 Maxentius seized control of Rome with the backing of the Praetorian Guard, hoping for the same recognition won by Constantine. Galerius refused but when he sent Severus to march on Rome, Maximian decided to come out of retirement and support his son as co-ruler.

The first great Christian churches were built at Constantine's expense, including the first basilica of St Peter on Vatican Hill, the Church of the Holy Sepulchre in Jerusalem, and the Church of the Nativity in Bethlehem.

Maximian still enjoyed strong support in the army and when his men began to desert, Severus surrendered and was later executed. Galerius tried to persuade Diocletian to return to office: he refused but persuaded Maximian to abdicate again. Unfortunately, Maximian did not know when to give up. He tried to seize power again in 310 but was captured by Constantine and forced to commit suicide.

To replace Severus, Galerius appointed his friend Licinius as the new Augustus in the west, refusing the title to his own Caesar, Maximinus. Maximinus responded by promoting himself to Augustus. Constantine had already done so. By 310, therefore, there were five Augusti ruling the empire. Galerius' death in 311 simplified this complicated situation. Then in October 312 Constantine advanced on Rome and defeated Maxentius at the Battle of the Milvian Bridge. Maxentius drowned when a bridge of boats he had built across the Tiber collapsed under the weight of his fleeing soldiers. Maximinus' death the next summer, probably by poison after he had been defeated by Licinius, left the empire divided between just two Augusti, Constantine in the west and Licinius in the east. In the same year, Diocletian died peacefully in his palace, aged 66.

313

THE TRIUMPH OF CHRISTIANITY ✦ Constantine believed that he owed his against-the-odds victory over Maxentius to the support of the Christian God. According to the story that the emperor later told to the Christian historian Eusebius, on the march to Rome Constantine experienced a vision. Looking up into the sky he saw a cross of light over the sun together with the Greek words *En touto níka*, 'through this sign you shall conquer'. Constantine did not understand the meaning of the vision until the following night when Christ appeared to him in a dream and told him to use the sign against his enemies. Because of this Constantine ordered his soldiers to paint the Christian Chi-Rho symbol on their shields before they went into battle against Maxentius. Constantine showed his gratitude to God in 313 when he issued the Edict of Milan, which granted toleration to Christians in the Roman empire and freed them from the threat of persecution. He persuaded Licinius, who was still a pagan, to issue a similar edict in the east.

PREVIOUS PAGES **Big game hunt.** *Detail of a late 3rd-century mosaic at the enormous Villa Romana del Casale at Piazza Armerina, Sicily, showing a big game hunt in North Africa to capture wild animals, including gazelles and ostriches, to be killed in mock hunts in the Roman arena. The villa the mosaics were found in belonged to Diocletian's co-emperor Maximian.*

OPPOSITE **The head from a colossal marble statue of Constantine the Great.** *Constantine was awarded his epithet 'the Great' by Christian writers who were grateful to him for legalizing their religion in 313 and for the imperial patronage that followed. In doing so, Constantine set Christianity on the road to becoming one of the great world religions.*

ABOVE **Constantine's victory over Maxentius** *at the Battle of Milvian Bridge in 313, depicted here in a fresco by the Italian artist Raphael (1483–1520), won him control of the western Roman empire. Because the battle was followed by the Edict*

four depicting incidents from the life of Constantine commissioned by Pope Julius II in 1508–9 for the Hall of Constantine in the new Vatican palace in Rome. The fresco shows the critical moment of the battle, when Maxentius' retreating troops caused

Constantine, in fact, went much further than tolerating Christianity: he actively promoted it. The first great Christian churches were built at Constantine's expense, including the first basilica of St Peter on Vatican Hill, the Church of the Holy Sepulchre in Jerusalem, and the Church of the Nativity in Bethlehem on the traditional site of Christ's birth. Pagan Roman emperors traditionally had religious duties, performing sacrifices to the state gods; Constantine saw his role no differently and soon became involved in trying to resolve the bitter theological disputes that split the church. To this end he called the first general council of the church to meet at Nicaea in 325. Thanks to Constantine's patronage, Christianity began its transformation from a minority religion of the urban poor and commercial classes to the state religion of the Roman empire.

324

THE NEW ROME ✦ Constantine's ambition was to be sole ruler of the Roman empire, and Licinius' revocation of the edict of toleration for Christians provided Constantine with the ideal pretext to march east and overthrow him. Christians were far more numerous in the Greek-dominated east than in the still overwhelmingly pagan west and Constantine found plenty of support. Following Licinius' defeat and execution in 324, Constantine decided to mark his break with Rome's pagan past by founding a new eastern capital for the empire, named Constantinople after himself, on the site of the ancient Greek colony of Byzantium on the Bosphorus straits. Constantine's choice of site was an inspired one. Constantinople (Istanbul, Turkey) was a natural stronghold. Situated on a peninsula it was surrounded by sea on three sides and the landward approaches were strongly fortified. The city was also at a crossroads of major sea and land routes, making it a natural commercial and communications centre. While Rome's population was now in decline, settlers flooded into Constantinople, attracted by its commercial and administrative opportunities, official financial incentives and offers of free bread for the poor.

361–3

PAGAN REACTION ✦ Thanks to continued imperial patronage by Constantine's successors, Christianity steadily increased its influence in the Roman empire. However, those who remained loyal to paganism feared that abandoning the traditional gods, who had served Rome so well in the past, would bring disaster to the empire. One of these was the emperor Julian (r. 355–63). As a member of the imperial family, Julian had been brought up a Christian but he secretly converted to paganism while studying philosophy in Greece. When Constantine died in 337, the empire was divided between his three sons, who became joint Augusti. By 350 only the youngest, Constantius II, was still alive. When Constantius appointed Julian as his Caesar in 355 Julian continued to hide his true beliefs, declaring himself publicly as a pagan only when he became sole Augustus on Constantius' death in 361.

Julian began an ambitious plan to restore paganism. Recognizing the organizational strength of the Christian church, he attempted to set up a pagan church with a regular priesthood. Pagan priests would imitate the Christian clergy by organizing charity for the poor and encouraging wealthy pagans to make donations.

OPPOSITE *The Emblem of Christ Appearing to Constantine* by the Flemish painter Peter Paul Rubens (1577–1640) depicts the moment of Constantine's conversion to Christianity when he saw a cross of light over the sun and the words 'through this sign you shall conquer'. As Constantine later told it to the Christian historian Eusebius, he did not understand the significance of what he had seen until, in a dream the following night, a young man (Christ) appeared to him and told him to make a copy of the sign as protection against his enemies' attacks. Constantine did as he was told and as a result ascribed his victory over his rival Maxentius to the intervention of the Christian God.

To set an example, Julian made food available from imperial stores. He revoked all the financial and judicial privileges Constantine had granted the church. By withdrawing legislation against heresy, Julian cynically ensured that the church was soon split by acrimonious theological disputes about the nature of Christ. It is not clear how successful Julian's attempt to restore paganism might have been given time. In 363 Julian led a campaign against the Persians during which he was fatally injured in a skirmish, possibly by a resentful Christian in his own army. Julian's successor Jovian (r. 363–4), hastily chosen by the army, was a Christian, as would be all his successors, and the Christianization of the Roman empire resumed its course.

376

GOTHS ALLOWED TO SETTLE IN THE ROMAN EMPIRE ✦ Around 370 a terrifying new force arrived in eastern Europe, throwing the German tribes into chaos and beginning a train of events that led to the eventual collapse of the Roman empire. This new force was the Huns, a Turkic nomad people from the Eurasian steppes. The most powerful of the German peoples at this time were the Goths. They were divided into two branches, the western Visigoths, who settled in Dacia after driving the Romans out in the 3rd century, and the eastern Ostrogoths, who ruled a vast kingdom in Ukraine. The Romans were, at first, pleased when they learned that the Ostrogoths had been crushingly defeated and conquered by the Huns. Their pleasure was short-lived for the defeat of Ostrogoths created a refugee problem for the Romans that they could not handle.

Rather than submit to the Huns, the Visigoths, the western branch of the Goths, decided to abandon their lands and seek asylum in the Roman empire. In the late summer of 376 around 200,000 Visigoths set up camp on the north bank of the Danube while their leaders negotiated terms for entry with the Romans. The emperor Valens (r. 364–78), who ruled the east, had already committed most of his forces to a war against Persia and he knew that he could not prevent the Visigoths from entering by force if they chose to try. Valens therefore tried to put a positive gloss on the situation. Population decline was having a severe economic impact and leaving the army short of recruits. This allowed Valens to present the admission of the Visigoths as an opportunity to strengthen the empire. They would be settled on vacant land in the Balkans, bring uncultivated land back into production, provide recruits for the army and pay taxes. Thousands of defeated Germans had been successfully settled

OPPOSITE **A 13th-century Byzantine painting** *from Ohrid in Macedonia of St Mercurius, a Christian soldier in the Roman army who was martyred during a persecution of Christians by the emperor Decius in 250. The last persecution of Christians took place under the emperor Diocletian. By the end of the 4th century it was the pagans' turn to be persecuted, their practices banned and their temples destroyed or taken over for use as churches. However, pagans were never subjected to the violence meted out to Christians under the pagan emperors.*

ROMANS AND BARBARIANS

The transition from Roman to Germanic rule in the western empire was a surprisingly orderly process.

The Romans agreed to settle the Germanic tribes as 'federates', that is, allies of the empire. This meant that even though they had their leaders, they were legally subjects of the empire.

Federates were settled in accordance with laws introduced by the eastern emperor Theodosius II (r. 408–50). They were billeted on landowners, whose estates were divided into thirds for sharing; the landowner got first choice of the thirds, the federates got second choice, and landowner kept the final third. Only the Vandals, who conquered their lands around Carthage outright and did not enter a federate agreement, went in for the complete expropriation of estates. Recognizing the new political realities, Roman landowners accepted the newcomers with reasonably good grace. The Roman writer Sidonius Apollinaris, who had Burgundians billeted on his Auvergne estate, complained of the stench of the rancid butter which they used as hair gel, but he also left an admiring description of his encounter with a Frankish prince. The continuity of Roman administrative institutions was encouraged by the practice of allocating the tax revenues of a province to the upkeep of federates settled in it.

As a minority among the native population, the Germans felt vulnerable to assimilation and loss of identity. To prevent this, the Germans continued to live by their own laws, while Romans under their rule continued to live by Roman law. They forbade intermarriage between Germans and Romans. Religion was a major obstacle to assimilation. Most Germans converted to Arianism, a form of Christianity Romans regarded as heretical. Arianism became both a badge of Germanic identity, creating a religious gulf between them and their Roman subjects, and a political statement. The emperors claimed sovereignty over the church, so becoming an Orthodox Catholic was seen as a sign of submission to Rome.

in the empire over the previous 200 years but the Romans had always been in complete control. Valens' decision was a dangerous one because the Visigoths had not been defeated by Roman arms, because their leadership was intact, and because he did not have the troops to control the Visigoths if things went wrong.

378

BATTLE OF ADRIANOPLE ✦ The

resettlement of the Visigoths was catastrophically mishandled by corrupt officials and early in 377 the Visigoths rebelled and went on a plundering spree. In the general disorder other bands of Germans crossed the Danube and joined in. In spring 378 Valens made peace with Persia and returned to Constantinople to gather forces for a campaign to subdue the Visigoths. Valens' advisers urged him to wait for the arrival of reinforcements with the western emperor Gratian (r. 375–83). However, Valens did not want to share the glory of victory with anyone else and in August he marched against the Visigoths, who were now camped near Adrianople (Edirne, Turkey). Valens was in such a hurry to deal with the Visigoths before Gratian arrived that he failed to carry out proper reconnaissance and he was unaware that their cavalry was not in the camp.

Valens tried to negotiate the Visigoths' surrender but general battle broke out when some Roman soldiers launched an unauthorized attack on the camp. The battle went the Romans' way until the Visigothic cavalry unexpectedly returned and attacked them from the rear. The Romans were routed with heavy casualties and Valens was killed. For four years the Visigoths ravaged the Balkans until they were pacified by Valens' successor Theodosius I (r. 379–95). The price of peace was high. Unable to inflict a decisive defeat on them, or expel them from the empire, Theodosius allowed them to settle as semi-autonomous *foederati* ('allies') under their own leaders in 382.

ABOVE **A Germanic horseman** *armed with a spear and shield, from the Hornhausen Stone, a 7th-century grave slab from Hornhausen near Magdeburg in eastern Germany. Although the Visigothic cavalry played a decisive role in the defeat of the Romans at the battle of Adrianople, Germanic warriors usually preferred to fight on foot, even if they had ridden to the battlefield.*

391

CHRISTIANITY BECOMES THE STATE RELIGION OF THE ROMAN EMPIRE ✦ In 381 Theodosius began the active persecution of paganism, banning pagan sacrifices and divination, and destroying many pagan temples. His western colleague Gratian followed suit, giving up the traditional title of *pontifex maximus* (chief priest), which all Roman emperors since Augustus had held, and removing the Altar of Victory from the Senate house in Rome. Loyal pagans held Gratian responsible for Rome's subsequent defeats by the barbarians because of this act. Between 389 and 391 Theodosius issued a series of decrees which prohibited paganism. The remaining pagan temples were closed, pagan holidays were abolished and performing pagan rituals even in private became illegal. The last recorded celebration of the ancient Olympian Games was in 393: it is likely that Theodosius abolished them because of their pagan associations.

395

ROMAN EMPIRE PERMANENTLY DIVIDED ✦ After the disaster at Adrianople, manpower shortages forced the Roman army to become increasingly dependent on German mercenaries, many of whom rose to high rank and became politically influential. In May 392 the western emperor Valentinian II was murdered at the instigation of Arbogast, a Frankish general who, for many years, had been the power behind the throne. As a barbarian, Arbogast realized that he could not become emperor himself so he nominated a Roman friend, Eugenius, as emperor of the west. Although he was nominally Christian, Eugenius made moves to restore paganism, earning him the enmity of Theodosius, who invaded Italy in 394. After Eugenius was killed in battle in September, Theodosius became, briefly, the last emperor to rule both the eastern and western halves of the Roman empire. In January 395 Theodosius died of heart disease at Mediolanum and the empire was divided between his two young sons Honorius (r. 395–423), who became emperor of the west, and Arcadius (r. 395–408). This time, the division proved to be permanent but this did not mean that the empire ceased to be a single state because laws passed by one emperor were automatically valid in the other half of the empire. However, in the long run, this arrangement disadvantaged the western half of the empire because it could now no longer automatically draw upon the resources of the wealthier and more populated east.

406

THE STORM BREAKS ✦ The arrival of the Huns in eastern Europe set almost the whole of the Germanic world in motion. As the Huns extended their empire westwards, the tribes in their path packed their belongings into wagons and fled in search of safer territories, often displacing other tribes from their lands in the

ABOVE **Theodosius I (379–95)** *was the last emperor
to rule both eastern and western halves of the
Roman empire. Theodosius completed the process of
Christianization begun by Constantine the Great by
making Christianity the sole legal religion in the Roman
empire. This image of Theodosius is from a missorium, a*
*large ceremonial silver plate, 29 inches in diameter, which
was made in Constantinople to mark the tenth year of
his reign. The emperor is shown with a halo. Though this
represented sanctity, the practice of depicting gods, heroes
and rulers with haloes began in pagan times and was
adopted into Christian art only in the 4th century.*

IN NOMINE
XPI·VINCAS
SEMPER·

·NORIO·SEMP·AVG

PROBVS·FAMVLVSV·C·CONS·OR·D·

D·N·HONORIO·SEMPER·AVG

PROBVS·FAMVLVSV·C·CONSOR·D·

process. Many tribes aspired to settle in the Roman empire, as the Visigoths had succeeded in doing in 376, but, despite the pressure, the Roman frontier defences held firm until the winter of 406–7.

On the last day of 406, a coalition of Vandals, Sueves and Alans crossed the Rhine near Mogontiacum (Mainz, Germany) and invaded Gaul. As they spread out and plundered the countryside, 'all Gaul was filled with the smoke of a vast funeral pyre' wrote the Roman poet Orientus. The dominant figure in the Roman empire at this time was Stilicho, a German general whom Theodosius had appointed regent to the young emperor Honorius shortly before his death. Stilicho's priority was, however, protecting Italy from the Visigoths, who had rebelled again over their treatment by the Romans, and he did nothing to protect Gaul.

Gaul was rescued from the Vandals and their allies by Constantine III (r. 407–10), a general who had been proclaimed emperor in Britain. Constantine withdrew the field army from Britain and began restoring order in Gaul. In 409, hounded by Constantine, the Vandals, Alans and Sueves crossed the Pyrenees and invaded Spain. Constantine did not follow them. He had quarrelled with his generals and would soon be overthrown and executed. After years of migration and war, the Vandals, Alans and Sueves were desperate to settle down. In 411 they divided the Spanish provinces between themselves. There was nothing the Romans could do about it: by this time they had even more serious problems to worry about.

OPPOSITE **An ivory consular diptych** *depicting Theodosius' younger son Honorius I (r. 395–423) who became emperor of the west in 395. His martial pose is appropriate to the troubled times, but Honorius, in fact, never led an army in person. Such diptychs were luxury writing tablets commissioned by newly appointed consuls as gifts for their supporters.*

ABOVE **A map of Britain from the *Notitia Dignitatum*,** *a document setting out the battle order of the Roman army at the beginning of the 5th century. The map shows the forts under the command of the Count of the Saxon Shore, the commander charged with protecting Britain from pirate raids by the Saxons from northern Germany.*

410

THE GOTHS SACK ROME ✦ Following the collapse of the Rhine frontier, Stilicho tried to win over the Visigothic leader Alaric by offering him the rank of general in the Roman army, and a province and subsidies and grain for his people, in return for a promise of troops to fight in Gaul. The deal was acceptable to Alaric but not to most Romans. Honorius seized the opportunity to rid himself of his domineering regent and ordered Stilicho's execution for treason. Unfortunately for the western empire there was no one of similar ability to replace him.

Still determined to win a better deal for his people, Alaric invaded Italy in November 408 and laid siege to Rome. Over a year of fruitless negotiations followed: Alaric lifted his blockade when progress appeared to be made and imposed it again when talks broke down. Fighting was not an option for Honorius: he needed to save his troops to regain control of Gaul. Despite his strong position, Alaric was conciliatory, dropping his demands for a generalship and gold and asking only for the province of Noricum (now part of Austria) and a grain subsidy.

After the Romans tried to ambush him at a parley, Alaric's patience finally ran out. On the night of 24 August 410 the Visigoths broke into Rome through the Salarian Gate. They faced little opposition. The sack which followed was surprisingly restrained, with relatively little wanton destruction or killing. Most of the Visigoths were now Christian and they left many church treasures behind. After three days Alaric withdrew. The sack of Rome exposed all too starkly the decline of Roman

ABOVE **Germanic warriors attacking a house** *on a whalebone panel from the Frank's Casket, a bone chest manufactured in northern England during the 7th century. The short inscription in the Germanic runic alphabet names the defending archer as* *Egil, referring to the hero of a now lost legend. The imagery on the casket mixes incidents from Germanic and Roman mythology with Christian scenes. The casket is inspired by ivory caskets made in the later Roman empire.*

power. Not since the Gauls had sacked the city exactly 800 years earlier had a foreign enemy captured Rome. Though Ravenna, in northern Italy, had been the capital of the western empire since 402, the city of Rome remained a potent symbol of Roman might, and its fall caused shock and dismay throughout the empire.

Safe in Ravenna, Honorius still refused Alaric's demands. Frustrated, Alaric led the Visigoths into southern Italy, meaning to invade Africa, but he died before the year was out. His successor, Athaulf, turned around and took the Visigoths to Gaul. Almost unnoticed in the midst of these dramatic events, the Britons expelled the Roman administration and began to run their own affairs.

On the last day of 406, a coalition of Vandals, Sueves and Alans crossed the Rhine and invaded Gaul. As they plundered the countryside, 'all Gaul was filled with the smoke of a vast funeral pyre'.

429–35

THE VANDALS CONQUER NORTH AFRICA ✦ In 415 the Romans reached a deal with the Visigoths. In return for lands in Aquitaine, the Visigoths launched a genocidal campaign against the Vandals and their allies in Spain. The Sueves held out in the mountainous northwest but the Alans were all but exterminated. The Vandals survived but suffered heavy losses. In 422 the Romans and Visigoths launched another campaign against the Vandals. It failed to exterminate them but the Vandals' new king Geiseric knew that it was only a matter of time before they were attacked again and decided to move on again, this time to North Africa.

In May 429 Geiseric gathered the Vandals at Tarifa, near Gibraltar, and over the course of a few weeks they were ferried across the narrow straits to Tangier. Geiseric's move took the Romans completely by surprise and the Vandals faced only small garrison in North Africa. Geiseric's objective was the rich agricultural provinces of Byzacena and Numidia and the port city of Carthage. The only provinces of the western empire still untouched by war, they were the major source of

319

OPPOSITE **A mosaic of the baptism of Christ** *by John the Baptist, surrounded by the Twelve Apostles, in the dome of the 6th-century Arian Baptistery at Ravenna, Italy. Arianism was a Christian sect to which many Goths* *and Vandals belonged. Regarded as heretics by Orthodox Christians, separate churches were built for them to worship in. Mosaic art flourished in the late Roman empire, belying its popular image as a time of cultural decline.*

tax revenue for the western Roman government as well as the main supplier of grain to Italy.

After their landing, the Vandals moved east, meeting no serious opposition until they reached the city of Hippo (Annaba, Algeria) in June 430, which fell only after a year-long siege. A major force was sent to Africa and Geiseric was driven back into Mauretania, which became an official Vandal settlement by treaty in 435. With Geiseric still within easy striking distance of Carthage the Romans could not afford to relax their guard but a Visigothic rebellion left them no choice. Geiseric saw his chance and seized Carthage in October 439. Recognizing the seriousness of the situation, Aetius, the master general of the west, gathered a huge expeditionary force in Sicily in 442 but it never sailed. Aetius had to withdraw his troops to face an invasion by the Huns. To maintain grain supplies to Italy, the Romans had no choice but to agree to a humiliating treaty recognizing Vandal possession of Carthage.

Of all the setbacks suffered by the Roman empire this was by far the most serious. Without the revenues of Africa, the west was not financially viable and its future was bleak. To make matters worse, Geiseric used Carthage as a base to launch destructive pirate raids on Italy and Sicily. Once, when his helmsman asked against who they were sailing, Geiseric is reputed to have replied 'against whoever God is angry with'. In 455 Geiseric even sacked Rome itself.

The campaigns of Attila the Hun map showing the following labels:

FRANKS
Coblenz
Trier
Metz
Troyes
Catalaunian Plains 451
ALAMANNI
HUNNIC HEARTLAND
N
Milan
Verona
Aquileia
Pavia
Padua
Ravenna
Singidunum
Ratiaria
Sirmium
Margum
Viminiacum
Naissus
Sardica
Philippopolis
Marcianopolis 447
EASTERN ROMAN EMPIRE
Constantinople
Rome
Thessalonica
Sestus 447
WESTERN ROMAN EMPIRE
Thermopylae
Carthage
VANDAL KINGDOM

Legend:
441–3
447
448
451
452
Attila's Empire c. 450
Roman Empire c. 440

0   200 km
0   200 miles

434–53

THE SCOURGE OF GOD ✦ Despite being ultimately responsible for the empire's problems, the Huns initially maintained good relations with the Romans. The Roman master general Aetius had spent part of his upbringing with the Huns, forging a close relationship with their king Ruga and his sons Bleda and Attila, who succeeded him as joint rulers in 434. After he was appointed master general in 430 Aetius relied heavily on Hun mercenaries in his campaigns to restore Roman control in Gaul. Relations changed after the Vandals captured Carthage in 439.

OPPOSITE *St Leo the Great Going to Meet Attila* by Francesco Solimena (1657–1747) depicts Pope Leo I meeting Attila the Hun at Milan in 452 to offer him tribute in return for his withdrawal from Italy. Attila did withdraw, but it is likely that he did so not so much because of the pope's intervention but because of the famine that was ravaging Italy at the time, which caused supply problems for his army.

ABOVE **The campaigns of Attila the Hun**. Attila's early campaigns targeted the Balkans in the eastern Roman empire. He forced major territorial concessions and payments of tribute from the Romans but he was unable to take Constantinople. Frustrated, Attila attacked the western Roman empire, where his campaigns were equally destructive but also inconclusive. Attila was planning another campaign in the Balkans when he died in 453.

REACTIONS TO THE DECLINE OF ROME

For pagans, explaining the decline of Roman power was easy: Rome had lost the support of its traditional gods by embracing newfangled Christianity. For Christians it was a more difficult question to answer.

The empire had become Christian as God surely wanted; why, then, was he allowing so many calamities to befall it? The North African theologian Augustine of Hippo (354–430) provided the answer in his work *The City of God*. Augustine argued that history moved with a purpose, but it was God's purpose, not humankind's. God had allowed the growth of the Roman empire to aid the spread of Christianity but it was a sinful state and now that it had achieved its purpose God was allowing it to be destroyed. The fall of Rome, therefore, did not really matter. Ultimately, God's instruments were not earthly cities but the community of believers who had dedicated themselves to the mystical city of God.

BELOW **A 13th-century canon** *of the Augustinian Order, St Agostino Novello. Augustine is best remembered for his theological work* The City of God *but his writings on living in a religious community were also very influential, guiding the way cathedral clergy lived together until the 11th century. In 1059 a separate Augustinian Order of canons (clergymen living in a community) was founded for clergy who wanted to live a more monastic life.*

The obvious weakness of the empire after this disaster was just too tempting and in 441 Attila led an invasion of the eastern empire, ravaging the whole Balkan region and forcing the cancellation Aetius' planned campaign against the Vandals. As his fast-moving columns of mounted archers swept across the countryside, plundering, burning and killing, Attila began to earn his terrifying reputation as 'the Scourge of God'. Attila ravaged the Balkans again in 443, advancing to the walls of Constantinople, which he judged to be impregnable. When he ravaged the Balkans for a third time in 447, Attila was sole king of the Huns, having murdered his brother in 445 or 446. In 451 Attila turned west and invaded Gaul. Aetius allied with the Visigoths and Franks, who felt equally threatened by the Huns, and with their support he fought Attila to a standstill at the Battle of the Catalaunian Plains on 20 June. Attila retreated in good order: Aetius and his allies were too exhausted to pursue him. Aetius judged that Attila would now be ready to negotiate peace and he was caught off guard when Attila invaded and plundered northern Italy the next year. Then, in spring 453, Attila died unexpectedly: he had drunk himself unconscious at a wedding feast, suffered a severe nosebleed and quietly drowned in his own blood. As Attila's numerous sons fought over their inheritance, their German subjects rebelled, and, at the Battle of Nedao in 455, they overthrew the Hun empire.

THE SWEETEST PLEASURE

To the strong man what is *sweeter than with his own right hand to seek for his revenge? It is one of the greatest boons which nature gives us to glut our souls with vengeance.*

ATTILA, AS RECORDED BY THE GOTHIC HISTORIAN JORDANES IN HIS *HISTORY OF THE GOTHS* (1907 TRANSLATION)

468

THE EMPIRE'S LAST CHANCE ✦ Attila's death did not benefit the Roman empire. Fear of the Huns had given the Visigoths and other Germans who had sought refuge in the Roman empire a strong vested interest in its survival, which acted as a restraint on their actions. From now on they would be harder to control. Attila's death also led to the downfall of Aetius, whose reputation as the best man to deal with the Huns had made him the dominant political as well as military figure in the western empire. Now the Huns were gone, Aetius did not seem so indispensable. The young emperor Valentinian III (r. 425–55) deeply resented Aetius' influence and in September 454 he murdered him at a finance meeting. A contemporary writer commented that Valentinian might as well have cut off his own right hand for there was no general of comparable ability to replace him. Valentinian did not outlive him for long. In March 455 two of Aetius' loyal Hun officers killed him while he practised archery in the fields outside Rome. Valentinian had no male heirs and most of his successors were merely the puppets of ambitious generals who disposed of them as soon as they tried to assert themselves.

It was clear to the eastern emperor Leo I (r. 457–74) that the west lacked the resources to save itself. Peace on the eastern frontier allowed Leo to plan another

THE BYZANTINE EMPIRE

After the fall of the west, the eastern Roman empire continued to flourish and under the emperor Justinian (r. 527–65) even won back control of Italy and North Africa. Though they did not feel less Roman for it, the majority of the population spoke Greek rather than Latin.

As a result, after Justinian's reign, Greek gradually replaced Latin as the language of government and administration, as well as of the church and everyday life. Theological differences which emerged between the Greek Orthodox Church and the Roman Catholic Church further widened the cultural divide with the former western empire. In recognition of this, modern historians use the term Byzantine empire (from the old Greek name for Constantinople) to describe the eastern Roman empire. During the seventh century the newly Islamized Arabs conquered Egypt, Palestine and Syria, but their attempts to capture Constantinople failed. Confined to Anatolia and the Balkans, the empire survived, as much by diplomacy as military force, as a bulwark of Christendom in the east. However, a crushing defeat by the Seljuk Turks at the battle of Manzikert in 1071 sent the empire into decline, and the sack of Constantinople by crusaders in 1204 ended the empire's days as a great power. The final blow came when Constantinople fell to the Ottoman Turks in 1453. To the very end, Byzantine emperors continued to regard themselves as true Roman emperors.

324

RIGHT **This magnificent 11th-century mosaic** *from the cathedral of Hagia Sophia in Istanbul (Constantinople) shows the emperor Constantine IX (r. 1042–55) and his wife the empress Zoe making donations to the church, symbolized by the figure of Christ. After years of disputes, Constantine's reign saw the final schism between the Greek Orthodox and the Roman Catholic churches.*

expedition to drive the Vandals out of Carthage. For this Leo amassed, at the enormous cost of 64,000 pounds of gold and 700,000 pounds of silver, a force of around 50,000 troops and a fleet of 1,100 ships.

The Roman army was landed successfully near Carthage but things soon began to go wrong. The Roman commander Basiliscus granted Geiseric's request for negotiations but the wily Vandal king was simply buying time while he prepared a fire-ship attack which destroyed the Roman fleet at anchor. The Romans never recovered the initiative and withdrew, having suffered heavy losses. Leo had emptied his treasury to fund the expedition: there was nothing more the east could now do to help the western empire and its end was not long in coming.

474–6

DOWNFALL ✦ Success for Leo's Vandal expedition would have gone a long way to restoring the prestige and viability of the western empire, and perhaps even secured its long-term survival. The expedition's failure exposed the western empire as a hollow shell. The Visigoths, Burgundians, Franks and other German tribes who had settled within the empire began to carve out fully independent kingdoms for themselves. By 474, when Julius Nepos (r. 474–80) became western emperor, all that was left for him to rule was Italy and Dalmatia. Nepos was the last officially recognized emperor of the west. In 475 the master general Orestes overthrew Nepos and placed his own teenage son Romulus Augustulus ('the little emperor') on the throne as a puppet emperor. The eastern emperor Zeno (r. 474–91) refused to accept the usurpation and continued to recognize Nepos, who had escaped to Dalmatia, which he ruled until his death in 480. Romulus lasted barely a year.

Valentinian III deeply resented Aetius' influence and murdered him. A contemporary writer commented that Valentinian might as well have cut off his own right hand for there was no general of comparable ability to replace him.

Odovacer, a German officer in Orestes' army, led a mutiny of barbarian soldiers, who proclaimed him their king. Orestes tried to flee but was captured and executed in August 476. A few weeks later, Odovacer occupied Ravenna and deposed Romulus, whose life was spared because of his youth.

The deposition of Romulus Augustulus is widely seen as marking the fall of the Roman empire in the west but it is unlikely that anyone at the time saw things quite

OPPOSITE **A Vandal horseman rides out** *on a hunting expedition on his estates in this 5th-century mosaic from Carthage. After seizing Carthage in 439, the Vandals expelled the Roman landowning class and took over its estates. As happened in other parts of the western empire taken over the Germanic barbarians, life changed little for the common people; they simply paid their rents and taxes to new masters. This mosaic was executed by a Roman craftsman working for a Vandal patron.*

so clearly. Odovacer did not follow up his coup with a declaration of independence. He sent an ambassador to Zeno offering to recognize the sovereignty of the eastern empire. There was no need, Odovacer argued, for two Roman emperors: Zeno could rule the whole empire from Constantinople and he would govern Italy as an imperial viceroy. Zeno accepted this face-saving offer, which at least maintained the legal fiction that Italy was still part of the Roman empire. Odovacer maintained the Roman administration, the Roman Senate still met, and for the vast majority of his subjects life continued as usual. The people of the west only slowly realized that the Roman empire was no more. For the people of the east, the deposition of Romulus Augustulus had even less immediate impact. A Roman emperor still ruled at Constantinople and would continue to do so for another thousand years. Only when the Ottoman Turks captured Constantinople in 1453 were the last vestiges of the Roman empire extinguished.

327

3500 – 2000 BC	2000 – 1000 BC	1000 – 500 BC

MESOPOTAMIA

3500 – 2000 BC
- c.3500 BC Uruk in Sumeria becomes world's first city. First pictographic writing system.
- c.2900 BC Mesopotamian cuneiform script develops.
- c.2350 BC Earliest known law code issued by King Urukagina of Lagash.
- 2334 BC Sargon the Great founds Akkadian empire.
- c.2218 BC Fall of Akkadian empire
- 2004 BC Elamites sack Ur.

2000 – 1000 BC
- c.1813 BC Shamshi–Adad founds Assyrian empire.
- 1792 BC Hammurabi becomes king of Babylon.
- 1595 BC The Hittite king Mursilis sacks Babylon.

1000 – 500 BC
- c.1000 BC King David captures Jerusalem.
- c.958 BC Solomon's Temple in Jerusalem.
- 814 BC Phoenicians found Carthage.
- 729 BC Babylon becomes part of Assyrian empire.
- 680–627 BC Peak of Assyrian empire under Esarhaddon and Ashurbanipal.
- 626 BC Babylon rebels against Assyria.
- 612 BC Babylonians and Medes destroy Assyrian empire.
- 587 BC Destruction of Jerusalem by Babylonians.
- 539 BC Persian conquest of Babylon.

EGYPT

3500 – 2000 BC
- c.3200–3000 BC Hieroglyphic script develops.
- c.3000 BC King Narmer unifies Egypt.
- c.2649 BC Accession of King Sanakhte. Old Kingdom begins.
- c.2630 BC First pyramid built for king Djoser.
- c.2550 BC Great Pyramid of Khufu at Giza.
- 2134 BC Famine causes the fall of Old Kingdom.
- 2040 BC Mentuhotep reunites Egypt. Middle Kingdom begins.

2000 – 1000 BC
- 1640 BC Hyksos invasion. Middle Kingdom destroyed.
- 1532 BC Ahmose expels the Hyksos from Egypt. New Kingdom begins.
- 1504–1492 BC Egyptian empire at its greatest extent under Tuthmosis I.
- 1353–1335 BC Akhenaten, the 'heretic' pharaoh, attempts to impose a monotheistic solar cult.
- 1323 BC Death of the boy pharaoh Tutankhamun.
- 1285 BC Battle of Kadesh: Ramesses II fights the Hittites.
- 1070 BC Fall of New Kingdom

1000 – 500 BC
- 712–664 BC Egypt comes under Nubian rule.
- 525 BC Persia conquers Egypt.

Painted limestone bust of Akhenaten's senior wife Nefertiti (r. 1353–1335 BC).

PERSIA

1000 – 500 BC
- c.700 BC Achaemenes becomes first king of Persia.
- 550 BC Cyrus the Great begins Persian expansion.
- 546 BC Cyrus conquers Lydia and the Ionian Greeks.
- 539 BC Cyrus conquers Babylon.
- 525 BC The Persians under Cambyses conquer Egypt.
- c.515 BC Darius I begins construction of Persepolis.

GREECE

2000 – 1000 BC
- c.2000 BC Origins of Minoan palace civilization on Crete.
- c.1650–1550 BC Origins of Greek Mycenaean civilization.
- 1628 BC Eruption of Thera devastates Minoan civilization.
- c.1450 BC Mycenaean Greeks invade and conquer Crete.
- 1194–1184 BC Traditional Greek dates for the Trojan War.

Snake goddess figurine, from c. 1600 BC discovered in the Minoan palace of Knossos.

1000 – 500 BC
- 776 BC Earliest Olympic Games held in Greece.
- c.730 BC Sparta becomes most powerful Greek city state.
- 510–508 BC Athens introduces democratic constitution.

ROME

1000 – 500 BC
- 753 Legendary date for foundation of Rome by Romulus and Remus.
- 509 Romans overthrow monarchy and found a republic.

TIMELINE OF THE MAJOR ANCIENT CIVILIZATIONS

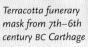

Terracotta funerary mask from 7th–6th century BC Carthage

Golden chariot from the Oxus Treasure, a hoard of 170 golden objects manufactured in different provinces of the Persian empire around 5th–4th centuries BC.

404 BC Egypt rebels against Persian rule.

343 BC Persia reconquers Egypt. Nectanebo II, the last native pharaoh of Egypt, is overthrown.

332 BC Alexander the Great conquers Egypt, ending Persian rule.

305 BC Greek general Ptolemy becomes king of Egypt.

30 BC Egypt annexed by Rome after the suicide of Cleopatra VII.

336–327 BC Alexander the Great of Macedon conquers Persian empire.

323–301 BC Alexander's empire breaks up following his death. Persia comes under rule of Greek Seleucid dynasty.

189 BC Battle of Magnesia: Romans defeat Seleucid king Antiochus III.

c.148–141 BC Parthians, under Mithradates I, conquer Persia.

53 BC Parthians defeat and kill Roman general Crassus at Carrhae (Harran).

Gilt bronze bust of the emperor Caligula (r. 37–41), the archetypical 'mad and bad' Roman emperor.

---

490 BC Battle of Marathon: Athenians defeat Persian invasion.

480 BC Xerxes of Persia invades Greece. Spartan last stand delays the Persians at Thermopylae. Athens defeats Persia at Salamis.

479 BC Greeks, led by Sparta, destroy the Persian army at Plataea.

460–445 BC First Peloponnesian War: ends inconclusively between Athens and Sparta.

447 BC Construction of the Parthenon begins.

431–404 BC Second Peloponnesian War: Sparta defeats Athens.

c.385 BC Plato founds the Academy at Athens.

338 BC Battle of Chaeronea: Philip II of Macedon conquers Greece.

146 BC Greece annexed by the Roman empire.

---

396 BC Rome conquers the neighbouring city of Veii, beginning its expansion in Italy.

Bronze sculpture, known as the Capitoline Wolf, showing Rome's legendary founders, the twin brothers Romulus and Remus.

272 BC Rome completes conquest of peninsular Italy.

264–241 BC Rome defeats Carthage in the First Punic War.

218–202 BC Second Punic War: Carthage, led by Hannibal, is defeated by Rome.

149–146 BC Third Punic War: Rome destroys Carthage.

48–44 BC Julius Caesar rules as dictator of Rome.

27 BC Augustus (Octavian) becomes the first emperor of Rome.

9 Battle of Teutoburg Forest: Germans defeat Rome.

43 Claudius begins conquest of Britain.

98–117 Roman empire at greatest extent.

235–284 Death of emperor Severus Alexander triggers instability in the empire.

313 Edict of Milan: Constantine the Great legalises Christianity.

378 Battle of Adrianople: Visigoths kill Roman emperor Valens.

395 Roman empire permanently divided into east and west.

410 Visigoths under Alaric sack Rome.

451 Battle of the Catalaunian Plains: Roman–Goth alliance defeats Attila the Hun.

476 Romulus Augustulus, the last Western Roman Emperor, is deposed.

INDEX

Page numbers in *italics* denotes an illustration/ illustration caption

330

PICTURE CREDITS

Quercus Editions Ltd
55 Baker Street
7th floor, South Block
London
W1U 8EW

First published in 2012

Copyright © 2012 Quercus Editions Ltd

A catalogue record of this book is available from the British Library

UK and associated territories:
ISBN 978 1 78087 321 3

Printed and bound in China

10 9 8 7 6 5 4 3 2 1

PROJECT MANAGEMENT: Elizabeth Stone
PICTURE RESEARCH: Caroline Hotblack
DESIGN: Austin Taylor
CARTOGRAPHY: William Donohoe
INDEX: Patricia Hymans